SPIRITED DIASPORAS

SPIRITED DIASPORAS

Personal Narratives and Global Futures
of Afro-Atlantic Religions

Edited by Martin Tsang

Foreword by Solimar Otero

UNIVERSITY OF FLORIDA PRESS

Gainesville

28 27 26 25 24 23   6 5 4 3 2 1

Library of Congress Cataloging-in-Publication Data
Names: Tsang, Martin, editor. | Otero, Solimar, author of foreword.
Title: Spirited diasporas : personal narratives and global futures of
   Afro-Atlantic religions / edited by Martin Tsang ; foreword by Solimar
   Otero.
Description: 1. | Gainesville : University of Florida Press, [2023] |
   Includes bibliographical references and index.
Identifiers: LCCN 2022056904 (print) | LCCN 2022056905 (ebook) | ISBN
   9781683403722 (hardback) | ISBN 9781683403838 (paperback) | ISBN
   9781683403968 (pdf) | ISBN 9781683403906 (ebook)
Subjects: LCSH: Black people—Atlantic Ocean Region—Religion—History. |
   Black people—Atlantic Ocean Region—Religious life and
   customs—History. | Afro-Caribbean cults—Atlantic Ocean
   Region—History. | Atlantic Ocean Region—Religion—History. | BISAC:
   SOCIAL SCIENCE / Anthropology / Cultural & Social | RELIGION /
   Indigenous, Folk & Tribal
Classification: LCC BL625.25 .S65 2023 (print) | LCC BL625.25 (ebook) |
   DDC 299.6/7—dc23/eng/20230608
LC record available at https://lccn.loc.gov/2022056904
LC ebook record available at https://lccn.loc.gov/2022056905

UF PRESS

UNIVERSITY
OF FLORIDA

University of Florida Press
2046 NE Waldo Road
Suite 2100
Gainesville, FL 32609
http://upress.ufl.edu

Contents

Figures

Foreword

"¡Indio bueno, Indio bravo, dónde vas con esa cruz? Voy al monte del calvario a entregársela a Jesús."[1]
—Verse, traditional Afro-Cuban spiritualist song "Indio Bueno"

In African Atlantic religions, spirits and deities move. It only makes sense that the individuals and communities that keep them serve as spiritual sojourners in a world that is complicated and connected culturally. This volume gathers the voices of practitioners to illustrate the intimacy and connection of each author's journey to a transnational set of practices that is also deeply localized. In examining the role of traditions like Regla de Ocha, Reglas de Congo, Espiritismo, Vodou, and Candomblé in their lives, the authors in this collection relate how African-inspired religions provide frameworks for how believers navigate their professions, spiritual selves, biological well-being, and chosen families. As with the Indio spirit that opens this foreword, the sojourners in *Spirited Diasporas* move through diverse routes of religions, cultures, and geographies that converge in likely and surprising ways. Practitioners write about the paths that pursuing African-inspired religions have taken them on, illustrating the living nature and material effects of bringing their spirits, divinities, and ancestors along with them.

The testimony you will find in the pages ahead spans the cultures and regions of Japan, the United States, England, Canada, Cape Verde, Cuba, Brazil, Haiti, Benin, Nigeria, and Louisianian Creole country. The voices you will hear are thus unique and diverse from points of origin and destination, yet each chapter tells a story of homecoming in motion. This kind of spiritual solace in the poetics of errantry is identified by Édouard Glissant as "the postulation of an unyielding and unfading sacred."[2] Glissant's articulation of "errant thinking" marks the global legacies of African slavery and the subsequent creation of Caribbean plantation systems onto world literatures, politics, cultures, and philosophies. The assemblages he suggests force us to rethink how we understand "the search for a freedom within particular surroundings."[3] *Spirited Diasporas* moves with such errantry, its authors irreverent in their search for spiritual freedoms in particular places and spaces that defy stereotypes of roots, routes, and traditionality. The sacred nature of the authors' journeys defies easy categorizations and reorients the textures of interiority and exteriority of travel as one of relation— with spirits, deities, and places.

Since African Atlantic religions are inclusive and can incorporate adherents of all races, ethnicities, nationalities, and cultures, the sojourners in this volume come from all corners of the Earth. Differences in gender and sexuality within the specific and varied contexts of the practitioners in this book highlight the unboundedness and efficaciousness of African-inspired religiosity in action. The intimate stories found here situate the multiple senses of belonging and reorientation that shape participation in the worlds of spirits, orishas, *lwas,* and ancestors. Chapters by Michael Atwood Mason, Terri-Dawn González, and Martin Tsang, for instance, provide a range of trajectories, experiences, and locations that will educate the reader on the diversity of spiritual lives created from African-inspired ways of being on the planet. Of particular note are the professional, artistic, and cultural movements that the travelers in this book make to create rich and varied existences in spirit, in diaspora. Further, the vivid images of shrines, offerings, and sacred art in this book illustrate this elaborate conglomeration in ways that are visually stunning and powerful. These views provide a depth to our consideration of the mobility and dwelling places made for spirits and deities by the authors and their religious families.

Spirited Diasporas is marked by the presence of the Yorùbá deity Oshún, also known as Ọṣun, Ochún, Oxúm. In diaspora, Oshún becomes all running rivers, and these currents mirror the ways our blood flows through our veins, the ways our bodies produce and absorb water. The personal stories presented in the pages to follow likewise reflect the microcosm of individual practitioners' internal paths and the macrocosm of African diasporic transnational flows. In each author's tale, new identities are constructed from deep histories of worship that illustrate the promise of spiritual, mental, and bodily rebirth. Oshún serves as one of the many guides to these transformations on the variety of roads traveled in this book.

The plurality of experiences provided in *Spirited Diasporas* does not lose sight of the historical, cultural, and political dimensions present in the practice of African Atlantic religions. The reality is that the history of slavery and racism profoundly shapes the nature of the deities, ancestors, and rites accessed for personal and communal power. In this book, the authors grapple with their positionalities through a reflexive engagement of their racial subjectivity vis-à-vis their religious identity. In doing so, we get a multivalent and accurate picture of the complexity of worship and belonging in contemporary African-inspired religions. Tsang is thoughtful in bringing this layered vision to light, to allow the reader to witness the mélange and flux of how people relate spiritual sojourns in a powerful and unexpected manner. In reading this book, we come to acknowledge the potency, sophistication, and presence of African-inspired religious cultures in our world today.

Solimar Otero
Indiana University, Bloomington

Acknowledgments

I wish to acknowledge my elders, family, friends, colleagues, and collaborators whose intellectual and emotional support made this book possible. The enthusiasm with which my project was received by those who heard it spurred me to reach out to the incredible individuals who have shared so much of themselves in the pages of this book. They each deserve a lot of applause for sharing their personal stories, and I commend and thank them for their openness and willingness to help positively shape religious understanding and tolerance. Collectively, the authors who collaborated on this book continue to inspire me—this book is theirs more than mine, and I am beyond grateful for their trust. I hold space for and acknowledge the deities, ancestors, spirits, family, and elders connected to all participants in this volume and humbly offer my thanks for allowing this collective endeavor to come to fruition.

My unreserved gratitude goes to Stephanye Hunter, editor extraordinaire, who has supported me and the project from its inception and who gave me the insight and encouragement to see the bigger picture and need for such a work. To Alexander Fernández, Alá Leké, who influenced this work in countless ways, I say *bendición* and *modupé*. By forces both seen and unseen, I was guided toward some incredible, life-changing, and life-affirming people. I hope that this small offering serves to better illuminate our world.

This book is dedicated to the memory of Afolabí, *ibá é, t'orun.*
Ashé.

Introduction

"Why Are You Here?"

MARTIN TSANG

It was 1997 and I had just arrived after a nine-hour flight from London Heathrow to Detroit Metropolitan Wayne County Airport, and the stern immigration officer was asking me the purpose of my visit.

"I've come to explore an African religion I have read about on the internet," I said, honestly and without thinking. *Why didn't I just say "Disney World"?!* The officer paused for a split second, lifted his hand back off the stamp on his inkpad, and gave me a scrutinous gaze. He was probably thinking, *What the hell is this Chinese-looking, British-sounding kid really going to do in Detroit?!* "Come with me," the officer said, placing my passport in a red folder and standing up. Red is never a good sign in such situations. I tried not to pass out from nerves and willed my now jellied legs to work to keep up with the man.

It was March 1997; I was nineteen, looking disheveled from the long flight and a complete bag of nerves and excitement. A religion I had only heard about and not experienced was calling to me, and arriving in America was the culmination of years of reading, dreaming, and saving money from summer work so that I could travel to find out more about the orishas, the humanlike yet supernatural gods and goddesses of the Yorùbá people of Southwest Africa whose global spiritual imprint had been made, in large part, through the horrors of the transatlantic trade in enslaved Africans. The orishas and other deities originating on the African continent have thus been prayed to and adored by devotees for centuries, in all sorts of locations and attracting all sorts of adherents. One potential member was me, undergoing the unlikeliest of spiritual sojourns that began in Mount Clemens, Michigan.

After many follow-up questions, the officer allowed me to enter the United States. It was my first time traveling alone, and while I delve into my journey in my chapter later in this book, I remember vividly how I was feeling upon arrival. The officer's question about what I was doing there had been something I was asking myself, and within a short time I would see and experience firsthand something that had been something I had read about, thought about, and longed for. Would I find what I had hoped? Would the orishas accept me? Would I be turned away or accepted? After getting my suitcase and finding my way out of the emptied baggage hall, Afolabí was there to meet me. We hugged and grinned. We had been corresponding daily through AOL chat rooms, by email, and via eye-wateringly expensive transatlantic phone calls. It was so good and comforting to finally meet him in person. He cracked a joke, and immediately I felt so much better. On the hourlong car ride to his house, we continued chatting like old friends, while my eyes were peeled at all the new landscape that was both wildly unfamiliar and familiar, thanks to American TV. I happened to arrive on the day his goddaughter, Babaladé, would be celebrating her priesthood initiation anniversary in his house. While spotting the iconic red stop signs and yellow school buses, and keeping up conversation and staving off tiredness, I was also processing that I would soon be among a whole house full of practitioners celebrating the orishas. I was beside myself! A natural introvert, I willed my shyness and insecurities to retreat and told myself that these were the type of people I would want to hang out with. My heart was hammering as I had read that at such a celebration, a special altar or throne is set up temporarily where the priest's orishas are placed, in the form of large, lidded vessels containing the consecrated emblems of the various orishas that a priest acquires for worship through initiation. Not only would I meet orisha priests, but I would also literally be face-to-face with the sacred!

I remember entering the lobby where Afolabí's orisha family members were milling around, eating pasta and cake, and they all greeted me warmly. These were real, living human beings who seemed sane and normal and were gathered in a shared love of the orishas. In the living room there was a majestic throne bedecked in shimmering white cloth and beads in honor of Obatalá and all of Babaladé's orishas, their respective vessels adorned with gorgeous textiles and large, multistrand beaded necklaces called *mazos* that took my breath away. I rang Obatalá's silver bell, his *agogo*, and was guided in how to prostrate with my head to the floor in front of the altar, called *moforibalé*, and was lifted by Babaladé and Afolabí. I instantly felt at home, and so began my journey, like so many others in this book, on the road to discovering my personal, perhaps out of the ordinary, connection to the divine.

Why Are We Here?

This is a collection of narratives of the sacred as written by individuals encountering Afro-Atlantic spirituality through initiation. The book helps open fresh dialogue on the diversity and inclusivity of these global religions from personal perspectives. These experiences of contemporary practitioners of African-centered religions reimagine plural ritual diasporas as spaces for contact, mobilization, and agency. More and more people are searching for tangible connection and initiation to the divine and are traveling to embrace and learn, transforming their lives and in turn amplifying religious global connections in new and impactful ways. The contributions found in this volume exemplify the plural global realities of priests and adherents, allowing for individuals to affirm their practice and to make visible their presence within a worldwide religious landscape. By drawing together firsthand accounts of practices and practitioners relating to Haitian Vodou, Yorùbá orisha, Afro-Cuban Lucumí/Santería/Ifá, and Afro-Brazilian Candomblé practices, we can see the manifold dynamics of continuities and changes over time, space, and worldviews.

In essence, this book signals the diversity of African-based religious traditions both in terms of ethnicity and global occurrences. In so doing, these narratives of orisha and Vodou religions help make visible their contemporary, transnational frameworks that rely on physical travel, digital communications, remittances of money and goods, sacred material culture, knowledge exchange, and cultural brokerage. Individuals are increasingly turning to Afro-Atlantic traditions and seeking instruction and initiation in them, creating transnational networks of practitioners. This book offers glimpses into the previously uncounted and underdocumented valuable experiences of cosmopolitan adherents, revealing some of the motives and methods that fuel their spiritual development and desire to "convert" to traditions different from those faiths and experiences akin to their geographical or familial frames. Each chapter is written by a person willing to share intimate aspects of their religious lives, how they came to encounter and learn about the tradition they would later initiate, and the pathways they made in realizing and creating their own ritual communities.

Contributors to this volume include scholars, activists, LGBTQIA+ identifying practitioners, and artists, yet they cannot and should not be reduced to such simplified or detached classifications. They—*we*—wear multiple hats and can claim many identities. A growing number of adherents are anchoring new centers for Afro-Atlantic spirituality and practice across the globe, planting the flag in many locations that have historically been under-represented or hostile to Afro-centric spirituality. By sharing these experiences and advocating with pride for their beliefs, the practitioners doing this valuable work help undo the harm and erasure experienced through imperial, colonial, religious extremist, and cultural hegemonic regimes. Rather than perpetuating the idea that orisha and Vodou religions are localized to exoticized geographies or othered demographics, this book establishes with greater precision a contemporary snapshot of diverse people who have made these religions their own through their personal sojourns of searching, learning, and initiation. Thus, while the persons and stories are varied, we get a heightened sense of the religious momentum and mobility that cross cultural, linguistic, and economic borders and honor the deep relevance and generative power these religions have on an ever-growing number of people. Pluralism, movement, and connections have been and continue to be important factors in spiritual encounters of African religions discussed here. From the historical contexts of Afro-Atlantic and Atlantic-Creole cultures to contemporary practices, these religions in Africa and beyond have mobility at their core. Such movement, called *iranjo* in the Yorùbá sacrocultural context, can be evidenced in the rich visual and material traditions such as woodcarving. Praise poetry, history, journeys, and sculptures inform the concept of iranjo and in turn become a rich epistemological and artistic framework.[1]

The individuals who have sought initiation into orisha and Vodou religions explore their respective reasons for having traversed geographical, cultural, and linguistic distances and divides to practice and create new global communities of devotion. The volume is, therefore, autoethnographic in its approach. The core of each chapter reveals the "religious itinerary" or journey—of travel, learning, adaptation, apprenticeship, and initiation—of each participant, allowing for nuanced analyses: exploring where they live, how they practice, and how they bring knowledge and understanding of their chosen religious traditions to their distinct geographies. The contributors to the book were not raised in the religion they write about. Instead, they are spiritual sojourners undergoing initiation as priests, often requiring the acquisition of new languages, traveling for learning, and negotiating both local and global terrains and cultures to understand and become competent in religious praxis.

Such conjunctions of worlds and words generate telling reflections on the panoply of emotions and actions each person underwent in deepening their spirituality. We benefit from reading each personal encounter and initiation experience as they pull into focus broader aspects of religious precepts and perceptions that have beguiled many. The writers reveal telling points of intersection, whether they are tension points or experiences that really put their differences (or sameness) into relief.

Studying Religious Routes, Networks, and Circuits

Religious lives speak to the plurality and idiosyncratic nature of forming and forging pathways for ritual practice, especially in geographical settings that emerge as important contemporary centers for spiritual experiences. Marloes Janson reminds us that pluriform religious movements require a framework that moves beyond traditional dichotomies, especially since one can only really identify as a member of Religion A and not Religion B, when in practice a person navigates and creates from both A and B and beyond. Janson notes that individuals often develop a pathway of religious practice in daily life that eschews narrow and separatist ideas of religions and conceptualizes these encounters and convergences as assemblages.[2] In Janson's ethnographic analysis of mixing Christian, Islamic, and "Yorùbá" religious practices in Lagos, framing such work in terms of an assemblage approach "overcomes not only the compartmentalized study of religion along theological boundaries but also goes a step further by dissolving religion as a bounded and distinct category."[3] Such a dissolution is useful in terms of thinking through the limitations of denoting Afro-Atlantic spiritual practices as religion and pitting them against the established and privileged religions that the term normally connotes.

Taking a broader Afro-diasporic perspective—including the religions of Brazil, Cuba, Haiti, and elsewhere—there has been a seismic shift in theoretical orientation over the decades, paving the way for a new ontology of the diaspora.[4] No longer are these religious traditions, systems, and lifeways considered "primitive," nor are they treated as having their foundations enshrined within a pristine and static past. Within the last two decades, discussions of diasporic Afro-Atlantic religions have increasingly become situated within the context of complex and dynamic politics, scales of economies, and international networks of communication and movement that serve to disrupt nation-state boundaries and the assumed lived realities of immobile, religious complexes. The forces of global trade and information exchange have caused a de-emphasis of the African diaspora as being comprised of neat, geographically bounded units of culture to be studied in isolation; instead, discussion centers on individuals actively engaging in modes that Kevin A. Yelvington frames as translocalism.[5]

Stefania Capone, writing on the ideas of power and tradition in Afro-Brazilian religions states that the tireless search for an idealized or essentialized idea of African tradition in Candomblé is a means to different ends. Capone cites the early work of Nina Rodríguez, for whom surviving African elements reified the primitive and inferior characteristics of Afro-Brazilians. Rodríguez's view contrasts with that of another early twentieth-century scholar of Candomblé, Roger Bastide, who argues that the ability to remain true to an African past and to cultivate those Africanisms in the diaspora became a positive sign of social and cultural cohesion.[6] "Black memory" for some Candomblé practitioners and terreiros (temples) thus becomes a sign of faithfulness to one's origins and notions of ritual purity, while moving away from these origins, in terms of incorporating European and Christian symbolism and syncretism, can be read as signs of betrayal caused by a loss of collective memory.[7] The concept and claiming of tradition in Afro-Atlantic religions is an important factor that has prevailed in scholarship and the search and desire for authenticity.[8] Thus, the signaling of religious constructs of being African, faithfully, and unchanged, especially in ritual, are echoed and reinforced in attendant academic studies. Such scholarly works may turn a blind eye and an ear toward European and American—especially Christian—influences, saints, and vernaculars and thus present biased histories. Afro-Atlantic religions and their scholars have entertained and cocreated complex histories and ritual pedigrees that manifest in terms of origins in the African continent and adaptation, addition, and preservation in the diaspora. Many early Black Atlantic sociological studies dealing with claims of authenticity and tradition by researchers of diaspora utilize the concept of collective memory, following Maurice Halbwachs,[9] whose work argues that individual memory is impacted by and impacts cultural realities. More specifically, collective memory can have a tremendous impact on all aspects of life, with the construction of a symbolic space that is situated within a material space, and the construction of these spaces leaves little room for cultural contact, routes, and networks. Rather, these diasporic religious were thought of as operating in isolation, cut off from what was considered the "homeland" as well as being distinct and wholly unconnected from similar and cognate diasporas. For Capone, writing on Afro-Brazilian diasporic religiosity, one can observe circuits between the different African American religions through the lens of the individual, and it is in celebration of this rich tributary that the chapters are offered here. Through networks and agile circuits, practitioners make use of and extend available contacts, both local and global, and these pathways pulse with exchanges of all kinds that help nourish and sustain spiritual practices across time and space. Such routes demonstrate how individuals and communities are unbounded realities and can be cast as protagonists in a sort of religious terrain where practitioners encounter notions of heritage, change, and creativity. Some of the prevailing concepts that religions of African descent encompass relate to the origins of ritual knowledge. Language use, songs, rhythms, narratives, and ritual procedures are some of the ways in which practitioners discuss their practices as faithfully preserved and transmitted via the African slave trade through multiple lineages of practitioners. Conversely, Afro-Atlantic religions are also discussed in terms of the ways they incorporate—or reject—Catholic, European, and other identifiable foreign influences.

In Cuba and its diasporas, the foundational work of Fernando Ortiz Fernández legitimated and promoted the study of African presences in the social sciences. Ortiz's work must be situated within a tableau of applied social theory that sought to address the racism and oppression encountered in explaining the nature of Africans taken to the "New World" via enslavement. Ortiz's contribution of mixing described in his idea of *ajiaco*—a culinary analogy that consists of a thoroughly Cuban product from diverse creole ingredients—thus a cultural stew with elements from Asian, indigenous, African, and European elements—was greatly influenced by scholars such as Melville J. Herskovits, whose work on cultural relativism paved the way for the scholarly study of the impact on forced migration and African cultural, social, and intellectual prowess. A critical analysis of Herskovits's work reveals multiple discourses on Africa at work in Latin America and the Caribbean; his many conceptual contributions laid the foundations for what Andrew Apter calls the "syncretic paradigm."[10] One such discourse was to be found in the manifestations of popular consciousness, in religious idiomatics such as Brazilian Candomblé, Haitian Vodou, Cuban Santería, and Obeah in Jamaica.[11] Yelvington explains that in Cuba, Ortiz became co-opted by *afrocubanismo*, a literary and artistic movement popular in the 1920s in which he was a central and legitimizing source for the movement because of his status as white lawyer cum politico. Overcoming and revising his early accounts that had racist undertones and motivations of criminalizing African practice in Cuba, Ortiz became a dominant international figure in emerging social science fields of studies that brought attention to Black culture and religion in the so-called New World.

Occupying the apex of this imagined hierarchy of knowledge production were the northern European and American Enlightened intellectuals, and occupying the lower rungs of the ladder were other cultures, to a greater or lesser degree, united in that they were viewed and imagined as possessing "less sophisticated" cultural processes and social structures. With the onset and exposure to superior cultures, the less developed intellectual frameworks would be examined in contrast and comparison to the ethnographer's own intellectual developments and notions of culture, a process by which all other cultures were deemed inferior and porous to the superior knowledge and capabilities of the more hegemonic, Western influences. Early scholarship on Afro-Atlantic religions has tended to portray such practices as anachronistic to the culturally modernizing experiences of industrialization.[12] In this way, we should proceed with caution or heightened appreciation that the very terms employed here—including *Lucumí/Lukumí, Candomblé*, and, to some extent, *Vodou*—by practitioners and scholars alike are recent religious identifiers, themselves reliant on and invoking the equally modern construction of a homogeneous Yorùbá whose forebears would not have participated in such imprecise ethnic lumping.[13] J. Lorand Matory, whose work on Afro-Brazilian Candomblé offers significant insight into this debate, powerfully argues for a revision of long-held assumptions that diasporic populations are reproductions of stable, nonchanging structures that are portals or reflections of a "pristine past."[14] Palmié and Matory call for a new anthropological strategy to be implemented in the study of Afro-Atlantic religiosities, one that serves to restore the "subject or agent to the narrative."[15] Such a framing departs from trying to understand the African diaspora in terms of aligning either with continuity or embracing change and shifting the discourse away from ideas of origin stories and ritual practices preserved from an imagined precolonial and transnational past.[16] The chapters in this volume offer insight and further evidence into the limitations of scholarly scribed framings of isolated and remote Afro-Atlantic religions and help advance our understanding of how the very actions and methods of modernity, technology, and materiality are not in opposition to spirituality but actively assist in forming and framing their visibility and discoverability, today.

The Deity Is in the Details

It is impossible to include a comprehensive description of each of the Afro-diasporic religions here. While they encompass many languages, philosophies, deities, and precepts, there are overarching similar features that span all expressions. All the religions explored here are premised on the belief in a supreme deity who does not interact directly with humanity. Rather, the intermediary deities and spirits—orishas, *lwa, vodún,* and *nkisi*—as well as the ancestors and other realms of being, are close to the worshipper. Initiations are ways of accessing the divine and directing spiritual energy strategically, bringing together communities of elders and practitioners to effect rebirth. These initiations and communities create strong spiritual family bonds that respect hierarchies of age, both physical and initiatory. Priests of each tradition may undergo initiation for their own deepening of faith as well as to help others. Healing of mind, body, and spirit underlies all ritual aspects, with the prolonging of life in good health underpinning the reason for all practice. These many and varied religions involve complex forms of communication through divination systems as well as trance, possession, and mediumship. Divination requires proficiency and training and is carried out at crucial times of the person's life to seek counsel and assistance at important junctures, crises, and as issues or occasions arise. There is information that can only be ascertained through divination, such as the determination of one's guardian deity, and thus divination plays an indispensable role in much religious practice.

One steadfast feature of many US urban landscapes are the numerous *botánicas* (religious goods stores) that cater to Afro-Cuban, Haitian, Dominican, and other diasporic religious and spiritual worldviews. These stores become meeting spaces for diverse traditions and seekers to find materials as well as networks and practitioners. These stores also broach territory that goes beyond the purely commercial or material in focus and are a common entryway for seekers to find religious contacts. As Joseph M. Murphy's research shows, botánicas often host ornate altars in their stores that integrate and honor spirits from disparate religious traditions, thus transforming the space where "the economic basis of the botánica is only partly retail merchandise and more fundamentally, consultation."[17] Botánicas and specifically their spiritual consultants offer services to help individuals deal with a battery of issues, life situations, and choices. Botánicas also serve as spaces to connect with local practitioners and community members, and many will offer spiritual consultations and related services that act as entryways

Figure I.1. A religious goods store in Havana, Cuba, called a *botánica* in the United States. Photograph by Martin Tsang, 2017.

for seekers interested in learning more about various Afro-Atlantic traditions. For many who (re)turn to Afro-Atlantic religious practices, these botánicas can play important roles in their spiritual lives, and the density and visibility of such stores can indicate the populations of practitioners who support them. The appearance of new stores that refer to these religions in their names and with the types of goods carried can also indicate currents of communities and practitioners in diverse and unexpected locations.

The Orishas: (A)Nago Deities

As religions born from the shared histories of enslavement, colonialism, and industrialization, Lucumí and Candomblé are two well-known and established religions that feature similar practices, rituals, and materiality, yet for the most part, they have developed independently of each other, creating parallel but separate trajectories, each with its own unique makeup of ethnosacred parts. Matory describes Candomblé as "an Afro-Brazilian religion of divination, sacrifice, healing, music, dance, and spirit possession." He states that "the only rival to its beauty is its complexity."[18] As deities that defy borders and are both local and transnational, the orishas and orisha traditions (as well as their origin stories) are known by or delineated by plural names on all sides of the Atlantic. For example, Matory notes that the wealthiest Candomblé terreiros in Salvador da Bahia self-identify and use the terms *Quêto* or *Nagô*. In this context, *Quêto*—also spelled *Kéto* and *Kétou*—refers to a Yorùbá-speaking town that straddles the People's Republic of Benin and Nigeria, creating multiple interpretations and inclusivity for practices derived from both kingdoms. *Nagô,* the second term that Matory points to and explains in the Candomblé context, can refer "either to a specific Beninese Yorùbá group or, in Beninese parlance, to the Yorùbá speakers."[19] The Brazilian Nagô both crystallizes and offers interpretive license as to what Yorùbá concepts the term alludes to. *Nago* and its variations, such as *Anago,* are employed in Haiti and Cuba to refer to Yorùbá-inspired traditions, deities, and practices.

Lucumí, also known as Santería, or *la regla de ocha* (the rule of *ocha/orisha*), is one of the most academically popularized and influential Afro-diasporic religions, as measured by the prominence of this subject and its space in scholarly literature. Lucumí was cultivated in Cuba by enslaved and free Africans of Yorùbá and Fon descent (from what is today southwestern Nigeria and the Republic of Benin). The Lucumí religion consists of the veneration of ancestors and the worship of orishas. It is henotheistic, organized around the core belief of one supreme yet remote god, called Olofín, Olórun, or Olodumaré, and the presence of intermediary deities, called orishas.

These practices of the ethnic groups that comprise the Yorùbá and their neighbors have become colloquially known as Santería, la regla de ocha, or simply *la religión.* Lucumí is steeped in ritual practice and performativity and includes initiation, singing, dancing, animal sacrifice, divination, and possession. A key concept of the Lucumí worldview is *ashé,* the name given to the unseen energy that motivates all things, a life-sustaining and healing force akin to the East Asian concept of *qi* or the South Asian concept of *prana.* Ashé is considered universal. Not only does it give form to every knowable thing, both abstract and concrete; it also surrounds, penetrates, and connects them together. It is this quality of ashé that is the backbone for concepts such as karma, continuous creation, and reincarnation. Everything—animal, vegetable, mineral, thought, action, emotion, spoken word, idea, or deed—has its own ashé.

Beyond (but also at times within) the realms and margins of the orishas, the lwa, nkisi, and vodún are mediators between the supreme god and humankind, including the ancestors. A worshipper develops his or her own unique and personal relationship with one guardian or tutelary deity through initiation, offerings, and service, determined through divination. Divination is a form of communication, as are possession and trance, that helps promote betterment and healing, often with the deepening religious practice through directed veneration, offerings, and initiations. Each deity governs specific domains in nature, animals, and foods and presides over different aspects of the human life cycle. The deities may speak through divination patterns and have signature colors, numbers, music, mannerisms, gestures, and so on. Often, they are treated and described as cherished and exalted family members—as mothers and fathers.

Much academic work from the 1920s on the religious ethnography of Afro-Atlantic religions charted and attributed the various Catholic correspondences of each deity. A saint has been assigned to each orisha or lwa. For example, Yemayá, the orisha of motherhood and water, associated with the color blue and the number seven, is syncretized with the Catholic Virgin Mary under the title Nuestra Virgen de Regla (Our Lady of Regla). The Vodou lwa Maîtresse Manbo Erzulie Fréda Dahomey is often represented with a chromolithograph of Mater Dolorosa, the depiction of the weeping Virgin Mary also known as Our Lady of Sorrows. While a worshipper may venerate a Catholic statue or image, the actual initiations and majority ceremonies have little Catholic interaction or symbolic use, especially in their respective sacred spaces of the Lucumí *igbodu,* the Vodou *djèvo,* and the Candomblé *ronkô,* wherein transformational initiation ceremonies are performed.

The initiation as a priest or *olorisha* in Nigeria, Brazil, or Cuba requires the initiate to undergo a ceremony directed on the body, especially the Orí or head of the person. During a period of seclusion,[20] the head is ritually prepared to receive the ashé of the orisha by being shaved, painted, and "loaded" with herbal medicine. The process is made possible by the community direction of ashé. Carole Boyce Davies defines *ashé* as the power "to be" and by its ability to move "across two large discursive fields: that of spirituality and that of creativity."[21] Through the manipulation of ashé, an initiate's head is creatively and spiritually connected to the orisha, an act that is only undone after death through mortuary rites performed on the body.

In both Candomblé and Lucumí, following the priesthood initiation ceremony, the person is considered an *iyawó* (junior bride/wife) of the orisha. The status of junior wife is not gender differentiated according to the sex of the person; the term is applicable to both male and female initiates.[22] The iyawó takes certain measures to indicate their elevated status, and the one-year-and-seven-day-long period of being an iyawó is a crucial gestation period in which the person is learning to live with the ashé of the orisha in their life. Iyawó are protected from the depletion of ashé and from the pollution coming from the mundane world by wearing white, bathing regularly, keeping their heads covered, and by not frequenting certain places such as cemeteries or jails where they may be exposed to harmful or volatile energy. The total number of orishas is unknown and forever changing. Priests will often give a numerical figure of four hundred plus one, with four hundred signifying a multitude of orishas and the plus one being the ability for future orishas to be discovered.

Afro-Cuban Ifá Divination and Priesthood

Ifá is a specialist branch of orisha worship. Ifá initiates are men called *babalawo* whose patron orisha is Orunla or Orunmila. Babalawos are specialists in divination and perform ceremonies, initiations, and services for worshippers, their families, and members of the public who are often introduced to the religion by receiving a divination, described in English as a "reading" and in Spanish as a *consulta*. A signature of Ifá practice is the initiation of the warriors where an adherent will receive the consecrated, activated material representations of four orishas: Eleguá, which often takes the form of a cement head with cowry features; Ogún and Oshosí, represented by implements in a metal cauldron; and Osun, represented by a metal rooster on a chalice who guards the life of the worshipper.

Figure I.2. Several sets of warrior orishas: Eleguá, Ogún, Oshosí (in cauldrons), and Osun. Havana, Cuba. Photograph by Martin Tsang, 2006.

Vodún and Vodou

From the fifteenth century to the close of the nineteenth century, colonial empires enslaved an estimated twelve and a half million Africans.[23] Four broadly defined ethnic groups who were enslaved were the Bantu, Ibo, Yorùbá, and Ewe/Fon. The largest of these groups forcibly taken to the Caribbean were the Bantu/Bakongo of southern and central Africa, bringing with them the worship of nkisi, the deities under the name of Palo that originated in the environs of Angola and Zaire. Europeans enslaved Ibo and Ijaw people from southeast Nigeria, and among them were the Efik, who established the confraternity of the Ekpé/Ejagham, known as Abakuá in Cuba. Between 1750 and 1800, European and American traders forcibly enslaved the Ewe-Fon of the Kingdom of Dahomey (now the Republic of Benin) who represented a sizable ethnic group to be taken to the Antilles. The British and French turned the Bight of Benin into a major center of the transatlantic slave trade, and from those ports, Europeans trafficked Ewe-Fon people to Haiti, Cuba, Brazil, and many other colonized countries for their plantation labor. The Ewe-Fon preserved their worship of Vodún. Dahomean Vodún (along with Bakongo ritual knowledge) is the foundation of Haitian Vodou. Similarly, in Cuba, the worship of Vodún spirits is known as Arará, from the word *Alada,* from the port on the Bight of Benin where the enslaved peoples embarked on the vessels that transported them across the Atlantic.

Vodún are worshipped by the Ewe-Fon as well as the Mina and Mahi of Benin, Togo, and Ghana. Vodún are influenced by and influence the Yorùbá or Nago people in present-day Nigeria. The word *Vodún* means "spirit" and refers to the deities and religion as especially linked to the quotidian life and royal rule of the kingdom of Dahomey.[24] The extensive two-volume study of Dahomey by Melville J. Herskovits details the ways that Vodún deities are organized into three distinct pantheons: Vodún of the sky, principally the two gods Mawu and Lisa; the Vodún of thunder, centered around Hevioso; and Vodún of the earth, presided over by Sakpata.[25] The matriarch of the Vodún pantheon is Naná Burukú, who gave birth to Mawu, the female creator aspect, and her consort, the male Vodún Lisa, to form the deity Mawu-Lisa. Always coupled, Mawu-Lisa are the sum of creation and are represented by the moon and the sun. In many founding myths of the spiritual dynasty, Mawu-Lisa is considered the parent of all the other Vodún. First born to the creator couple was Sakpata, also known as Dada Zodji, and his wife, Nyowhe Ananu.

Leslie G. Desmangles recounts that "anyone who has visited Haiti at least once is likely to have heard the maxim that Haitians are 100 percent Catholics and 90 percent Vodouisants [Vodou adherents],"[26] indicating the dual and often overlapping spaces and roles that Catholicism and serving the spirits of Vodou plays in everyday life in Haiti. Vodou spirits are termed *lwa* in Haitian Vodou and belong to nations of deities, including the Rada and Petwo, who have different characteristics of respectively being cool and hot as well as being composed of deities from different enslaved subgroups, namely Dahomean and Kongo. Worshippers may undergo *kanzo*, or initiation to various levels. *Manbo* and *houngan* are the titles for female and male priests who can preside over and care spiritually for adherents, called *ti-fèy* (little leaves). The senior rank of priest is designated as *houngan* or *mango asogwe*, referring to the conferment of the *asson* (sacred beaded gourd rattle) during initiation.

Vodún and especially Haitian Vodou have been grossly misrepresented and demonized in popular press. Often portrayed using vulgar racialized tropes, Vodou as a religion bears no resemblance to many essentialized and stereotyped mainstream depictions, creating fear that in turn is used to justify bigoted acts of violence against the religion's practitioners. Through close and intricate networks of spirits and practitioners, Vodou provides practical assistance, healing, and community. Well-established Haitian diasporas in the United States, Canada, and France have *sosyetes* (societies led by manbo and houngan), conducting ceremonies and initiations in those locations as well as maintaining transnational ties by traveling to conduct rites and fulfill spiritual obligations that are indelibly tied to the land of Haiti.

Palo

The Bakongo/Bantu ethnic group of central Africa gave rise to a system of ancestor (*nkisi*) and deity (*mpungo*) reverence in Cuba as introduced by enslaved people from the Kongo region, especially Angola. This Afro-Cuban religion is generically referred to under the umbrella term *Palo* or *Palo Monte*, and depending on lineage or doctrinal differences, it can also be known as Briyumba/Brillumba, Kimbisa, or Kinfuiti, with provinces such as Matanzas or Cienfuegos known for having one or more of these distinct *ramas* (branches) of Palo, each with its own set of initiations, priesthood titles, liturgies, practices, and rites. Just as Palo and Lucumí are derived from separate geographically situated and ethnically distinct communities

Figure I.3. An outdoor hut housing a Palo Mayombe *prenda/nganga*. Sagua La Grande, Cuba. Photograph by Martin Tsang, 2009.

and cultures in Africa, so too are their Cuban and Cuban diasporic ritual spaces maintained in separate areas of the house cum temple. Similarly, Afro-Cuban interreligious hierarchy maintains that Palo initiations called *rayamiento* (scratching) and Tata and Yayi Nganga (father and mother of the foundation) occur prior to the Lucumí priesthood initiation. A Lucumí worshipper cannot initiate in Palo in these ways once having undergone the Lucumí priesthood rites.

Espiritismo

Also called *misa blanca*, Kardecian Spiritism, and Cordon Espiritual, Espiritismo originated with the published works of Allan Kardec (1804–1869), a French-born Theosophist whose works have served as manuals for spirit contact and outline the performance of séances. His writings have become extremely popular in Europe and colonial Latin America and the Caribbean. Kardec's opus *The Book of Spirits*, first published in French in 1857,[27] reflects the author's interests in Hindu and Buddhist religious philosophies that were rapidly gaining in popularity in Europe as the original texts were translated into European languages.[28]

Figure I.4. A *bóveda* with glasses of water, flowers, cologne, prayer book, and candles set up for a spiritual *misa* (mass). Miami, Florida. Photograph by Martin Tsang, 2018.

As well as being a stand-alone practice, many practitioners of Afro-Cuban religions are also Spiritists and mediums. As the term *misa* (mass) suggests, Spiritism takes the form of séances as a key part of its doctrine and practice. There are no titular initiations in Spiritism; however, there are ceremonies such as the *misa de coronación,* a type of séance or mass often conducted before the orisha priesthood initiation ceremony where mediums focus on the development of a person and that culminates in a symbolic act of coronation or crowning of a person's spirit guide to the person.[29] The misa is performed in a style described as *mesa blanca* (white table), where the focus is a table draped in a white cloth with glasses of tap water placed on it. The glasses of water are conductors or loci for spirits of light that are drawn to the misa through songs and prayers. Candles, flowers, incense, and colognes are used during the misa for various spiritual actions, including to attract the spirits and perform cleansings. A basin is placed on the floor in front of the table with fresh water, cologne, and flower petals with which participants cleanse themselves at various points during the reunion.

A Spiritist develops their mediumistic and clairvoyance/clairaudience abilities by working with their spirit guides. Within the household, practitioners of Espiritismo will maintain a permanent shrine like the mesa blanca for the veneration of their ancestors and guides. The space or altar with glasses of water, photos, and other items dedicated to one's guides is called a *bóveda* and is separated from Lucumí orishas, often located in a different room if space permits. Guides are revealed through mediums in masses and can take distinct ethnoracial characteristics such as *la gitana* (gypsy) and *el Congo* (Kongolese) who collectively form within a person's *cuadro espiritual* (spiritual quadrant or framework). A medium who has established strong relationships with identified spirits may work with them for the benefit of other people. Such a strong relationship may be given material form, such as the addition of a doll, often bearing similar features of the guide to represent them. The doll is dressed in clothing fitting the guide's likeness and will live in the house, often close to or on the *bóveda*. In addition to clairaudience and clairvoyance, the spirit guides may manifest through possession.

In some Lucumí lineages, mediumship development practices derived from European Kardecian Spiritism are supremely as well as independently practiced. Misas frequently form part of the pre-Lucumí priesthood initiation preparations to develop the person's mediumship, connection, and protection. European-derived Spiritism has been popular in many Latin American and Caribbean religious practices, extolling the multiplicity of diasporic religious experiences.

The Contributors and Their Ritual Texts

Vivid comparative reflection by the authors here helps us appreciate different conditions of knowing. Our contributors are particularly attentive to writing about the full sensory experiences of their ritual endeavors both in terms of ceremonies and initiations and community-building more generally. We can read about sense-observations that engage body performative and affective aspects of ritual and see how sacred experiences are often completely overwhelming in their engagement of the senses.

The chapters in this volume are condensed ethnographic pieces that examine different epistemic spaces in first-person prose. Each contribution respectfully draws out intimate details of relatable and surprising moments of spirituality that also respect and preserve ritual privacy and codes of ethics when it comes to sensitive and proprietary religious information. The religions described here are unified in that each creates conditions of knowledge by *opening* spaces and situating them within the practitioners' experiences rather than being limiting and *closing off.* Such a volume as this is only the beginning in the momentous and much-needed task of revealing the many and diverse persons who seek out and practice Afro-Atlantic religions. By no means is this book a comprehensive account of the entire global landscape of such religious practices. I view this book as a testament to trust, and hopefully it opens pathways for further practitioners and seekers to tell their stories too.

The contributors have generously shared their stories in their own words and focused on what is most meaningful for them to describe at this moment. We as readers are fortunate to catch glimpses into how ideas of race, ethnicity, gender, and sexuality interplay with religiosity in very personal circumstances and life choices. We see that ritual realms may overlap or that a person may practice or identify with more than one or multiple faiths and religions. In recognition of the need for more contributions and to treat the Afro-Atlantic as an inclusive space, the present volume does not contain representations of practitioners' stories from every important center of worship. Included on this list are practitioners who adhere to Trinidad and Tobago worship and attendant practices from across the Antilles, Winti from Suriname, and more. The book leans heavily toward the orisha-worshipping religions, especially those of Afro-Cuban heritage, which reflects the network of friends, priests, peer recommendations, and colleagues who agreed to being part of the work. Indeed, within the religions represented here, we can detect the work of several key protagonists, including Oshún, revered goddess of the river. Her name and priests flow throughout the pages, which is a testament to her global presence and power. So too like Oshún's rivers, these multiple religious practices—Afro-Brazilian Candomblé, African Vodún, Haitian Vodou, Afro-Cuban Lucumí and Ifá, Palo Monte, and Espiritismo—flow across the globe. Knowledge by and about their practices, priests, and deities helps open new channels of understanding and discovery to new audiences and becomes ever more prominent across expanding terrains.

The Plurality of Languages, Words, and Definitions in Afro-Atlantic Religions

Two potential pitfalls of a volume such as this are the dangers of generalization and confusion. For the reader encountering Afro-Atlantic religions for the first time, the multiple religions, the nonstandard naming conventions of the practices, in addition to the variety of languages, vocabularies, and spellings, as well as regional and generational differences can be starkly overwhelming. While individual stories are drawn from distinctly labeled Afro-Atlantic religions, they do not operate in a vacuum, and neither do the practitioners. How do we adequately represent or convey the spectrum of religious experiences when they can differ wildly in both time and space? How do we capture words from a variety of languages, many of which are creolized or vary regionally, without inadvertently confusing the reader encountering these religions for the first time? An example of the confusion can be given in the name for the deities of the Yorùbá, which in the tonal language would be òrìṣà. In Cuba, the influence of Spanish has rendered the pronunciation of òrìṣà as both *oricha* and *orisha* and sometimes even *orisa*. In the òrìṣà practices of Brazilian Candomblé, the impact of Portuguese means that one would hear *orixá* uttered by practitioners there. Further, practitioners in Latin America and the Caribbean who read widely, travel, and learn from multiple sources may choose to use òrìṣà rather than one of the Latinized versions, as it may feel more attuned to how a person fluent in Yorùbá would spell it. In the individual chapters that follow, editing of foreign words has been undertaken to minimize unnecessary variations in spellings. Each chapter author has decided which of their terms can be aligned with spellings throughout the book without losing meaning, and they have also identified words that should retain the author's spelling preferences so that personal meaning and emphasis are conveyed. Given the multiple languages' ritual terms and concepts, English translations are included in the body of the text where words first appear, and a glossary of terms follows the last chapter.

1

Pelerinaj—Pilgrimage

ALEX BATAGI

My involvement in *sèvis lwa,* also known in Haitian Vodou as "serving the spirits," did not necessarily begin by conscious choice, but certainly not by total chance. Unlike many *blan* (outsiders) who arrive at the proverbial door of the temple seeking the lwa, I was only seeking to gain more insight into how other people live their lives. No one was more surprised than I when it became clear that my initial attendance at a ceremony celebrating the elevated dead in the religion was a threshold that had been waiting for me and that, like all things in Vodou, had been made visible and accessible at exactly the right time.

Growing up White and Protestant in suburban New England in the 1980s, I had little exposure to any religion outside of the Baptist denomination I was raised in. When I was a child, my faith followed that of my parents; a parent brought me and my younger sibling to church each week, and we attended Sunday school while my parents sang in the choir or went to Bible study. There was vacation Bible school during the summers, and stories were read from a children's illustrated Bible. We placed Baby Jesus in the crèche, lit advent candles before Christmas, and went to church early on Easter.

As I grew older, my faith was further shaped by the changes in my parents' faith; they had a deep conversion experience and made the decision to pursue a theological degree and ordination in the denomination in which we were members. The church became how we related to each other, as it was the predominant language in my family, and as a young teen, I began to pursue what in hindsight was a search for an understanding of myself.

I attended an Evangelical summer camp and, at fourteen years old, had my own radical conversion experience that led to me undergoing a believer's baptism, or full-immersion baptism, at the church my family and the camp

Figure 1.1. An *iliminasyon* (illumination) or enlightenment ceremony for Sosyete Nago, Jacmel, Haiti. Photograph by Alex Batagi, 2016.

staff attended. I became more involved with church activities, including attending a national Evangelical youth conference, engaging at school with faith activities sponsored by Focus on the Family (a conservative Christian media outlet), and returning to that same summer camp as staff.

That summer at camp was the first time I had ever lived away from my family for any significant period and was the first time I had ever been able to explore who I was away from my family. For many teens around my age, that might have been a positive or memorable time, but for me it was a deeply painful and tearing experience. While working at the camp that had shaped my religious identity so much, I began to question both that identity and the precepts of White Evangelicalism that were shaping my day-to-day experiences in a religious community. My formative moment of deciding to leave that faith community came during an incident in which a fellow staff member was required to stand up at an all-staff meeting and apologize and acknowledge a rumor that some of the young campers had spread regarding the implied "fact" that he was gay.

I did not fully understand at the time why this was so abhorrent to me, but it was only a year or so into the future before I was able to recognize my own sexuality and, eventually, my own gender-nonconforming identity. It is a unique form of despair, particularly for a young person, to realize that who you are stands outside of what is deemed acceptable in the faith you have been raised in since birth. This was my first experience with death, in that each opportunity to change or make a different choice is another opportunity to have a part of yourself die, inwardly. These radical transformations of self and life were lost on a grieving, lonely teenager, but they are not lost on the priest who looks back on those memories.

As a young adult, I was disillusioned with organized religion and put myself in the mindset of being an agnostic. Instead of anything religious or spiritual, I dove into understanding who I was in the wider world as a queer, gender-nonconforming individual. I largely ignored all things spiritual until I had the opportunity not to and found myself in a social circle with a variety of polytheists, many of whom also found a home on the LGBTQ+ spectrum. Seeing that other people like me, in one way or another, had meaningful spiritual and religious experiences put enough of a crack in my own antireligious armor that I was able to have my own experiences: to explore what it meant to be a spiritual adult outside of a traditional church and to learn to listen to what is often unseen.

The first time I was explicitly presented with information on Haitian Vodou was via a library book of unknown origin. At that time, I wasn't interested in practicing Vodou but only learning about a religion I was unfamiliar with. I believed—and still do—that it is important to be curious about the world and about other people's customs, as this is what defeats and deconstructs White supremacy and colonialism. For me, however, this had unintended consequences and led to me being presented with a series of thresholds and, in some ways, continual experiences of growth as death to the self.

The initial threshold I crossed came via the then-uncommon medium of Facebook. In 2012, spiritual communities had not yet exploded across social media as they have now, and it was a bit thinner then, in terms of available outlets to seek information. As it was, I wasn't seeking information about Vodou specifically but was pursuing different interests in American folk magic. I joined a Facebook group for discussion, and several days later I received a message from someone whose profile information listed what was clearly a religious name and title. Even in those Wild West days of Facebook, occasionally I would be contacted by a Spiritualist offering unsolicited services or stating that one's ancestors needed immediate ceremony, so I was skeptical about these out-of-the-blue messages. But my skepticism quickly turned to surprise as I discovered that these messages were not from a stranger but were from a friend I had met almost a decade prior and had lost touch with. Our lives had grown and moved in very different directions; I had sought out mysticism via an understanding of polytheism, and he had found his way to Haitian Vodou and completed his initiation as an *oungan asogwe,* the most senior level of the priesthood that confers full faculties for the conduction of ceremony, devotional activities, work for clients and *ti fèy* (spiritual children), and all that those areas of the religion entail.

After lots of catching up and eventually chatting about his experiences in sèvis lwa, he suggested that I attend a ceremony coming up at his spiritual mother's temple in Boston, Massachusetts, for Gede, the family of spirits understood to be the elevated dead in the religion. I was happy to accept this invitation with my philosophy of curiosity in mind. I would be able to experience something that was rarely accurately represented in the media, and I was thinking that I may come away with some interesting memories to reflect upon.

My friend was not going to be able to attend that ceremony, so I would be going alone without knowing anyone else there. In retrospect, there was clearly something special at work. I am quite introverted and somewhat shy, particularly in unfamiliar settings and in situations where I may not have a touchstone of a familiar face to accompany me. I certainly wasn't in the practice of going to religious events by myself in a community and religion I had no familiarity with and whose protocols I did not know. However, at the time, these thoughts did not even occur to me as a concern, and I excitedly made my plans to attend the all-night ceremony in the Mattapan neighborhood.

My biggest concern was how I would be received when I got there. What little I knew about Haitian Vodou had informed me that there was some Roman Catholic influence, and I was a bit worried that as a visibly queer and gender-nonconforming individual, I would be turned away or somehow found lacking, either because of my queerness or because I would not be wearing the same clothing as other assigned-female-at-birth individuals. I can realize now that this was my own fear brought on by my religious upbringing and baggage influencing my perception, particularly because my friend who initially extended the invitation is an out gay cis man, but it was certainly something I worried about in the days leading up to the *fèt.*

My fears were unfounded and the fèt itself became its own threshold. I was welcomed warmly and I stayed the whole night, enjoying the songs I didn't know, the orishas holding up the entire energy of the ceremony. As I prepared to leave when I thought the ceremony to be over, I learned that it was far from coming to an end. I was almost out the door and was pulled to the side by Gede, who was in possession of the lineage head of the house

I was visiting. I spoke no Haitian Kreyòl and Gede spoke no English, but one of the house members graciously translated. Gede told me emphatically that he had been walking with me for a long time and was happy I was there to see him. He asked if I would I come back and see him again. This was a situation I was entirely unprepared for; after all, I intended only to observe for a night and go home. But in that moment, I knew the value of an agreement with a spirit—even if I wasn't sure exactly what that fully entailed. When you are faced with that sort of question, you want to say yes, and so I did. I told Gede that I would be happy to return, and he nodded briefly, shook both my hands, and went on his way while I went on mine.

Gede had extended his hand and opened the door and brought me to its threshold. I found out later that Gede was welcome at all ceremonies, regardless of the function or the spirit(s) being honored, and that he can (and does!) largely arrive whenever he pleases; thus, my agreement to return and see him again had a bit of a catch to it. If Gede can arrive whenever he pleases, then I should make some effort to be there when that happens. I sat with this for a while and realized that he had set the hook for me to return to ceremonies regularly, and I had unknowingly bitten.

This was the beginning of my journey toward Ginen. If I am honest, I dragged my feet a lot. I did return to ceremonies regularly because I keep my promises and heard from spirits each time that this is where they wanted me to be and that the other places I was seeking spiritual fulfillment could not help me. I took that with the attitude of "uh-huh, that's nice" and kept it moving, spiritually speaking. I did not want to form ties with anyone or anything, and I was content with my own version of being a spiritual dandelion seed in that I went wherever the wind took me and was hesitant or not ready to put down roots. I had certainly done the more comfortable intellectual work of reading the information that was available on the religion and browsing burgeoning Facebook groups discussing how different people served the lwa, but I quickly learned that the religion couldn't live on a page, paper or otherwise, and my best option was to continue to put myself in the physical place where the lwa lived. My friends outside of the religion were and remain supportive and curious and were integral in the support of my initiation, whether financially or by providing me with rides to and from the airport or for extended shopping trips to gather what I needed.

In those small moments of the lwa encouraging me to open myself up to the possibility that there was something in Vodou for me, I was missing the significance of that and where it could fit in my life. I was struggling a lot in more ways than I could recognize or openly discuss and was barely scraping by personally and professionally. I felt trapped in a job that did not pay me enough that I could even look for other work, and my health was failing me significantly, yet almost constant doctor's appointments could not pinpoint what exactly was wrong except that what was happening in my body added up to something that was unsettling for my doctors and for me. I felt spiritually dry and as though I had hit a wall with my understanding and practice of polytheism, and I felt that my life was without direction or purpose yet that there had to be something bigger and better out there for me. I was miserable but also pretty damn stubborn. Things might have been bad, but it was *my* bad, and I could manage it all on my own.

However, I am true to my word, and so I kept going to ceremonies under the slightly misguided assumption that I could keep my promise and access these ceremonies without any further personal investment. Someone who is less stubborn than I may have decided that those messages from spirits might need to be explored with a trusted priest and might need divination—direct means of communicating with the lwa and understanding their will and requirements—to ascertain what exactly the spirits might have to say to me and to clarify my involvement and path. I, however, was more invested in my own ideas about my life than in listening to what anything else might have to say to me. I am grateful that the lwa humored me and saw fit to walk with my own self-determined ideas of what might be asked of me.

After patiently waiting for me, the lwa made things begin to tumble forward. A lwa arrived in possession during a fèt and asked me for *maryaj lwa*, a ceremony in which selected lwa arrive in possession to marry their spouse, complete with a priest pronouncing traditional vows, an exchange of rings, and sharing food. During the fèt, the lwa placed my hands between the hands of my now spiritual mother and solemnly washed us both with his perfume, indicating that he was literally placing me in her hands and thus under her spiritual care and guidance. Gede arrived that same night to tell me that I had obligations to him that I could not ignore, and several months later, another lwa arrived and told me that what I needed could only be found in the *djevo* (initiatory chamber). This meant becoming a Vodou priest.

Saying that I was unhappy about this would be a massive understatement. I initially had been able to accept maryaj lwa to meet the obligations the lwa wanted from me without making any other binding agreements or taking on any responsibility within the religion, but initiating into the religion seemed completely unreasonable to me. In being a pastor's kid, I was aware of the burden of clergy and absolutely wanted nothing to do with

Figure 1.2. A celebratory *vèvè* for Milokan, representing all nations of Iwa, Baptem, Sosyete Nago, Jacmel, Haiti. Photograph by Alex Batagi, 2016.

that. Further, there were much deeper concerns on my end. Why would someone like me—a queer, gender-variant White person—be involved in a majority Black religion? How could I be involved in an initiatory process that had a gendered outcome, in that you are made a *manbo* (female priest) or an *houngan* (male priest)? Where would the money come from to pay for the necessary ceremonies, and how was I going to go to Haiti to do it, as all initiations take place *nan peyi a* (in the country, Haiti) when I hadn't ever traveled internationally, didn't even have a passport, and spoke not one bit of Kreyòl?

This proposition and its attendant reality overwhelmed me. Shortly after *kanzo* was asked of me, Manbo Maude, the lineage head of Sosyete Nago, the Vodou house or community I had been attending ceremonies at for two years, went to Haiti for the house's yearly cycle of initiation and ceremonies celebrating the lwa who support the lineage and all its ti fèy (Vodou initiates or members of a particular sosyete). I spent that summer alternately crying about what my life had turned into once I agreed to marry the lwa and consulting every single diviner I knew to see whether there was a way out of what was being placed in front of me. In short, there was not.

When Manbo Maude returned from Haiti, I asked to talk, and we met for a long time. It was a conversation that I was very nervous to have. After a lot of consultation with others and a lot of prayer in front of my very small and very bare table for the lwa I felt I barely knew, I had come to a place where I realized that I did need external help changing my life and that the lwa had not yet let me down, even though what they asked felt unimaginable. I had no reason to say no, and so I was ready to say yes, but with two conditions: the lwa would need to help me find the money to complete all my ceremonies, and I would walk away if the only option was that I would be made a manbo, as I was assigned female at birth but have never aligned my identity with that label.

I told Manbo Maude that I wanted to do kanzo but felt that I could not live with being made a manbo as it felt as if I would be betraying myself to do so. The two-second pause before she responded was easily the longest two seconds of my life. I was still holding onto the fear that someone like me had no place because of who I am and who Bondyé had made me. Despite Manbo Maude never being anything but kind and welcoming and never even blinking when I came to all her ceremonies in pants and with my head uncovered, I was certain she was going to dismiss me out of hand and tell me she could not help me.

Her response quite honestly changed my life. She shrugged as if this was the most unimportant thing in the process and said, "Then I'll make you an houngan." This was such a nonissue for her that the next thing she did was ask me if I was hungry and start plating up *diri ak pwason* (rice and fish) for me. She left me with the impression that I was not the first transgender or gender-variant person to show up at her door needing the medicine the lwa can provide, but indeed I was the first, and she was willing to take a risk on me to help me save my own life while I followed the lwa into the djevo.

Kanzo is a word that really communicates an idea. It is not translated easily, but it can approximately be described as "initiation" or, perhaps most accurately, "trial by fire." It is an intense and intimate process of death, transformation, and rebirth done with the mutual hands of the lwa, the presiding houngan or manbo, and the community in and around the *lakou*. In an assemblage of ceremonies stretching up to several weeks or, in some areas of Haiti, a month or longer, an individual is prepared and cared for in a descent *anba dlo* (under the water) to the realm of the lwa while the presiding priest and their household complete physical and spiritual work to align their soul with the intentions the lwa have for them. For the individual undergoing kanzo, it can often be a surprisingly difficult process. It is long and can feel complicated, particularly when, as my *parenn* (Vodou godfather) coached me, it is a process done *to* you rather than *with* you.

At the end of the period of seclusion in the djevo, each new ti fèy is lifted from their long sleep by their now-parent. Each new initiate is first brought out of the initiation room, the djevo, in all-white clothing representing

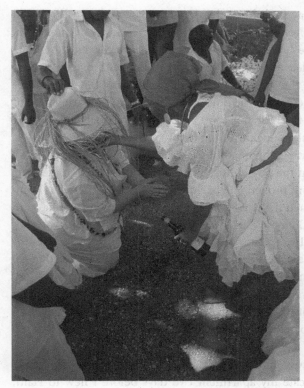

Figure 1.3. The author with Manbo Marie Maude Evans during the *Leve Kanzo* ceremony, Sosyete Nago, Jacmel, Haiti, 2016.

newness and purity, and a long fringe of *Ayizan* (palm fronds) is hung in front of the initiate's face to obscure their identity, as their journey is not yet complete. Later, the coolness of white clothes is replaced with clothes in bright colors and patterns for *baptem*, the ceremony where the new initiates are baptized and given their new names. It is after they receive their names that the palm fronds are lifted and their faces tipped up for all to see.

The ceremonies are complete, and they take a new place in the community. Each initiate now bears a new title; for some it is *hounsi*, an initiated member of the lakou; or oungan or manbo *sou pwen/si pwen*, a priest who can work for the lwa and for clients but may not confer the asson to others; or an houngan or *manbo asogwe*, who is a priest with full faculties to conduct all ceremonies and confer the asson onto others. Some houngan and manbo may be lifted with additional duties assigned to their initiation, such as *ountogi*, who is initiated specifically as a ritual orishamer; or *la plas*, an individual charged with the protection of the lakou, both practically and ritually. Still others may find themselves gravitating to other roles within the lakou, such as *houngenikon,* an individual who is a master of *chante lwa,* the songs sung for the lwa during ceremonies; *medsin fèy,* an individual with a mastery of the leaves and roots used for healing and magic; or even *mama* or *papa ounyo,* the individual charged with caring for the initiates while they are in the djevo and who does everything from preparing food to assisting in ceremony to enforcing good and appropriate behavior among the newly made hounsi, houngan, and manbo.

I went into this trusting only that if I did kanzo and hated it, I never had to go back. I embodied the pop culture mantra of "fake it 'til you make it" and found myself being proverbially stripped bare before I left for Haiti. The lwa were determined that I would rely fully on them, and so I gave up everything to follow them. When I was at the most difficult moment of not knowing whether I would be able to make it to Haiti for these ceremonies, I bought my plane tickets as insurance because that meant I had to go. Once I was there, my needs—transportation to and from the airport, food, lodging, and the day-to-day things—would be taken care of. My spiritual mother made sure that what I had paid for the ceremony would cover all the ceremony and associated needs; I only needed to bring myself and my clothes.

For me, even that was difficult, but the lwa held me up through it all. When I needed to vacate my apartment two days before I flew to Haiti, friends suddenly offered up storage space for my belongings. In the wee hours before I was to fly to Haiti, an Uber car driver arrived to help me move the last of my clothing to my friend's home, and it was a lwa in disguise: a beaming Haitian man dressed in blue jeans and a blue plaid shirt who just happened to be from the town I was going to. When my connecting flight was canceled and I would have to remain in the airport for twenty-four hours before I could go to Haiti, a flight crew gave me a pass to an airport lounge where I could finally get a little sleep. Each step of the way, my lwa held me up.

I arrived in Haiti having quit a failing job and abandoned an apartment and most of my belongings, and when last-minute finances fell through, I sold my car to afford the trip. Among a plane full of White missionaries, I arrived in Port-au-Prince with a suitcase filled with clothes still damp from being hastily washed and with no idea where I would end up or what I would come back to when I returned to the United States.

The seemingly simple acknowledgment that Manbo Maude would make me an houngan had been transformative and had allowed me possibly for the first time to trust a religious authority, but my real moment of full conversion from "fake it 'til I make it because I can just leave" to "I am going to spend the rest of my life learning and understanding this" came while I was in the womb of the djevo. While all details of what transpires inside that initiatory chamber are private and not to be shared, I can say that there was a moment after a ceremony was completed where it was almost as if my entire head was cracked open. I had this sudden and profound realization of the gravity of what I was doing and what had gone into my being able to reach that exact moment in time. It was not only the size and scope of the ceremonies and the community supporting that work, but the reality that my sacrifices and effort to be there had been met by incredible sacrifices and effort on the part of the spirits who I suddenly realized loved me beyond all comprehension and all ability to measure. I cried a lot leading up to and during kanzo for a variety of reasons, but significantly that was the first time I have ever cried out of gratitude and love.

When I was lifted from the djevo and rejoined the world, I was a different person, and the changes were tangible for me. During the process of initiation, I experienced what can only be described as miraculous healing for many of the health issues that were otherwise going to take my life in the not-too-distant future. I will never be the picture of perfect health, but I have never returned to the same state that I was in when I entered the djevo. I came away knowing and feeling that I was valued and was welcomed as a whole person without needing to change or alter who I was in order to deserve that. I found myself understanding that having roots was not a bad thing, and that family could be created through ties other than blood.

Perhaps the biggest change I came away with was knowing that my life now had purpose and that whatever happened, I was not alone in the world. As I have grown in my relationships with my lwa and with my spiritual mother and family, this has been cemented as a core part of my life. Conversion addresses not only spiritual and religious practice but also how we live our lives and what we do with the practice outside of the temple and sacred spaces.

Kanzo was only my beginning; I returned to Haiti the following year and completed my maryaj lwa there, on the ground that is the home of the spirits whom I strive to love as deeply as they love me. For me, this was an opportunity to begin to understand what vulnerability and being open and receptive means. The lwa held a mirror for me to see that I kept myself closed off and held back from potential harm that now may never manifest. They asked me to trust them and to keep my heart open, and so I have, even when it is a struggle and I want to close the doors and lock them.

This sometimes-painful practice has not gone unrewarded. In remaining available in this way, I have been able to start a new career that I excel in and that also has the dual purpose of fulfilling me and serving the people whom the lwa love as their own children. My identity as an artist was able to reawaken after a long sleep, and my work feels fruitful and rewarding. Perhaps most surprising was that my initial trip to Haiti introduced me to the man who is now my husband. A relationship was something I had convinced myself I did not desire, and yet the lwa challenged me to be vulnerable in a new way and have seen fit to provide a partner who sees me and loves me not despite who I am but *because* of it.

In exchange for these blessings and all these opportunities to grow, they have only asked for my fidelity. I deepen my spiritual practice by returning to Haiti and the temple as often as possible. I am also active in the temple that my mother maintains in the United States. To love them more fully, I have worked hard to learn Kreyòl, the language of the majority of practitioners and that of the gods in Haiti. To remember where I was before they found me and to remain transparent and humble in my growth, I have blogged about my experiences in the religion continuously since 2013. With my lwa, I have cocreated a life that brings them as close to me as possible while not closing the gate on what new opportunities and adventures they may bring to me.

My goal was never to be where I am right now, but I can't imagine anywhere better. What once was something I was only willing to tolerate has since become a part of me that I can't live without. I arrived as this closed-off, baggage-bearing person who didn't want other people and found religion poisonous, and the lwa granted me space that allowed me to see that they could change things, if only I let them. Nothing could have prepared me for what that meant, but it is in that lack of preparation that I found the grace of Ginen and the strength of the lwa. I am only a little leaf attached to a *gwo pyebwa* (a big tree) whose roots reach all the way to Ginen.

2

Death and Rebirth in African Vodún and Haitian Vodou

PHILIPPE CHARLIER

I was born in the town of Meaux, which lies to the northeast of Paris. My father is a doctor and my mother a pharmacist, and I followed in their scientific footsteps. In addition to becoming a medical doctor, I have trained in forensic science, anthropology, and paleopathology, the latter of which is the study of disease in ancient human and nonhuman remains, including those excavated from archaeological sites. I have built my career examining life, death, and the afterlife from a variety of angles, and I have always been fascinated by the circle of life. At the age of ten, I performed my first excavation—and found a human skull. Maybe that was an early portent of things to come, or maybe the experience served as a guide. I went on to study archaeology and art history at the Michelet Institute and later worked at the forensic medicine department at Raymond Poincaré University Hospital, a teaching facility in Versailles.

I have been fortunate enough to examine the remains of several historical figures, as well as the remains of those purported to be historical figures. To date, I have studied the remains of King Richard I, or Richard the Lionheart; Agnès Sorel, the mistress of King Charles VII of France; the children of Tutankhamun; and various relics of Louis IX, the only canonized king of France, which are now scattered throughout France. I was also able to confirm that the relics once thought to be of Joan of Arc were not, in fact, genuine. However, I was able to authenticate the presumed head of Henry IV. Conversely, in 2017, I confirmed previous findings that a jawbone fragment held in secret Soviet archives did in fact belong to Adolf Hitler.

As a doctor of medicine, of science, and of letters, I apply a variety of methods and interdisciplinary understanding to my research. I have supervised multidisciplinary teams and taught in France, West Africa, and other regions. In 2018, I was appointed as the Director of Research and Teaching at the Musée du quai Branly–Jacques Chirac in Paris, a museum that contains over three hundred seventy thousand indigenous works and cultural objects, mainly from Africa, the Near East, Asia, Oceania, and the Americas, from around 10,000 BCE to the twentieth century. I have authored books on rituals, ghosts, and zombies, and I have garnered a reputation for "allowing the dead to talk." Currently, I am the director of the *Terre Humaine* collection at Plon, a French publishing house famous for releasing ethnology and anthropology classics, including *Tristes Tropiques* (1973) by Claude Lévi-Strauss.[1] The following is my personal journey of encounters with Vodún religious practices in Benin and Haiti and their transformative power in my life and work.

Benin: My Call to Vodún

In 2006, when I was a medical intern at a university hospital in the north of France, I spent my days surgically excising and examining cancerous lungs, opening formalin-fixed intestines, and examining appendixes under a light microscope. In the sad and difficult monotony of this daily life, I got to know my work colleague, a Beninese student named Luc Brun. As my companion in mysteries and someone who shared in the emotional and psychic toil of our work, we became fast friends. Luc hailed from Parakou, in the northern part of Benin. When he finally returned home after acquiring his advanced degree, he invited me to come and teach medical anthropology at his university. To me, Parakou itself wasn't especially interesting, and my teaching-filled days in Benin passed quickly. But three days before returning to France, Luc told me that he had an ancestral home in Abomey, further south. Abomey was the capital of the Kingdom of Dahomey from the early seventeenth through the nineteenth centuries, and thus one of the most sacred and culturally rich cities in the country.

We immediately decided to board the night bus, and by dawn we had arrived and were blissfully seated at the foot of a giant tree in the garden of Luc's vast family compound—structures that must have been built at the turn of the twentieth century. My days in Abomey were incredible, a total revelation: I spent my time roaming the city, visiting the royal palace and Vodún temples, and being overwhelmed by the religion and Beninese culture. My senses were ignited. This initial stay was far too short, and as my Air France flight finally took off for Paris, it was a real effort to adjust and mentally prepare myself for the life and work that awaited me upon my return home. My mind was still very much lingering in the sacred shrines of those seemingly timeless Vodún temples.

Back in France I had one burning desire: to return to Benin as soon as possible. From then on, every year, I made a point of going back to Abomey, feeling called by the spirits. The need was visceral, and the call was unequivocal. There are few places where I feel perfectly at peace and in my element: the Greek Islands—especially Naxos and Eastern Crete; Emilia-Romagna, in the north of Italy—especially in Bologna; and southern Benin. I was able to return annually to Benin by teaching university courses and conducting my own research projects. There, as I walked through the alleys of fetish markets, offered libations on the tombs of the ancient kings of Abomey, and honored the memory of the Amazons who resisted the French military at the end of the nineteenth century, I felt as though I was following in the footsteps of the gods. I was fully present, taking in everything with all my senses and my soul. And ultimately, I was undergoing a spiritual transformation.

There was something inexorable about my being called to Vodún. I wanted to see and feel, totally feel, and understand. It seemed to me that the best way to interpret these rituals that encompassed life, illness, and death was to confront them spiritually while diving right into them. During one of my trips, after leaving class, a student came to see me. He was in his fourth or fifth year of studying medicine at the University of Parakou. I had previously expressed to him my wish to attend a Vodún ceremony and had explained that my knowledge was limited to what I had gleaned from reading widely on the subject, including testimonies from unreliable authors (sensationalizing adventurers or Catholic clerics with their noxious gaze). My frustration was real, my expectations immense.

I still remember the moment he called out to me as I left the classroom, my binder of messy notes wedged under my arm. With two or three friends he approached me, calling out: "Professor Philippe!" There were still a lot of students in the classroom, and it was late in the afternoon. Many would soon be meeting up in an open bar (*maquis*) to drink a Fanta, a Beaufort beer, or a nonalcoholic Malta. The student told me:

Professor Philippe! We have given a lot of thought to your account. And we know what you need. My brother Franck is a high-ranking worshipper. He's okay with you getting closer to Vodún, but you shouldn't just attend the initiation. You must live it. If you agree, next year, you too will be initiated.

We ended up in the maquis, like the others. Luc Brun joined us a little later. There they explained to me what I already knew. That you don't have to struggle, that one must accept what is stronger and larger than us when given the opportunity. I was curious, eager, and, above all, ready. I had to quench this thirst for knowledge and religious experience. After all, I could only be a better teacher by knowing inside what I sensed outwardly about my teaching. Thus, I incorporate into my pedagogical philosophy the suggestion of additional dimensions in objects and art, whether from sub-Saharan Africa or elsewhere. I encourage my students to look beyond the surface when examining an object or work of art and to try and find (perhaps feel?) the inherent sacredness in art. Alongside the idea of the sacred, I ask students to ponder how such objects are related to ritual and I ask them to go beyond notions of beauty or the aesthetically pleasing and to include the mundane or everyday materialism into this frame. I ask students to adopt different lenses—cultural, spiritual, philosophical, and so on—when working. I encourage them to reflect on and perhaps try to sense the vitality of an object, no matter what it may be; human remains, for example, shouldn't be thought of or viewed as just extracted abstracted pieces of body or dead remains, but rather as entities with meaning, having an animation, having something more than a mere past purpose.

Transformation: Sakpata, Ritual Death, and Rebirth

That year in France was a long one, but it finally passed. Buying my plane ticket to Cotonou was like a deliverance. That year, in 2013, at the age of thirty-six, is when I died ritually. A new breath was imparted to me, and my eyes opened differently. I was consecrated to Sakpata, a venerable deity of the earth and of healing, medicine, and divine justice. He rules over communal illness and could either heal or, if offended, bring about epidemics. For the ceremony, my skin had been incised and prepared to carry the energy of this formidable spirit, as well as to bring about my oracular sign of Fa divination (an art that is widespread south of the Sahara), which characterizes and determines my present existence and future trajectory in life. I shared ceremonial libations under the auspices of the Sakpatasi—his high priests—who toasted me on the accomplishment of my initiation with a warm welcome that signaled acceptance into the community. To cement this pact, I also received the insignia of Sakpata, his sacred beaded necklace, which was placed around my neck by my new spiritual family. In my death and rebirth, I had shed blood, and blood was shed for me.

The ceremony was powerful, arduous in parts, and different from anything religious I had experienced before that moment. Through these rituals, and in a very real way, Sakpata fused with my soul: he is a father, a king, a noble warrior who takes pride and care over his children, and I continue to learn the intricacies of venerating him, the ways to call him, his devotional songs, and how to maintain contact with the religious lineage who graced me with his energy through consecration.

I cannot reveal many details of the actual ceremony as they remain confidential, much like patient-doctor relationships. I do remember the sleep and food deprivations, wearing nothing but a loincloth that was almost as white as my skin, while bare-chested and barefooted. I was sequestered in an initiation abode that had a compacted floor of red laterite—one of Sakpata's colors and materials. My ritual time was spent making offerings in the sacred forest. Many of the ceremonies for Sakpata are conducted in the dead of night. We would exit the chamber and enter the sacred grove for these special, sacred night walks—processions that were accompanied by dance, percussion, and songs. I remember those looks, those salutations, those hugs. This initiatory whirlwind seemed suspended in time, but in a pleasing way: within that chamber and that sacred forest, time stopped its rhythmic ticking. Sakpata's intense, hot energy was like flames that licked and curled and crackled in the dark. It all made sense and felt familiar. I also recall and can see myself lying on the cool floor of a chamber in the stillness of dawn, eagerly anticipating the days and nights ahead, knowing that with every moment in this sacred, healing space, I was transforming, becoming something different from and yet even more myself.

As important and alive as religious objects and icons are, to me it is the essence and experiences of the spirit that touched me the deepest during my ritual time in Benin. Vodún is quintessentially a marriage of the physical and invisible dimensions of human experience, and while I underwent a carefully supervised ritual rebirth, a critical part of the process was the consecration of sacred materials that would become the foci for my personal devotion. There was a creative aspect of the initiation process where my deities and tools were crafted and in whose material forms the divine was made present.

Of the objects that were brought into tangible existence during my initiation, one is a small movable altar for Legba, the Vodún god of communication between the worlds, that I carry with me when I travel. I carried my Legba nestled in its bespoke wooden box with me back to France, and he makes the best travel companion. Legba ensures safety during travels, and

I make frequent libations of red palm oil to keep him happy as he is also owner and bearer of chaos when overlooked. I also received a belt made of goatskin that contains medico-spiritual preparations or charms called *gris-gris* to ward off harm from the wearer. Oh, and there was the wrought iron ritual ring that I received. Worn on the left hand and a protection and sign of affiliation, upon seeing it my wife was momentarily convinced that I had remarried in Benin! But for me, it is the spiritual that is the most important aspect, not the material. Following my initiations, a spirit regularly presents themselves to me in my dreams—which are another form of peremptory communication of the divine alongside divination and possession—and when this spirit appears to me, I know to pay close attention because it will reveal important events that will play out in my waking life in the days following the visit. The spirit has advised and prepared me for both good and bad moments in my life, and I am grateful.

Without hesitation I can say that this initiation changed my life. It fundamentally altered my senses in some way—maybe it retuned them? I began to see and make my way differently in the world. In my new way of seeing, I felt I had the tools within me to consider life and orient myself and my purpose in the world. My initiation revealed the animate nature of my surroundings: in Vodún, hardly anything is considered inert or without some sort of animating force behind it. Through this orientation I began to sense spiritual circuitry, a sort of invisible energy that circulates everywhere, at times cresting and dispersing but infinite. Vodún rituals help crystallize and call on specific energies—those attributed or contributed to by deities and ancestors. But this energy can also be stolen, captured, or diverted to the wrong hands. I know that this sense of vibrancy and animate forces in the world is not new or unique to Vodún. But to me, before my experience, it was more of an abstract concept than a perceived reality. Afterward, I saw how fundamental this awareness is for those seeking to understand the full complexity of the world.

Being initiated into Beninese Vodún was my first step in an ongoing journey, something that went well beyond the simple label of personal experience. My initiatory and apprenticeship activities didn't end there. The experience prompted me to seek out membership in several adjacent secret societies, and I went through the stages of membership or induction into their priesthoods. I learned the mechanics and philosophy of Fa divination. Based on binary signs that are produced and revealed by the priest, and using prepared seeds, chains, or shells, it involves a vast body of oral wisdom divided into chapters (*Du*), relating to its 256 possible combinations.

Chief among these initiations was my admittance into the cult of *Egungun*, an ancestral masquerade fraternity that brings treasured elders back to the community by sacred acts. Although Egungun performances concern the dead, they are about more than just contacting the other world; they have important social functions in matters of the living, and they demonstrate, viscerally, that our distance from the departed isn't so great a divide. Some Egungun ancestors, for example, have acquired a postmortem status comparable to that of protective deities of the home. Such elevated elders are called upon by their families and communities during Egungun ceremonial outings, as they are known to deliver important messages to the living. They are also a sight to behold, as Egungun arrives in the specially prepared, dazzling costumes worn by initiates, whose bodies, while in costume, are temporarily occupied by the visiting dead. In a village Egungun outing, you will see a group of enrobed spirits: twisting, turning, speaking with their signature deep voice from the beyond, and surrounded by attendants and music. Onlookers can venture close to them, but it is dangerous to get too close lest the departed whisk a person away. The community is brought together by such events, and everyone is reminded of how much they depend on those ancestors who went before them and continue to rely on wisdom and counsel from those who mean them well.

In Search of the Dead in Haiti

I traveled to Haiti in 2014 to investigate the ritual undead *zonbi* (which unfortunately gave rise to the stereotyped and dramatized Hollywood zombies that we see in movies), a phenomenon first introduced to wider North American and European publics in William Seabrook's racialized and sensationalized book *The Magic Island* (1929).[2] My initial trip was planned solely to undertake an anthropological survey of zombies; however, once in Haiti, I was totally and happily immersed and enamored by the country. I discovered a great deal more there than I had ever imagined possible, especially in the sumptuous and complex rites of life and death in Vodou and the spirits or lwa who inflected the country so deeply that they never felt far away. I felt unbelievably lucky and beyond privileged to experience such richness in ritual daily. I have returned twice so far to the island to continue my studies of Vodou. At the time, I knew a little about the Haitian community in France, and the French in Haiti, but our links developed considerably afterward, spurring several other work and research trips. I was received and embraced in the courtyards of Vodou temples like a brother as the community acknowledged and validated my initiation in West Africa. Having been initiated in Benin, I had acquired a sort of intermediate status between the Haitian Vodou initiate and the ancestors. As such, alongside the *houngan* (Vodou priest) Erol Josué, I was permitted to enter the *djèvo* (Vodou initiatory chamber) to handle prepared spirit bottles that held the souls of certain members of the community—either dead or still living— and could see, taste, touch, hear, and breathe contemporary Vodou traditions that were like my experiences in Benin. Since my initiation in 2013, I have come to learn and appreciate how Beninese Vodún and Haitian Vodou fully, and at times overwhelmingly, engage all of one's senses.

Despite having a well-established Haitian diaspora, Vodou is not very well known in France, or it isn't very visible among most of the population. When we talk about it or see it on TV, it is the stereotypical mess of *voodoo!* that is promulgated by the sensationalist global media and designed to give goosebumps and send the heart racing rather than creating a forum for African-centered dialogue or to understand Black experiential worldviews of spirits, the community, and the ancestors. There is still a great deal of educational work to be done in France and Europe in this regard.

As someone who works in a museum and is confronted with myriad assemblages of art and cultural materials from Africa and elsewhere, the ways of seeing and interacting with objects that I learned in Benin and Haiti has given me what I call a type of *Vodún vision*. I have developed a deep appreciation for the energy contained or present in presumed inanimate, static objects. It has somewhat changed my outlook. As such, I believe that there is a vitality in everything. This spirited vision can be called *circulating energy*, and it informs how I appreciate and have respect for the objects around me and that inhabit this world alongside us, pulsing with an indescribable force that feels good to contemplate upon. French cultural anthropologist, explorer, and writer Jean Malaurie wrote of a shamanic vision of the universe.[3] Accordingly, I embrace the idea of an absence of inertia. To my mind, it is the same kind of vibrancy inherent in human corpses or Byzantine icons, or a marble representation of Aphrodite or a Shiva Lingam from Rajasthan. Thus, far from being inert *things*, there is something that animates them, discreetly. In any case, they demand our consideration and our thoughts. Nothing is totally inert. Nothing. It is because we do not easily see or perceive its vitality, energy, and mobility that it is easy to dismiss.

With each initiation level I experienced, the philosophy and symbolism of dying and being reborn were revealed to me with correspondingly greater complexity. In Vodún there is typically a public, external feature of a ritual, and this face is grafted onto its esoteric, or hidden and private, aspects. By this I mean that Vodún is outwardly identified by a plethora of ritual symbols, clothing, gestures, and materials, yet there are entirely different ways of reading their relevance. Its symbolism has multiple layers of interpretation, and that is a key part of its magic. A casual observer may see an object, or view a part of the ceremony, and not grasp the beauty, depth, and complexity of what is being conveyed. It is a visual, verbal, and material language, hidden in plain sight, all the while connecting the living to the unseen worlds of the dead and the deities.

For those of us who have undergone initiations and followed the path of successive rites, it is as if we have been placed within a boundless center of learning, where doors open onto other corridors, themselves lined with further portals to pass through and explore. The progression within Vodún sometimes happens incrementally. At times the divinities reveal themselves with very human appearances, and other times they represent deeper commonalities. They can express moral characteristics or even abstract philosophical concepts, in ways that go beyond anthropomorphically realistic or historically situated figures and narratives.

Being an initiate can also be very frustrating, as one's religious education happens only when the elders and deities want to teach, and only when they deem the candidate ready and worthy, not when the student thinks they have earned it, or—God forbid—when they demand it! A word of warning to the impatient, Western-educated seeker: a direct question can be ignored or answered with ten more questions. In those cases, just when you think you are on the verge of grasping something, you can feel like you know even less than you did before.

Since my initiation back in 2013, I have given much thought to the unseen and to perceptions of the world around us. I think that Vodún can instill a way of sensing or becoming more sensitive to the invisible and the evanescent. When I see and participate in Vodún ceremonies, immersed in the sensorium that includes the divine and the dead, I get an impression of, or perhaps a heightened sensitivity to, the multiple layers of meaning anchored to various material forms, including statues, shrines, and practices. I feel a certain impression or echo of the porosity between realms: just as we use science and other tools to see and interact with our material world's complexity, Vodún contains a wisdom that equips the initiate to navigate barriers or see through appropriate filters or lenses as circumstances arise.

As a forensic investigator, archaeologist, and anthropologist, I do not think my religious initiations detract from my Cartesian-based training or my pragmatic mindset. Firmly rooted in science beforehand, so I remain. However, and crucially, I now know the limits to my knowledge. Or, better put, I know that my knowledge has frontiers, and I try to cultivate a sensitivity and openness to exploring and expanding them. I recognize that the human mind has its limits; there are concepts or events that, even with the strongest will in the world, are impossible to fully comprehend though any one paradigm. There will always be anomalies and the utterly unexplainable.

Texts, Anthropology, and Interpreting Sacred Experience

I like to say that my initiations have added a prismatic perspective to how I see and understand the universe. These sacred experiences changed my fundamental approach to grasping death's meaning. My thinking has pivoted from viewing death as a stage that is the opposite of birth. In my long and complex history of working with death, dying, and the body, while training in hospitals and elsewhere, I have sought to unravel some of the mysteries and intricacies of death. And after encountering and directly confronting Vodún rituals of death in Benin, I came to see death in a complete continuity with life. It is a change of state that does not correspond easily with outright disappearance or an abrupt end. Similarly, my initiations changed my way of grasping the meaning of ritual objects—not only practical objects but also those explicitly imbued with sacred meaning and elemental energy—and thus objects that are sacred in themselves. Just as people die, so can objects become desacralized, or returned to a state of sacred inertness, something that requires well-codified ceremonies and can be potentially dangerous for officiants and their entourage if not handled appropriately.

From my experience, the path of Vodún is a long one, and for me it is not over. At least I hope not. There is still a long way to go and so much to experience: shrines to explore, divinities to discover, legends to hear, and elders to meet. I have wanted to leave a written testimony of my Vodún journey and what it has taught me, which led me to write an anthropological book called *Vaudou: l'homme, la nature et les dieux* (Vaudou: Man, nature, and the gods).[4]

Publications for a general comparative anthropology readership can often trend toward haphazard and sloppy cultural interpretations. Thus, I wanted my own book on Vodún to follow the best of the anthropological writing tradition: integrating careful hypotheses on rituals and objects gathered from radically different contexts, always respecting their contextual particularities. Just as Noh masks of traditional Japanese theater, spatial symbolism in Gothic cathedrals in central France, or the organization of funeral offerings and banquets in Etruscan necropolises in northern Italy all had their historical specificity, so I worked consciously to avoid intellectual opportunism and to treat Vodún in its full context. But at the same time, I treated the project as one where Vodún could open a portal to deeper understanding of our world. That book, my Vodún initiations, my career, and even writing this chapter have all been steps for me in a larger journey, starting from a home base, a fixed point, a bit like a Benin village square, where one could find the shrine of To-Legba, but with the destination yet unknown. All I know is that I will now be able to shine with the blessings of the deities and the ancestors.

3

Crossed Paths

On Becoming Both Anthropologist
and *Omo Orixá*

GIOVANNA CAPPONI

Early Signs: Anthropology, Drums, and Orishas

My anthropological (and spiritual, as I would discover later) journey started with an almost obsessive interest in music and percussion during my adolescence. The boring, 4/4 rhythmic patterns of Western pop music were not very satisfying to me. Instead, I liked to listen to West African tunes (from Mali, Senegal, Burkina Faso), and I would spend all my pocket money on orishas, rattles, and percussive instruments of every sort. My admittedly young imagination would infuse these sounds from distant countries with a certain exoticism. The memory of these early, exoticizing associations has continued to haunt my thinking, writing, and career, ever since my first university lesson on postcolonial theory.

Still, there was not much sophistication to be expected of a teenager growing up in a provincial town on the Italian Adriatic coast. My exotic imaginings were both reinforced and challenged during our holidays, when my father and I would join an old friend of his—a photojournalist working for *National Geographic*—on his trips overseas. For me, these travels doubled as expeditions to collect instruments, music tapes, and language books, all of which were extremely precious in a predigital streaming era: a sitar from Jaisalmer, a sistrum from Lalibela, a didgeridoo from Perth, and other treasures.

In 2002, when I was fifteen, a new teacher came to my school. His biology classes were unmemorable, but his passion for music was contagious. Amedeo—his name—worked as a science teacher by day, but he performed

as a percussionist by night and gave music lessons as a side-career. He organized a *batucada*[1] workshop at school, and I soon became one of his most
engaged students. Being specialized in Afro-Cuban style, Amedeo soon
convinced me to buy a set of congas. And here began an intense, confusing period, made up of long, obsessive afternoons spent attempting circular
patterns on the claves, weaving beads around *shekere* gourds, and learning
by heart the intoxicated chorus of rumba tunes. In his scrupulous explanations of Afro-Cuban intricate rhythmical patterns, Amedeo would reference the ritual use that those patterns had in their African context, still very
much present in the diaspora. Since I kept asking questions about these
usages, showing early signs of anthropological interest, one day he gave me
a book he had brought back from Cuba. It was a Spanish photocopy of *Los
orishas en Cuba* by Natalia Bolívar Aróstegui,[2] carefully wrapped with plastic ring-binding.

From then on, my musical afternoons would alternate with attempts to
translate the book with a pocket dictionary that omitted most Cuban Spanish vocabulary. I was fascinated by the descriptions of the orishas, their
characteristics and their favorite food. Two orishas were particularly attractive to me: one was Obatalá, the creator of the world and of all human
heads, the king dressed in white; the other was Erinlé, the river orisha of
fishing and herbal medicine. This process of identification is what Vagner
Gonçalves da Silva has called a "seduction game."[3] Humans approaching
Afro-diasporic religions tend to soon start asking themselves: which one
would be my *orisha de cabeza*, the guardian of my head and spiritual identity?

Amedeo, a fervent Christian, kept repeating to me not to get too involved in those things, "otherwise you will be stuck with silly taboos, like
'you cannot eat chicken or go to the beach.'" Indeed, his mentor and music
teacher, one of Italy's best professional percussionists, was one of those who
"got too involved." His name was Roberto "Mamey" Evangelisti, a tall, slim
man with polite manners and a severe expression, whom we would invite
once or twice a year for rumba workshops. Originally from Rome, Roberto
spent half of the year in Cuba fulfilling musical and spiritual commitments.
As he led our rumba ensemble session or explained the rhythms on the *batá*
orishas, we could glimpse black and red bead necklaces (the colors of the
orisha Eleguá) peeking out from under his shirt collar.

One day, Amedeo gave me a pirated copy of a compact disc. He had
originally given it to another student, who did not appreciate it very much.
He told me, "It is Brazilian music from the seventies, I think you would

like it." The CD contained the album *Os Afro-Sambas* by Baden Powell and Vinícius de Moraes, a classic masterpiece of Brazilian popular music. Almost every song contained a reference to the orixás, the Brazilian counterpart of the Yorùbá deities I had read about. And thus, alongside my Afro-Cuban musical explorations, I began studying Afro-Brazilian music. Along with other music students, I had joined a couple of percussion street bands led by Amedeo. We would rehearse *Afrosamba, batucada, frevo,* and other genres, and would perform them at town events around Ancona.

When I was not playing, I was training in the Brazilian martial art of capoeira with one of the first groups present in Italy at the time. The name of the group was Capoeira Ogûm, the orixá of warfare and metal. I found myself trying to translate once again, but this time it was song lyrics and capoeira chants, and this time the pocket dictionary was Brazilian Portuguese. Without realizing it, the orishas, in their multiple diasporic forms, started populating my imagination: popping out of song lyrics, being evoked by clave patterns, and appearing in the rare online content I could find in that primitive and utopian era of the internet. One day, while trying to find information online, I stumbled upon the website of a cultural association called Association of the Diffusion of Candomblé (ADICA).[4] It was in Piedmont, more than five hundred kilometers from my hometown. The rudimentary ADICA website had only a few uploaded images, a few explanations about the orixás, and an updated calendar of annual festivals and events. But its unassuming communication lingered in my mind.

First Dance

In 2006, I left Ancona and moved to Bologna to attend the university. My still unresolved exoticizing tendencies led me to choose anthropology as my core discipline. Unfortunately, my conga orishas were too big and loud for my shared student apartment, and soon I got bored playing alone, without the support of Amedeo's lessons or the batucada bands. Gradually, my hands were reaching for anthropology books more than percussive instruments, and my first exams challenged my perceptions and worldview in unexpected ways. I became a bit more conscious of my prejudices and my (post)colonial projections of otherness. This new perspective was the beginning of a lifelong process of deconstructing many feelings and ideas I had held in the past. My nascent anthropological awareness, together with regrets of having abandoned my musical hobby, made me even more curious about Afro-diasporic religion.

One year later, I found myself puttering around the internet, looking for Santería or Candomblé temples or practitioners in Italy, when the ADICA website popped up again. I decided to send them an email. A few weeks later, someone got back to me and provided a phone number. I called and arranged a visit to the *terreiro* (temple) for the following week. On that morning, I took a train to Vercelli, where a tall man in his forties, Pai Mauro, the *babalorixá* (Candomblé priest) of the Candomblé house, picked me up at the station. He kindly offered to drive me to Arborio, where the temple was located, to show me around. I entered the terreiro, in this instance a country house surrounded by rice paddies, with a tidy garden where one could notice a few *assentamentos* (receptacles of the spiritual entities) partly hidden by the vegetation. The *barracão*, the indoor space where the celebrations were held, was large and somber, with small, framed pictures of the orixás and clean, white tiles on the floor. Pai Mauro had me sit in a room with some bookshelves, a coffee table, and two chairs. I asked a few questions about aspects of Candomblé that were still very unclear to me: the different roles and hierarchies in the religious community, the taboos of novices, the characteristics of the orixás. I soon noted how Pai Mauro, an Italian man with a pragmatic approach, spoke of his spiritual "sons," but also of his "clients."

Until that moment, I had had no idea of the relationship between Afro-diasporic religions and magico-religious practices—of these religions *as* magico-religious practices—a theme that became so central in my academic research and was an essential, widely explored issue in the literature. Indeed, Pai Mauro's primary occupation was attending to clients with problems to solve (from financial issues to romances) and performing rituals for spiritual healing, prosperity, and the like. Later I would discover that, both in Europe and Brazil, Candomblé practitioners come to Afro-diasporic religions by means of a variety of other inquisitive worlds, including tarot reading, bioenergetic healing, Reiki, ufology, but also politics, illness, and personal crisis. As Mattijs van de Port observes, what these engagements all have in common is the contemplation of the existence of different realities and realms of possibilities.[5]

However, as I told Pai Mauro, I had no problems to be solved at that moment: I was twenty years old, I was healthy, and I had many interests to pursue. My interest in Candomblé at the time was a mixture of anthropological and personal curiosity, and I was there to understand more about this world. "Let us see, then," Pai Mauro said, and removed the white cloth from the coffee table, revealing his *jogo de búzios*, a divination set with

Figure 3.1. Pai Mauro de Ayrá and his first initiate, Tiziana de Oxalá, after a ceremony. Photograph by Giovanna Capponi, 2015.

cowrie shells. In this first session, the orixá who responded was Oxum, the river goddess of femininity, love, and fertility. I was a bit surprised, as I did not recognize myself in the few (very stereotypical) descriptions I had read about this orixá. However, here started a game of constant alignment with my personal deity, looking for signs of Oxum in my own traits. I left the Candomblé house a bit puzzled, but I decided to come back for the next celebration. After all, despite my mixed feelings of attraction, skepticism, and curiosity, I still wanted to see the orixás dance.

Their next public event was in May 2007. Following Pai Mauro's instructions, I arrived on a Thursday afternoon. I was unsure of what to expect. It was the *festa* of Oxalá, the father of all the orixás, the deity of peace, whiteness, and purity. I participated in different parts of the ritual—those permitted to the noninitiated. On Sunday morning, the day of the public festa, while the rest of the outsiders were arriving and taking seats among the audience, the members of the religious community found some festive clothes for me and threw me in my first *roda* (ceremony in which devotees dance in a circle). I will not indulge in the details of that first dance. I remember feeling ashamed, surprised, excited, and slightly nervous. I tried to mimic the steps of the people around me as I recognized the Afro-Cuban rhythmic patterns I had studied years earlier being played on the atabaque orishas. I also remember my first contact with a very old Oxalá, who hugged me and left me on the floor in an emotional state while a snail (Oxalá's votive animal) was crawling undisturbed toward the middle of the room. Indeed, I was experiencing precisely those mysterious coincidences that populate most accounts of people experiencing the "magic" of Afro-diasporic religions.

A Contested Head: Identification, Foreignness, and Bodily Experience

For a couple of years after attending the Candomblé ceremony, I perceived that first encounter with the world of the orixás as a sort of one-off experience. I moved to Barcelona to study. I became busy with the challenges of living in a new country, and I started exploring other realms and opportunities that my field of studies opened for me. However, there was something unresolved about that brief experience. Questions that I could not fully answer kept coming back in my mind. As soon as I moved back to Italy to complete my degree, I decided that the terreiro of Arborio would become the focus of my bachelor's dissertation. I spoke about it to Pai Mauro and I started to attend Candomblé ceremonies as part of my research practice. That proved to be not only an excellent first fieldwork experience but also a space to start familiarizing myself with the language, etiquette, and social structure of Candomblé. Most importantly, I slowly became aware of and started to incorporate the sensorial dimension of its rituals: the chants, dances, gestures, and smells, all integral parts of the religious practice. This process of embodied learning continued well after completing my degrees, as I would sporadically attend Candomblé ceremonies with a mixture of anthropological and personal interest.

During the years in which I was learning how to conduct myself in that unusual space, I started developing a stronger identification with the deity who had answered my first *jogo de búzios*, the orixá Oxum. The identity-making process is typically led by and constructed together with the Candomblé community, whose members often comment on and make jokes about one's behaviors, personality, and attitudes, based on the characteristics of his or her orixá. This game of pairing humans and gods plays with stereotypes and archetypes, but it also has the power to discipline Candomblé followers and point out their human imperfections. One day, an *ekede* (high-ranking female initiate) and daughter of Oxum herself started making jokes about my messy curls and said: "With your hair in that state, you cannot be a daughter of Oxum! Maybe you are a daughter of Logun Edé!" By alluding to the fact that I was not displaying the stereotypical feminine traits of vanity and beauty associated with Oxum, the ekede suggested I was probably more connected to the orixá Logun Edé; also written as Logunedé or Ologunedé, this orixá, child of Oxum and Oxossi (the hunter god), is depicted as an androgynous deity because he retains both the feminine and masculine traits of his parents. A few years later, a second jogo de búzios confirmed that the guardian orixá of my head was indeed Logun Edé. Every person has an orixá who is like a parent, overseeing and caring for the person throughout their life, and ultimately determining which priesthood the adherent can be initiated into. At that moment, my social and personality traits and those of my orixá finally aligned in the eyes of the religious community. Indeed, it is common for Oxum and Logun Edé, orixás with similar energies, to swap places and "fight" for the same human head.

In 2014, I started a PhD in London, focusing on human-environment and human-animal interactions in Afro-Brazilian religions, and I came back once again to the terreiro in Arborio as a researcher. As I continued reading about the topic, more aspects of Candomblé cosmology and its worldview started to make sense to me. I also immensely enjoyed participating in its rituals, despite the long, exhausting nights spent preparing the offerings, the difficult gestures and postures required of low-ranking novices, and the bewilderment that these experiences sometimes brought about. One day, Pai Mauro's spouse, a Brazilian *mãe de santo* (Candomblé priestess) and Iyalaxé (high-ranking position of responsibility in the temple) of the temple, told me, "A Candomblé house needs all types of different energies." In her view, the disputes, conflicts, and sorrows experienced in the terreiro, together with its joys, fun, and calmness, all served to fully embrace the orixás as natural forces of the most diverse kind. I think it was precisely this aspect of Candomblé's worldview that started growing on me: the inclusion and sublimation of everything that is made available in life, the high biodiversity of energies, the multiplicity of material elements and lived experiences that are incorporated and valued.

Through all this time, I had slowly transitioned from casual guest to community participant. Noninitiated participants in the Candomblé hierarchy are called *abian,* which defines a status of preinitiation whereby someone is considered part of the community while still not allowed to participate in its secret rituals. This status felt very comfortable to me as a researcher, as I was concerned that closer involvement would put my anthropological perspective at risk. At that time, nothing worried me more than being criticized by my academic peers for getting too close to the object of my study. But at the same time, I was terrified of being accused by members of the religious community of gaining illicit access to its religious secrets for the mundane purposes of my research. These double-edged ethical questions haunted me for years—until a series of events forced me to reconsider the importance of a researcher's own experiences and involvement, aspects that Western academia had refused to explore for far too long.

In June 2014, an Italian woman, daughter of Oxum, decided to be initiated into the Arborio Candomblé house. As part of my fieldwork, I followed the whole ritual process from beginning to end. The initiation requires the novice to spend a week (or more) in seclusion, to have his or her head shaved, and to perform a series of offerings. One day, during a ritual dance called *perfuré*, in which the novice is taken out of the seclusion room to learn the different dance steps of the orixás, something strange happened to me. As the ijexá rhythm played on the orishas, I felt an intense heat hitting my head. This energy was powerful, like sound waves coming out of a huge electric speaker. My eyelids became heavy, and my head became light. It was a beautiful feeling, which I could not compare to anything I had experienced before, yet my heartbeat increased to a worrying speed. I started sweating, and my arms and legs started tingling. Slowly, these sensations faded away, leaving me in total bewilderment. Had I just experienced a form of trance possession? Was that feeling a sign of Logun Edé (my orixá guardian) wanting to dance with his mother, Oxum? Was my anthropological detachment failing me?

About a year later, when I had almost convinced myself that my previous experience had been caused by a sort of "fieldwork stress disorder," my orixá manifested again, this time in the middle of a public celebration dedicated to Oxalá. As I was standing aside, enjoying the festa from a safe corner, the same feelings of dizziness came to me, but this time they were even stronger. I froze and started trembling, unable to move, with my eyelids cemented closed. I remember the mãe de santo coming and taking me to dance in the roda. I also remember feeling somehow ashamed, as that intimate contact with my orixá was being exposed during such a public ceremony.

That event was the beginning of a very strange and confusing period. The Candomblé community had started pressuring me to formalize my ties with my orixá. However, I was still confused and worried about what a full initiation would mean for my life and research. The blessing of those close encounters with the invisible world started feeling like a curse. I had trouble explaining what had happened to me, to either my partner or to family members and friends. And I still had no idea how to resolve my ethical predicaments in ethnographic terms. How was I to maintain critical objectivity as a researcher, safeguard the religious community's protected knowledge, all while trying to understand my own embodied experiences? The lack of initial support in both my social and academic environment compounded my own feelings of foreignness. Indeed, the distant world I had imagined through books and music as an adolescent now had a heavy immediacy with real consequences. No one had prepared me for how to handle them.

Becoming Both Iyawó and Researcher

Part of the distress of that period was because my anthropology fieldwork was not yet complete. I had focused the first part of my research on the Italian case study while only conducting limited, preliminary research in Brazil. Before making any more decisions, I felt I needed a fuller understanding of the complex and diverse world of Afro-Brazilian religions. But how could I involve myself with this different world while still feeling so foreign?

In October 2015, I went to São Paulo, where most of my contacts were located. I soon realized I needed to vastly expand my research ties. I started to attend every Candomblé or Umbanda ceremony as well as every festa, public event, activist group meeting, or conference talk I came across. These experiences helped me enormously in situating the Candomblé house in Arborio within a broader picture. The diversity of ritual forms, social organizations, traditions, and hierarchical rules I encountered gave me a better idea of the complex world of Afro-diasporic religions in Brazil. All of this was great for my research, but it also became essential to my own personal understanding.

Most importantly, I had the privilege of meeting wonderful people, including those who were both anthropologists and active Candomblé followers. They became close friends and showed me that it is possible to participate in the enchantments and pleasures of Afro-religious practice without losing one's critical perspective. Collaborating with "native anthropologists," or "insider researchers," has been to date one of my most transformative experiences and one that guided me in decolonizing my perspective as a researcher.

Figure 3.2. Giovanna makes an offering at the river with anthropologist and initiate friend Patrício Carneiro Araújo. Photograph by Valéria Santos, 2015.

Yet during my months in Brazil, the impact of my *foreignness* continued to be part of my daily reflections. My physical features and European accent carried historical power relations, expressed in stereotypes and assumptions. Reflections on these sorts of associations often come up in ethnographic accounts by researchers who have confronted their own otherness in the field. However, in my case, my foreignness also reshuffled the correspondences and associations that my interlocutors held between humans and gods. Most of my interlocutors surmised that I was a daughter of Yemanjá, the goddess of the ocean. Indeed, many studies of the Brazilian Yemanjá and her Caribbean and African counterparts describe her as somewhat "white," or at least "coming from abroad." A Brazilian Candomblé priest once told me, "They say you are a daughter of Logun Edé because you are skinny, you look like a hunter! But here I see Yemanjá in you." Often, in Brazil, my accent and foreignness seemed to hold greater relevance than any other traits.

These reflections sparked even more questions in my journey. Eventually I came back to Italy, and in September 2016, after the official completion of my fieldwork, I was initiated as an *iyawó* (novice) of Logun Edé in the terreiro of Arborio. Among the different experiences that led me to this decision, my anthropological and ethnographic readings played a fundamental role. I had spent months reading accounts describing researchers' personal involvement in their fieldwork, and not only in Afro-Brazilian religions. I read biographies of British anthropologists who converted to Catholicism and books on trance possession in various types of Spiritism, including one by an anthropologist who had been "slain in the Holy Spirit" while researching Charismatic Christianity. The transformative engagements I was reading about were not only spiritual or mystical but political and physical

Figure 3.3. Giovanna de Logun Edé. Photograph by Sara Clamor, 2017.

as well. They could manifest when researchers experienced trance possession but also when they took sides in a protest or when they got food poisoning somewhere far from home.

In a sense, for me, these anthropology books took the form of multiple "bibles," in which I sought relevant "passages" to help me understand and describe my experiences in a nuanced way. Each ethnography was a sort of love story with a lesson to be learned. Ironically, it was these solitary acts of book-reading that allowed me to trust in ways of understanding that were only accessible *beyond* books. These scholarly accounts showed that research was not just a neutral ground for intellectual hypotheses, but a space to dwell in, with its own life and expansive wonder, bewilderment, and insight.

At the same time, as I developed a stronger participatory feel for the community's rituals and understandings, my decision to become initiated as an iyawó was a comfortable one. I trusted my sense of which sorts of activities and understandings could be academically shared and which layers of knowledge were beyond expository analysis or public communication. With deeper practical awareness as both an anthropologist and iyawó, I realized that, even if the time allocated to my research might be coming to an end, I could not imagine my life without the enchantment and enjoyment I experienced during my close encounters with the world of the orixás.

4

The Scattering and Sharing
of Wisdom around the World

MARTIN TSANG

This chapter attempts to capture how I first became attentive to the orishas as a mixed-race young adult in the United Kingdom. Trying to find practitioners of an Afro-Atlantic religion far removed from any discernible community in England in the pre-internet era was daunting, to say the least. I am surprised I didn't take more wrong turns. The process of learning about these divinities and connecting with knowledgeable sources took all the ingenuity I could muster. Yet I was driven forward on this journey by a deep-seated feeling that I was looking for something strangely familiar. Maybe it was a past-life thing, or maybe it was the orishas trying to find me; after twenty years of being initiated, I still don't know for certain, though I am at peace with this ambiguity. Still, every time someone asks me how I became an *olorisha* or *santero* (names for an orisha priest), so many thoughts and flashbacks appear instantaneously in my mind. The following is an attempt to (hopefully with some humor and good grace) relate some of my experiences on this spiritual path. It is also my hope that in the process of reflecting and writing about these events, my relationship with the orishas will continue to deepen, bringing new insights into my life.

I was that weird shy kid who was more into playing in nature than playing with cars. I was obsessed with all animals, except spiders—although I did own a few tarantulas in my teen years. One of my earliest childhood memories is of my mother having to carry me down the outside stairs to the basement where my kindergarten was. There was no way those cobwebs or the hidden spiders that spun them would get anywhere close to me! My kindergarten was a typical one, full of playtime and naps, but the space in which it was located was unique. Every day, I would spend time in the basement of a Spiritualist church. Now, in my forties, I ponder whether the vibes raised in countless medium sessions above somehow, either subconsciously or spiritually, filtered into my development. Growing up, I was obsessed with religions—all of them, I was faithful to none. I was perhaps searching for the one that felt completely right. I enjoyed learning about different faiths as well as the occult and the supernatural, and with anything that was considered strange or taboo, I wanted to find out why.

The uniqueness of my kindergarten, however, did not seem out of place given the uniqueness of my life. I was born and raised in England to a Chinese father from Hong Kong and a Swiss-German mother. Both had independently migrated to the United Kingdom. My dad worked as a waiter in various Chinese restaurants, and my mum began learning English as a nanny looking after the children of a Swiss expat couple. They met in a Chinese restaurant where my father was serving, and he showed my mother how to use chopsticks for the first time. She, being from the quintessentially Heidiesque village, had originally thought the chopsticks were knitting needles. The rest, as they say, is history. My older brother and I grew up and went to school in the southeast of England in Kent, about an hour from London by car. Philip went the sporty school rugby captain route. I, however, was more bookish, a demeanor that aptly presaged my future career as a librarian.

Growing up as a mixed-race Asian-European person in England, especially if you look phenotypically Chinese as I do, is not without its challenges, and while I did indeed experience quite a bit of racism, I never took it lying down. My approach was largely influenced by my father's experiences. While he and I rarely discussed racism because of the deeply lodged feelings of shame it triggered, he did share with me a few incidents. One took place in a supermarket in London about twenty years ago. He recalled:

> Those bloody bastards! Three young men followed me around, calling me "chinky" and making monkey noises. I left but they followed me and followed me. I stopped and made sure that I had my back to the wall so that they couldn't get behind me. I put my hand in my pocket as though I had a knife and I stood there. They didn't know what I had in my pocket, and eventually they left me alone.

Because of racist encounters such as these, my father equipped me with strategies to protect myself. He would tell me, "Make sure you punch them in the nose. If you hit them in the arm or kick, that won't do much, but a hit on the nose will make their eyes water and you can get away." What is implicit in these survival instructions is that the only defense I could count on was self-defense. I mention all of this here as it appears that such survival strategies, racism, and outsider feelings are par for the course for those who have historically practiced Afro-Atlantic religions. Those devoted to the orishas are marked by difference and are marginalized because of their race or beliefs. Given hegemony's insidiousness, the root of such deep-seated prejudices is rarely named. Yet our society perpetuates these violent acts of exclusion, ones that have been going on for centuries and are experienced worldwide, not only in distant developing countries, as some would prefer to imagine, but also in seemingly "innocent" places such as schoolyards, supermarkets, and parks. The religion places great emphasis on protection from harm and promotes self-preservation, with the biggest taboo resulting from engaging in any thing, action, or behavior that would have the effect of shortening the person's life.

Despite my innate interest in the spiritual world, I grew up in a secular household. My mother had us baptized in the Catholic Church in her village, mainly as an easy holy insurance policy for fear that our immortal souls be wrested in purgatory. Given my burgeoning youthful interest in Catholicism, especially the saints—and how I was reading that they helped shield enslaved and freed Africans to practice their religions during the devastation of colonialism and enslavement—I started to see or read them differently, like a secret code. I had to work hard to convince my mother to come with me to church on the occasional Saturday in Kent. My mother had a secret, painful feeling about the Catholic Church. She came from a deeply Catholic family in which weekly mass was mandatory, and she and her siblings were forbidden from eating food until after mass, which meant that her younger sister would often faint. The final straw came years later as an adult, when my mother was giving birth to my brother and unbeknownst to her, her mother was dying back in Switzerland. They hadn't told her until after the safe delivery. Unable to travel for the funeral, she phoned the family priest who adroitly told her that it was wrong to be sorrowful for losing her mother; rather, it was best to rejoice in the knowledge that her mother had arrived at the kingdom of heaven. Despite those inarguably traumatic personal experiences with organized religion, my mother did her best to accompany me on my journey, and perhaps because of those same experiences, she barely batted an eyelid when I started buying more and more books and magazines on the supernatural and when I paid frequent visits to the local New Age store, Destiny's, in the nearby town of Rochester, once home to Charles Dickens.

Televisual Orisha Encounters

I remember watching TV with my mother when I was around thirteen years old, and there was a short segment on a travel show about the Oshún grove in Oshogbo, Nigeria. Preserved in part by the work of Austrian Jewish artist Susanne Wenger, who moved to Nigeria during the Nazi occupation, the natural grove was transformed by her immense sculptures of orishas and spirits. I was mesmerized; I didn't totally understand it, but something had awoken or clicked inside me.

Around that same time, my brother, who had recently turned eighteen, borrowed a VHS tape of *The Believers* and left it in the VCR. Naturally, on Saturday morning I watched it while everyone was still asleep. If you haven't seen it, *The Believers* is an incredibly bad mix of thriller and horror from 1978 and stars Martin Sheen. It's supposedly based on Santería in New York City and narrates how an affluent, white family gets embroiled in and ultimately challenged by all forms of terribly portrayed African and Caribbean witchcraft. Despite the ridiculousness and sensationalism of the plot and the confusing Hollywood portrayal of Santería (Was Santería for protection or harm in the movie? I'm still not sure), I was fascinated by the appearance of an Eleguá, the small cement head with features made up of cowrie shells. In one scene, the nanny places Eleguá under the child's bed and prays to keep the kid safe while he sleeps. In another scene, the parents receive a cleansing by a santero that involves shotgunning smoke on Eleguá as well as a rooster sacrifice complete with blood splatters and eerie music. The santero practices out of the basement of his store rather than his home, and I watched that scene over and over, trying to absorb every detail. On the umpteenth viewing, I noticed in the background of the sacrifice scene the various colored *soperas*—lidded ceramic vessels housing the physical attributes of the orishas. Although the film didn't really focus on them, I felt like I had seen a relative on screen. Silly, I know, but this weird outsider and superficial portrayal was the closest I could get to anything related to the orishas, and at the time, it was better than nothing.

As my interest in spirituality grew, I kept reading widely on all forms of religion. But something kept bringing me back to the orishas, and I had an indescribable need to learn more. During this time, I started to attend a Spiritualist church with my mother's friend Melvina, who read runes and with whom I could talk about all this stuff. It wasn't the same Spiritualist church where my kindergarten was located. In fact, there were three such independent churches within a short walking distance from our house, and they would all regularly hold psychic fairs and meetings. Eventually, I started selling handmade candles from a booth along with Melvina. It was a great way to get to know the community. I did try to broach the subject of Afro-Atlantic religions a few times, but I was recurrently met with indifference, which once again led me to books and magazines, scouring them for any content or clues about the orishas. Magazines imported from America devoted to new pagan and New Age book releases were pretty much the only tangible thing I had at the time that linked me to the orishas. In the back of these magazines were small advertisements for magical supply shops and even a couple of quasi-*botánicas* (stores that provide Afro-Atlantic religious materials and services). I would call or write them asking for a printed catalog, and thankfully at that time the US dollar/British pound exchange rate was almost $2 for £1. This meant that the money I made as a fifteen-year-old selling candles and working over the summer in my dad's Chinese takeout restaurant went far in fueling my Santería book-buying habit. I will never forget the excitement when a package from Mi-World Supplies in Hialeah, Florida, arrived at my home in Kent. It was crammed with all the available literature on Santería—the good (few), the bad (some), and the ugly (many!). I had dropped $200 and had asked them to send me every book they had on Afro-Cuban religions. Even though what I received was a hodgepodge of serious and sensationalist literature, I was smitten. I've kept those paperback books, which are now cracked and tattered, and for sentimental reasons I don't think I will ever discard them.

A Walk through a Textual Botánica and Beyond

One of the few gems included in the box from Mi-World Supplies was Georgetown University professor Joseph Murphy's 1993 book *Santería: An African Religion in America*. Murphy was writing in English about the religion, which was incredible. Spanish was a massive barrier for me at the time, as only French and German were taught at my school. My lack of Spanish-language skills thus led me to concentrate my quest for more information and contacts mainly from North American orisha practitioners, as I surmised they would be easier to encounter and understand. In chapter 3 of his book, Murphy begins his journey to find an orisha priest as many have: by asking in a botánica, a religious goods store that serves the Afro-Atlantic religious community with everything from fresh plants (from which the stores derive their name) to saint statues, tools, beads, incense, musical instruments, clothing, and much more. Now, I don't think I can quite convey how badly I wanted to visit a botánica back then. I read Murphy's chapter countless times, with its rich and enticing descriptions of the contents of the store, daydreaming what it would be like and conjuring the interior so clearly in my head that I was almost there. Within that short chapter, Murphy also included a double-page table of fifteen orishas, giving their corresponding saint syncretisms: their characteristics, favored numbers, emblems, colors, and foods. To me, it was a type of crib sheet for a test I didn't know I was studying for, but it clearly set out a lot of information on the orishas that was otherwise difficult to come by in one place.

Murphy describes his entry into the *ilé* of legendary pioneer babalawo Francisco "Pancho" Mora (Ifá Moroté) in New York and the preparations and initiation steps he undertook in Mora's orisha house. Through Murphy's prose, a blend of personal account and academic ethnography, I felt like I was in that brownstone building with him. I hoped that I would one day somehow emulate that same journey and perhaps even receive my *elekes* (orisha beaded necklaces that place the person under the care of a priest's orishas and signals their admittance into the ilé) and warriors (consecrated symbols of the orishas Eleguá, Ogún, Oshosí, and Osun, who protect the initiate). The beads and warriors are two fundamental initiations that an adherent can undergo and are short and beautiful ceremonies. I thought that those two initiations would be as far as I could ever go, considering I am not from the culture. I had also read that being initiated as a priest can cost thousands of dollars and was a huge commitment—dressing in white as an *iyawó* for a year and seven days, no human contact outside of family, strict curfews for the year, and so on—and that would be impossible to complete properly while living in the United Kingdom away from a supportive and understanding community. Plus, getting my hands on that kind of money seemed unattainable at the time.

Getting Online in Search of the Orishas

While I was dreaming of visiting a botánica, I came up with more inventive strategies to find orisha practitioners in the United Kingdom. I couldn't be the only one who wanted to find a practitioner, surely. I tried placing an advert in an occult magazine for pen pals and got a few very strange replies—enough to never try *that* again. In the meantime, I began noticing more and more snippets of information about the orishas on random television shows, or perhaps I was becoming more attuned to seeing them. I saw a segment on late-night television about a coming-of-age ceremony

Figure 4.1. Joseph M. Murphy's Eshú Eleguá, which he received in New York in 1978 from the babalawo Pancho Mora, Ifá Moroté. Photograph by Joseph M. Murphy, 2022.

held at the Oyotunji Village in South Carolina. In the CD liner notes for a London jazz band called Galliano, they give thanks to the orishas. Suddenly, I felt that the orishas were all around me, though they continued to be out of sight and just out of reach. On a whim around this same time, in the mid-1990s, I decided to call directory inquiries, the equivalent of 411 directory assistance in the United States. I asked for the "Africa Center" in London, hoping that such a thing existed. Not surprisingly, it did exist, and when I called and explained that I was interested in Yorùbá religion, the person who answered identified himself as a babalawo. For a second, I was absolutely elated. However, my enthusiasm was tempered when he kindly told me that he couldn't help, that there was no community in England to speak of, and that he belonged to a lineage in Ile Ife, Nigeria, where his elderly family quietly maintained the tradition. In a nutshell, he wisely warned me to be cautious, as legitimate priests do not advertise themselves as such and that the safest way to find someone to trust is through trusted, personal referrals who can vouch for the spiritual credentials of the person. Before we said goodbye, he gave me an important piece of advice: trust your Orí (one's spiritual and physical head and personal spirit). He told me my

Orí would deliver me to the place where I needed to go and that by trusting in it and listening attentively to its guidance, I could never go wrong.

At the age of sixteen, I took the hourlong journey by train to London to find an internet café so that I could get online and try to find people knowledgeable about the orishas. I paid five pounds for an hour at a place near Euston station and did some rapid searches mainly with keywords like "orisha." I naively wrote in the one and only orisha website that had a guestbook available at the time,[1] stating my purpose and my phone number (I didn't have email then). I also hastily wrote down the contact information from some of the other entries in the guestbooks. Through these efforts I did manage to speak to some people, mostly people from California. Years later, I would unexpectedly meet some of them. However, like my other phone calls, those I spoke with regretted that they could not help someone so far away and wished me luck on my journey.

About a year after this first internet search, I acquired my first home computer and a dial-up internet connection. Through the magic of America Online chat rooms and newly discovered daily email lists, I began participating and getting to know colorful online characters in the US orisha world. One of my new friends was a santero in New York who offered to host me and introduce me to his godfamily. After some emails and phone calls, I asked him if he could be my *padrino* (my orisha godfather) and give me the initiations of the beads and warriors. He agreed, and I booked my plane ticket to spend time with him, to be introduced to his orisha godfamily, and to receive those initiations. Hindsight being what it is, I now know that it is not the seeker who calls the shots in terms of what initiations they can or should receive. The orishas themselves, through divination, are the ones who would have had the first and last word on any steps like that in the religion. I guess I was learning to listen to my Orí, and for some reason, as the initial excitement of finding someone willing to guide me subsided, I began feeling unsure about whether this was indeed the right step to take. This feeling only increased as some of the questions I was asking about practical matters regarding the trip and what I hoped to accomplish were met with vague answers. As I sat with my growing doubt, I stumbled upon the website of a priest by the name of Afolabí.[2] His site had a plethora of well-written essays about the orishas and his experiences as a midwesterner Jewish punk kid getting into Lucumí. Afolabí's writing was witty, biting, and brilliant. I realized I had to contact him. Soon after, we started chatting and I let him know my plans and reservations (both personally and travel-related), and afterward, he made a few discreet inquiries through the orisha

Figure 4.2. Clayton D. Keck Jr., Afolabí, *iba é* priest of Yemayá. Also known as Shloma Menachem Mendel Rosenberg. Photograph by Martin Tsang, 2007.

grapevine on my behalf. This is how I discovered that the person I had been planning on visiting was not indeed initiated (which he had neglected to tell me directly) and that what he was planning to do was to "hand me over" to his godmother to initiate me. This news hurt like hell. I felt both embarrassed and betrayed.

In his generous style, Afolabí suggested that I change my plane ticket and fly instead to Michigan. He felt bad for being the bearer of bad news, and he let me know that he was planning on driving to Miami in a few months' time (he was afraid of flying). He invited me on the trip with him, stating that we could stop in Chicago and New Orleans on the way so he could introduce me to all the orisha priests that he knew, thus allowing me to gain a greater sense of the community and its diverse practitioners. I eagerly agreed. Three months later, I took my first trip to the United States and arrived at Detroit Metropolitan Airport at age nineteen. When a US Customs and Border Patrol agent asked about the purpose of my visit, I earnestly told the officer that I had found an African religion on the internet and I had come to be initiated. Given that my comment led to a half-hour "chat" with the officer, I now realize that I shouldn't have given such an innocent and open description. Simply saying I was going on a road trip with a friend would have sufficed! Despite this misstep, I finally made it through immigration and customs and found Afolabí was waiting for me in the arrivals area. He had come to pick me up despite it being his goddaughter's orisha anniversary initiation, which she was celebrating in his house.

On the drive to the festivity, I took a moment between our animated and excited discussions to attempt to prepare for what lay ahead. I realized that in no time at all I would finally be face to face with an orisha altar, a space that contained the consecrated embodiments of these divine energies on Earth. I was overcome with a mix of elation and wonder. When the moment of truth came, would it be close to what I had imagined so many times throughout the years? Would it prove to be what I had been inexplicably searching for all this time? Afolabí pulled up to his house, and when I stepped through the door, I found myself surrounded by the warmest, most diverse, and happy group of people I had met in a long time. They were all here for the orishas, celebrating another year of initiation in the life of one of the ilé's members. Afolabí, who was walking ahead of me, was greeted by his godchildren who had been looking for him. They took turns to *foribale* (pay respects by prostrating) to the orisha Yemayá he had crowned in his head by prostrating themselves in the ritual manner according to their own orisha and asking for both Afolabí's and Yemayá's blessing. After these ritual greetings were completed, I was led into the room where the orisha throne had been set up for the occasion. The throne was a sumptuous and grand production of orisha tureens draped in rich fabrics, beads, and accoutrements. It overflowed with offerings of food, sweets, and candles. In the place of honor was Obatalá, royal father of wisdom and purity. Finally standing face-to-face with the material embodiment of the orishas in front of this magnificent throne, my previous doubts and worries about whether I was on the right path or just imagining it in my head completely melted away. As I was instructed on how to salute by prostrating in front of the orishas, I silently gave thanks to the orishas and my Orí for guiding me to this moment.

The trip soon became a happy blur. Afolabí was a marvelous host, and we became fast friends; the road trip was beyond anything I had experienced before, and through it I also fell in love with New Orleans. The people I met during this visit, including and especially the godfamily and community who would take me under their wing, were all exceptionally generous, welcoming, and beyond patient with me. Their actions instilled in me a profound level of respect for all. The orishas are the epitome of love, and they insist on and instill humility and respect. A very good and wise friend once told me, "There is the family you're born into, the family you marry into, and the family you make." The orishas and the people in the religion are very much the made or chosen family for many. People become bonded through initiation and are made strong by facing life's problems with a clear head that aids them in trying to resolve problems, or at least make them better. As is the case for far too many, my childhood was far from ideal, and I think as a large part of healing generational trauma that can manifest in multiple ways—emotionally, physically, spiritually, and so on—the orishas ask us to do the heavy and difficult work. With their help, and often their lifesaving interjections, they are transformational.

Everyone Has a Guardian Orisha

One of the most exciting moments in the life of an orisha practitioner is when one learns who their guardian orisha is. Every person has an orisha assigned to help them achieve their fullest destiny while on Earth. Lucumí theology posits that everyone is born with a destiny made up of elements that are set in stone and elements that can be changed. Prior to their birth on Earth, an orisha chooses to become the guardian orisha of a person, depending on their destiny. The act of priesthood initiation is to fuse the energy of the guardian orisha symbolically and spiritually with that of the person. This bond, which lasts until death, creates new ways of communication and channels of help and advice that flow between the orisha and the person. This relationship, which takes a lifetime to develop, deepens and grows from the moment of initiation.

Lucumí practitioners actively worship around twenty to thirty orishas in total. In his chapter, Murphy lists fifteen orishas and their attributes. A handful of orishas are most familiar and popular, including Eleguá, Oshún, Obatalá, Shangó, Oyá, and Yemayá. These orishas, and perhaps one or two more, claim most guardianships over adherents—a process determined not by individual choice but solely through a sophisticated divination ceremony conducted by a well-trained ritual specialist. Imagine my surprise at the age of nineteen when I discovered that I was a child of Erinle,[3] a less-known orisha of the hunt, herbalism, and wealth. In other words, Erinle was the orisha who ruled my head, and should I ever become initiated as a priest, it would be to his priesthood. Because there are not many children of Erinle out there, this orisha is not mentioned or discussed as frequently as the others, nor is there an abundance of information about him.

When I received this news, I began a personal quest to find out anything and everything I could about Erinle. This was not an easy feat, considering that many priests I encountered had only cursory knowledge about his characteristics, rituals, and history. Then, I found the books of Lydia Cabrera, a Cuban artist and self-taught ethnographer who wrote multiple volumes on Afro-Cuban religions. Where many authors on Santería failed me, Lydia disclosed a cache of information, although it was largely interspersed as hidden jewels I had to diligently mine from an abundance of lines, pages, and volumes. Through narratives spread across several of her books, I was able to piece together a great deal of information about Erinle. For example, Lydia's work taught me that Erinle had intimate relationships with several orishas.

One popular example is Erinle's relationship with Yemayá. Yemayá, who gave Erinle his wealth and his knowledge, cast a spell on his tongue,[4] reinforcing the idea that Erinle depends on Yemayá for communication. This *patakí* (divination narrative/story) is often used to explain the Yemayá *oro* Erinle process of priesthood initiation, wherein a child of Erinle requires the mediation of Yemayá in their initiation, effectively casting Yemayá as a catalyst and placing her in a prime position in the confidential ritual process. As a result, Yemayá "speaks" for Erinle in the Lucumí initiation. On the third day of the priesthood initiation, when the life-defining divination ceremony is performed for the initiate, Erinle speaks through Yemayá's divination implements—sixteen cowrie shells (*dilogún*)—and not through his own tools.

In conversation, Lucumí practitioners in Cuba and the United States have told me that, yes, Yemayá and Oshún are two of Erinle's loves, but he also had intimate relationships with other, less-known orishas, Oba, and Otin. Then, in an almost whispered tones, they reveal that Erinle also had intimate relations with Oshosí, a fellow male hunter orisha. Both Yemayá and Erinle are associated with queerness, and Erinle and Oshosí are by no means the only orishas associated with same-sex intimacy. The worshipping of Yorùbá orishas on the Catholic feast days associated with the syncretized saint is one of the best known and most publicly celebrated aspects of Afro-Cuban Lucumí or Santería.[5] Given my early fascination with the saints, more so than the overarching religion, I recognized how public symbols can be interpreted in a variety of ways.

After consulting multiple sources, I confirmed that Erinle had a curious mix of characteristics. To Lydia Cabrera, devotees explained that he was *el medico divino* (the divine doctor), a physician and herbalist, but also a hunter and fisherman. Cabrera's words were redolent with the emotive stories elder orisha priests would similarly tell me over the years. These tales

Figure 4.3. Martin in Sagua La Grande, Cuba, conducting field research on the Chinese influence in Afro-Cuban religion. Photograph by Silvia Petretti, 2006.

recounted how Erinle was also the deity of wealth, how he was mostly described as beautiful rather than handsome, and how he was a sensitive and delicate deity for whom all ceremonies must be completed precisely and with unique finesse. Many mentioned his androgynous demeanor and his many loves, both male and female. Because of his many roles and his ability to occupy multiple spaces, Erinle is associated with the river, the sea, and especially where they come together, a confluence called *ibulosa*. Still, Erinle's domain is also the forest. In religious ceremonies, and during fieldwork on researching Chinese influence in Afro-Cuban religions, many testified to me of the love and affection they felt for this elegant and noble orisha. Some had proudly and touchingly fulfilled *promesas* (promises) to Erinle for health reasons, and in return Erinle performed miracle cures, aided fertility, and safeguarded pregnancies to term. While there are relatively few priests of Erinle, his many followers continue to celebrate the 24th of October, offering back in gratitude some of the abundance and prosperity he has manifested in their lives.

Spreading the Word on Erinle

In the proceeding years after having had my "head read," my incessant searching for information on Erinle coincided with the growth of the internet. An increasing number of websites, listservs, chatrooms, and discussion boards focused on Afro-Atlantic religions were popping up, and I decided to share with the cyber monde what I had gathered about Erinle. I made a rudimentary website on a free server and started with pages such as "Who Is Erinle?" and "Erinle Iconography." I put a lot of effort into it and was gratified by the responses I received and the encouragement to continue, as many people were getting in touch with me after having found the pages. It appeared that many were indeed searching for information on Erinle, just as I had been, and many couldn't quite believe that such a resource was out there, let alone made by a Brit.

I soon found myself, my site, and its many later iterations quoted or mentioned in several published books. I also met many people who had read the content and recognized me from the small author photo I had included on the site. Many websites were copying and pasting the information as well as translating it for audiences in Brazil and for Spanish-speaking audiences. Often, my entire site was copied and translated, word for word, and the photos I had taken and posted were reproduced. It was amusing to see the proliferation of a passion project taking on a life of its own. I was thrilled that some reliable information on Erinle was circulating on the internet, and I was elated to make such a contribution. I was also amused by the idea that now I was potentially influencing internet-savvy orisha worship in different traditions globally. To this day I wonder: What did those Candomblé worshippers reading something about Erinle in Portuguese think about it? Did they know where it came from? Did it affect their religious practice? Has some of my shared information made an impact on what was shared among practitioners on Erinle? While I eventually closed the website to concentrate on other projects, there are still pieces and versions of it living and circulating on blogs and pages created by priests and practitioners around the world.

In Difference We Stand

Learning about Erinle helped me learn a great deal about myself. Knowing that he governs fish and amphibians and that his partner, the orisha Abatan, is represented by the pond, I better understood my childhood passion for wildlife and freshwater. As a hunter and someone who dwells silently in the forest, Erinle teaches us the power of silence and the necessity of (a) retreat. Similarly, Erinle is a deity of both the land and the water, which is highly unusual, as an orisha is usually only part of one. This fluidity speaks of the ability to cross boundaries and norms. Female orishas are usually considered riverine or water-related orishas, and male orishas are often associated with the earth and contours of the land. Defying these norms, Erinle codeswitches and can dwell in both. He is also the caretaker and bastion for gender-divergent and queer people and is adored by all.

Orí as spiritual guide and personal deity of every human being also features as a protagonist in many of the pataki or important lessons and tales contained within the Lucumí divination corpus. In Ogbe-Di, one of the 256 possible combinations or chapters called Odu, we learn that *la sabiduría está repartida en el mundo* (wisdom was shared across the world), meaning that no one person has the monopoly on knowledge and that everybody has a contribution to make. Similarly, one must go out into the world to learn, and I presume that there is something to learn about the orishas in all pockets of the globe. To me, *ashé* (divine power) is the force behind wisdom that has been scattered by Olodumaré (God), and it may be this recognizable or familiar aspect that speaks to some of us drawn so strongly, and often inexplicably, to these religions.

Having Erinle as my orisha father has helped me revel in my own difference. As expressed in my discussion of racism, the world we live in can make the embodiment of difference painful. The orishas, however, provide us with the ability to refract and support all forms of humanity; they teach us to embrace difference and allow for the existence of many expressions of love and loving. My subsequent training as an anthropologist also trained me in theories by which I am now able to dissect and describe differences and otherness. It has also afforded me with a professional voice that I continue to use to disseminate knowledge on the orishas. My story affirms my belief that our work is most powerful when we allow ourselves to be open and curious. That first day in Afolabí's house when I encountered Obatalá and all the orishas for the first time, my Orí confirmed that I had indeed found what I had been searching for. To this day, I continue to work on edifying that trust.

5

Making *Ocha* in Havana

IVOR MILLER

As the son of a young university teacher, I was raised on the move: from Palo Alto and then Monterey Bay, California, to Beirut, Lebanon, from five to eight years of age, and Long Island, New York, until age ten. Eventually, we settled in Amherst, Massachusetts, where my father was a founding faculty member at Hampshire College, an innovative experiment in education that urges raising questions and finding solutions. Returning from Beirut, I realized the experience separated me from my classmates, and I never felt like a full "American" because living in a multilingual, religiously diverse city like Beirut instilled in me a desire for international dialogue. My father was raised in poverty and struggled to achieve a PhD in marine biology and genetics, while my mother was raised comfortably and worked as an elementary school teacher. We were decidedly white, middle class, and latently Protestant. Our overarching belief and convictions were in the value of education to solve problems while helping others along the way.

My first memories of a religious community were attending Easter celebrations in Beirut with my Lebanese foster sister and her Maronite family; I was visually overwhelmed by an abundance of flowers, candles, and small children dressed in fluffy lace as if they too were blossoming. Meanwhile, I had an innate sense that nature itself was sacrosanct. I often imagined forests as mystic spaces. When I learned about the Lucumí traditions of Cuba, with deities embodied in wind, thunder, hills, trees, rivers, and so on, this made perfect sense to me. After initiation in Havana, I experienced the multiple benefits of membership: being part of an extended face-to-face community with aims of mutual aid, having access to esoteric knowledge, and learning about underground systems established by forced African migrants who maintained historical narratives about their versions of the past. Whereas I was raised in an urban industrialized society with a great sense of alienation from the land, from small-scale farming, from extended families, the Lucumí tradition offered an antidote that brought me closer to nature, to community networks, alternative sources for historical narratives, and new tools for problem-solving. These are some of the reasons the Lucumí tradition expanded in the twentieth century from Havana and Matanzas to the entire island of Cuba and more recently throughout the globe. Because modern science and industrial societies are not able to solve existential problems of our species, many of us continue to search for answers, even through a practice that our recent European ancestors publicly rejected as "primitive" and "savage."

As a scholar, I understand that lived experience is a fundamental tool for learning. The experience of undergoing Lucumí rites of passage was transformative, not only for how I felt but also as to how others perceived me.[1] My status as initiate was essential for working with communities of African descent in Cuba who generously guided and taught me about their insights into the cultural history of the Caribbean's largest metropolis as well as the human condition.

Encountering the Orishas through the Art of Juan Boza: New York City, 1987

I met Juan Boza after seeing some of his paintings in an arts gallery in the South Bronx.[2] I was there to see the work of several local artists, the original subway painters who transitioned to painting their "signatures" on canvas for galleries.[3] Ritual signatures of Abakuá (a Cuban mutual aid society for males), I learned later, inspired some of Juan's colorful work. I called him, met him at his studio apartment, and we began what would become a bonding relationship, the center of which was his teaching me about the orishas.

As a photographer, I began to document Juan's work, and we spent many weekends photographing his hundreds of paintings and talking about Cuba. Juan, along with his *padrino* (initiation father), and several musicians who regularly play at New York area ceremonies, were Marielitos, some 125,000 Cubans who arrived in the United States in 1980, surviving the treacherous journey from Mariel, Cuba, on overcrowded boats with only what their hands could carry.

Inside his home, Juan created a world where the orishas filled his works with power. Even from the street below his apartment atop a brownstone building, one could see the rainbow-colored Christmas lights he displayed inside his window, a symbol of the orisha Oyá. It is customary in Santería

Figure 5.1. Juan Boza with his mother in Camagüey, Cuba. Photographer unknown. Ivor Miller archives.

for elders to guide noninitiates, and Juan became my teacher. When I brought him 35mm slides I'd taken of his work, he offered me one of his prints of Abakuá symbols. I chose one, but Juan suggested I take another symbol. It turned out that the first symbol was one of death and the second of initiation. In Afro-Cuban initiation systems, the uninitiated are ignorant of the codes and must be guided for their own protection. Symbols are icons of power that affect the bearer. At this precise moment, I became conscious that Juan had begun to act as my padrino. This symbol, Juan told me, is drawn during Abakuá initiations to attract positive power.[4] Juan had rendered the symbol his own by creating it as a bright-colored mask with eyes and a mouth that radiate life. Years later, as I embarked upon a lifelong study of Abakuá cultural history and became initiated into a lodge in Calabar, Nigeria, I often reflected upon Juan's gift as prophetic.

Juan was a santero who had "made saint" four years earlier in New Jersey.[5] His "guardian angel" was Yemayá, and, like her, Juan was generous and nurturing as he began to teach me about Lucumí tradition. He took me to ceremonies of two Afro-Cuban initiation systems practiced in the Bronx, Manhattan, and New Jersey, introducing me to the community and their deities. The first event I witnessed was a Palo Monte (Kongo-derived religion) ceremony in a working-class area of the Bronx, where percussionist Orlando "Puntilla" Ríos, also a Marielito, directed the music. Everybody in the cramped house was dressed in white, while a white dove fastened to the top eave of the door frame functioned to "cleanse" all those who entered.

I will not forget the time I first met an orisha in possession. We were at a Lucumí birthday party (*cumpleaños de santo*) for Juan's padrino, a priest of Oshún, in Union City, New Jersey; it was the anniversary of his initiation into Santería. There were about one hundred people there, as well as five percussionists and singers with *batá* orishas. During the ceremony, the orishas Oshún and Ogún "mounted" several people.[6] At one point, when Juan was dancing, he suddenly began to shake and quiver as if an electric bolt had struck him. The dancing *santeros* (orisha priests) behind Juan caught and held him, as he regained balance and walked away from the orishas. He explained to me that because his guardian Yemayá mounts (possesses) him easily, he usually prepares himself ritually to discourage Yemayá's presence, saying that it is an exhausting experience. On this day, he received a tiny cut across his forehead, explaining later that his *camino* (road or path) of Yemayá has elements of Ogún; whenever he is mounted, he is cut in some way, or "marked by the spirit," even when he isn't hit by anything visible.

Juan felt the presence of Yemayá, yet the ceremony was ending and participants were leaving. Just then, Juan became fully possessed by Yemayá: his round, wide eyes doubled in size, gazing upward, above the heads of the dancers. It seemed Juan's presence was diminishing, as if carried away by an undertow, as Yemayá emerged in his body. Juan's padrino escorted Yemayá/Juan to the altar in a back room to be clothed and attended to as a royal visitor in the customary way. After some time, Yemayá emerged with a large fan of peacock feathers in hand and a deep blue satin cloth tied around her shoulders. She walked slowly around the room filled with orishamers and dancers, fanning herself with great strength, yet somehow in slow motion. Dreamlike, Yemayá's fan seemed like a sea fan waving along the coral reef. Her mouth, like that of an underwater fish, silently opened and closed. Yemayá's nostrils inhaled huge amounts of air, sensing its life-giving force.

Yemayá was silent; only her deep breathing was heard. She approached participants, one by one, received their prostrations, and shared messages with them. Juan had not yet had the "ceremony of the tongue," a rite that would allow an orisha to speak through him; for this reason, Yemayá did not verbally speak. Instead, she was followed by a person who interpreted her gestures. Yemayá would motion and mime a phrase, then would emphatically nod "yes, correct" or "no, try again" at the interpretation in Spanish. Within an hour, about fifteen people were consulted in this manner, many of them eager to hear messages from the spirit world or advice about protecting themselves against danger. I was tired and ready to leave, but at the last minute Yemayá came to me, her fan waving like underwater flora rippled by a sea current. Her eyes—wide, unblinking, and bulging with knowing—gazed at me, her head slowly nodding. I stood there, unsure of what to do, unsure even of who confronted me: my friend Juan, the powerful sea goddess Yemayá, or a combination of both? Yet knowing Juan, his sincerity and gentleness, I knew I was in a safe place. I also knew I was entering a world far removed from my own and my family's experience.

Yemayá motioned and I understood that I was to remove my shoes. The interpreter took bunches of grapes from the altar and placed them at my feet; I was motioned to step on them, then a third helper smashed other bunches on the tops of my feet. I was handed two oranges and held them while Yemayá conveyed information from the spirit world. Slowly, after some unsuccessful interpretations, I learned that soon I would be given an opportunity to journey to another land and that I must go, for I would profit greatly from the experience. I was then told to rub the two oranges over my body in a cleansing motion, as they would absorb negative influences, and throw them away from me, into a street dumpster or a nearby river. Yemayá returned with her interpreter to the altar room, and a few minutes later Juan himself reappeared, exhausted, and signaling to me that he was ready to leave. On the way home, I had asked him about being mounted, and he said he remembered nothing of the experience.

The first night I stayed in Juan's studio apartment, he had a dream. When he awoke, he told me he had seen an angel in the doorway between our rooms. It was very tall with long white feathers and arching wings. The angel was struggling to enter Juan's room, squeezing its huge wings into the door frame, but couldn't quite make it. As Juan's dream might suggest, he had brought me to the doorway of Santería. Because of Juan, I later went to Cuba to learn about Santería in its homeland. At the time, living conditions in Cuba were particularly difficult because the Soviet Union was collaps-

Figure 5.2. Juan Boza *cumpleaños* throne/altar for Yemayá. Constructed December 1990, Brooklyn, New York. Photograph by Ivor Miller, 1990.

ing and could no longer provide Cuba with foreign aid. In response, Cubans suffered severe cuts in food, clothing, and energy rations. Fidel Castro coined the term "Special Period" to refer to these hardships.[7]

I arrived in Havana to study with the National Folklore Ensemble of Cuba (Conjunto Folklórico Nacional de Cuba), founded in 1962, to research and promote Cuba's folklore, primarily its African heritage. Yet during the 1959 Revolution, the Conjunto presented a culture of the past that the "progress of socialism" had allegedly "outgrown." Although most of the dancers, musicians, and teachers at the Ensemble were initiates of Santería/

Lucumí, Palo Monte, or Abakuá, the classes were structured to teach the mechanics of dance and orishaming but little about the actual ceremonies. Finally, a Cuban friend told me, "If you want to learn what the religion is really like, get out of the Conjunto and into the streets!"

Rubén: Havana

A few months later, I was back in Havana, where I met Rubén. A Cuban friend who considered Rubén a respected and knowledgeable santero took me to Rubén's cumpleaños de santo ceremony. Rubén is also an Obá Oriaté. Obás are highly trained and accomplished ritual specialists who direct a range of orisha initiations and ceremonies. Rubén was constantly called to all parts of Havana to conduct ceremonies. At forty-six years of age, he was young for an Obá. Rubén is an opera singer of English descent and was the first in his family to be called by the orishas. As a child, Rubén didn't believe in possession, he told me. That is, until he was himself mounted by his orisha. He tells me it's something he doesn't understand and can't explain. He says that at age nine a spirit guided him to the house of the woman who became his godmother, a daughter of Oshún, well known in Havana for her knowledge.

Rubén lives far from the center of Havana, at the end of a dead-end street next to railroad tracks. His house is humble and impoverished, needing many repairs, yet strikingly clean. One day we spoke on his back patio, sipping small cups of hot and sweet coffee above the railroad tracks of Ogún. Just then a majestic bird sailed high above us in the infinitely blue sky. Observing the bird, Rubén raised his open hands toward it, chanting in both Spanish and Lucumí: "bendición y salud, the blessings of Olofi." The bird lingered high above, staying motionless in the current, as if to absorb the words of praise. Rubén told me this bird is the symbol of his mother, Oshún, and it is a blessing for him when it flies overhead.[8]

Commencing the Ritual Process

While talking to Rubén (Abebe Osún), his *madrina* (godmother, his ritual elder) Esperanza, and other members of their ritual family, we arranged the date, place, and cost of my initiation.[9] There were many things to consider. Rubén said it was like building a watch with many tiny parts—each is important, and they must all fit together to work well. We agreed to begin on January 20, 1992. Esperanza mandated that the santero's fees be raised because the cost of living had risen. We made a list of the foods I must buy. Down the street, we encountered Aleida (Oshún Deí) at a ceremony for the initiations of two *babalawos* (priests of the orisha Orula who specialize in divination among other things). They were both twenty years old and from Colómbia. The father of one of them, Gilberto, was the first babalawo in Colombia.

Milagros (Ogún Deí), a priestess of the warrior orisha Ogún, was Aleida's daughter and Rubén's ritual sister. She agreed to be my *ojubona,* which she translated as "the eyes and the guide of the initiate," meaning that she would be my madrina. Returning to Aleida's house, a center for ritual activity, we talked about the fees and the date. We then asked Aleida's Oshún for permission to hold the event at her house. Her altar room was a potent space. The cauldron for Milagros's Ogún had a green and black beaded sash or *collar de mazo* hanging on it (a gift from a godchild in Venezuela). At the center of the altar was a picture of San Pedro. In another cauldron below was a detailed cloth doll used to "work" for a client.

Aleida took four pieces of *obí* (coconut used for divination) from her refrigerator and a gourd of cool water and approached her Oshún altar. Before greeting her orisha, she lifted the lid of the *sopera* (an elegant soup tureen) and laid it aside, so that Oshún would hear her properly. Rubén, Grisel, Aleida (all Oshún initiates), and I knelt on our hands and knees. Aleida sprinkled water on the floor as a libation while chanting "omi tutu, ilé tutu, ona tutu" (cool water, cool house, cool road). As Aleida began to conjure passionate and inspired words for her orisha, I felt the energy in the room rising and sweeping by, as if we were engulfed by an electric wind. She spoke to Oshún for a few minutes, with great respect and with the certainty that Oshún was there, listening and responding in all her power. Then Aleida tossed the obi. Three up, one down—Etawa! (Yes). She tossed again— four up—Alafia! We all thanked Oshún by touching the floor with both hands and then kissing it. Then Milagros had me kneel before her father Ogún. In her new role as my *ojubona* (initiatory co-godparent), she asked Ogún to bless and protect me. We hugged, and I walked into the night.

The Ocha Family

Initiation into an *ocha* family is a social process, as Santería involves creating extended ritual families for emotional support and problem-solving. The family I am joining (Rubén's ritual house) is an "ilé Oshún" because the elder santera is a child of Oshún. This ilé originates from Pogolotti, Havana,

Figure 5.3. Ivor with Gladys. Photographer unknown, 1993.

where lived the founding *iyalorisha*, a *mulata* named Isabel Rojas, known as "Bellita" and as Oshún Leyi in Lucumí. Bellita's madrina was Andrea Trujillo, Ewín Yimí, known as "Tití."[10] When Bellita was six years old, she made ocha and started her ritual house, or ilé Oshún, in her twenties. She died in 1985 at ninety-six years of age, carrying ninety years *de santo*. The ocha family is a network of people giving each other *aché* and passing on ritual knowledge.

El Derecho

I formally presented Rubén and his orishas with *el derecho* (a ritual fee) for the padrino's work in orchestrating the series of ceremonies required for ocha initiation. In my presence, Rubén put the envelope of 700 Cuban pesos (approximately US$28) upon his altar and took Oshún's brass bell in hand. Ringing it, he saluted Oshún, informing her that this was the derecho for the ceremony of consecrating my head for Shangó, who Orula had determined is my guardian angel. Rubén then gave me the bell, instructing me to prostrate myself to Oshún and inform her why I had come. I greeted

Oshún, then lay prone on the straw mat before the altar. Rubén spoke some words in Lucumí and tapped my shoulders, and I rose. Crossing my hands on my chest to touch opposite shoulders, as did Rubén, we embraced by touching opposite shoulders to each other, one side at a time.

La Vista

I was almost prepared for my ocha ceremony. The first *vista* (spiritual investigation) began on Monday. *La vista del ebó de la entrada* was the first ritual step on the path of ocha, to inquire into my preparedness for initiation and the offerings I would make to open the way for a successful ceremony. Rubén said that all must be calm before and during my ocha. I must avoid all conflicts and resolve my problems so that I'm not agitated.

On the day of my vista del ebó de la entrada, Esperanza (Okantomí) told me I was at "the door" of the saints. She took me down the road to Hans's house. Here, two babalawos of her *rama* (branch, or ocha lineage) were preparing to make the vista. Because I had received the mano de Orula (a divination ceremony that ritually links a client to Orula), Esperanza said that a babalawo must throw his divination chain (*opele*) for my vista. She likened it to going to a Western doctor before an operation who looks at the data and makes a diagnosis about what I can and cannot do for my health. Here Ifá would advise me about what I needed to do for success.

When Rubén came, I sat down with one babalawo, who divined with his opele. Hans recorded Orula's messages: Orula said that I was spiritually clean and needed only to sacrifice a rooster and a few small items to prepare for my initiation. Orula confirmed that I am a son of Shangó and that I should receive his wife, Oyá, during my ocha ceremony. The babalawos told me I must not enter any cemeteries before receiving Oyá.[11]

The Spiritual Mass

A few days later a spiritual mass was organized to investigate my "spiritual portrait" before initiation. Rubén and two middle-aged Black women came, and we all took seats in front of Rufina, the doll representing his principal spirit guide atop his *bóveda* (Espiritismo altar). The *espiritista* mass is another probing tool used to investigate one's preparedness for ceremony. Accompanied by the two women, Rubén recited a long prayer in Spanish. As we chanted, he passed around a bottle of Agua Florida, a type of cologne I had brought with me from the Botánica Shangó in New Haven. They said they hadn't seen anything like it in thirty years. We rinsed our hands, necks, faces, heads, and arms and snapped the energy onto the bóveda. Rubén had on a bright red shirt for Shangó, a blue handkerchief on one knee for Yemayá, and a yellow handkerchief on the other for Oshún. He lit a cigar, as did one of the espiritistas. After the chant, there was a concentrated silence. By and by a woman "observed" that there was someone envious of my relationship with Rubén. It was determined that this person was a mutual friend of ours, who introduced us. After the spirit was pacified, it left. We again rinsed ourselves with Agua Florida, snapped away the energy, and left.

Leaving the Throne

Because of the hidden nature of Santería in Cuba, only invited initiates can participate in the "birthing" ceremony of an iyawó and the orishas. This ceremony, the act of "crowning" an initiate with an orisha, is also called "making ocha." Participants are forbidden to talk about the ceremonies; therefore, I have not included any statements about my own initiation. This section begins when I left the "throne room," where most of the ceremonies take place over a period of seven days.

On the eighth and last day of the ocha ceremony, iyawós are customarily dressed in brand-new and elegant white clothes and guided by their *oju-bona* around the four corners of the marketplace or *plaza* (called Mercado Unico) in Old Havana.[12] Before the Revolution, an important part of this ceremony was to have the iyawó "steal" a piece of fruit from a market in the plaza to offer to the orishas. The vendors would knowingly turn their backs when they saw an iyawó coming, to allow the "theft." This act was an *ebó* (translated to me in this context as "good luck," but literally meaning "sacrifice") for the vendor who was "robbed." During socialism, there were no vendors at the market: all food was rationed at special shops. Thus, there was nothing to steal; the fruit was bought from another place.[13]

After my walk around the plaza with madrina Ogún Deí, we went to the church of Oshún (Iglesia de Nuestra Señora de la Caridad del Cobre) on Calle Salud, where we walked a slow circle inside the nave, greeting each statue of a saint. The priest asked me to remove my hat, and Ogún Deí apologized, taking off my hat. Although my head was shaven and must be covered in white for three months, out of respect for the rules of another powerful institution we adapted to the circumstance. Thus, there are fluctuating and competing forms of orthodoxy, or methods to exist fluidly within several distinct social traditions. Respecting the rules of the church is one example of this, and adapting to the authority of the Revolution is another.

After visiting Oshún's church, Rubén took me to the house of his madrina Okantomí. She was excited to see her new grandchild and said I looked lovely. I was introduced as a new member of the family to all santeros present. Rubén took me across the hall to meet the next-door neighbor Elsa, widow of the late *batalero* (batá orisha specialist) Jesús Pérez.[14] I was presented to her orishas, and we saluted each other. I was then presented to the other initiated neighbors. Suddenly, many doors were opening for me as I was surrounded by my ritual family.

Even though it was a tremendous experience, I was glad to be away from the confines of the throne. The iyawó suffers many hardships in the throne room, and the santeros told me, "To be a king is a great privilege, but it is also to be a prisoner, for the role carries its own responsibilities." Finally leaving Aleida Oshún Deí's house the previous day, I imagined myself a person freed from jail, seeing the sun, sky, and city with new eyes.

Before returning to the United States, I took my orisha to Rubén's house to be placed under his care. Rubén took me to his altar and presented me to his Oshún using my *orukó*, or my new Lucumí name (Oju Obá—the Eye of the King/Shangó), so that Oshún might know who the new iyawó was. Later I went to Grisel's house. Her *abuela* came to the door, and with a calabash of water in her hand, she poured a libation. With her welcoming prayers for peace and possibilities, I entered the threshold and went straight to the orisha room, where all santeros with me saluted the altar, presenting themselves with their Lucumí names, the same as I did.

The abuela told me many inspiring things: that as I was now "born" into a new life, I must release the past and move forward. She instructed me to follow very closely the path set out for me in my *itá*. I must be like a car on a highway, driving straight and carefully in order not to hit dangerous obstacles. She emphasized that doing this would allow me to become great, live calmly, and rule my own "kingdom."

All santeros observed that I was "cool," that my head was "cool," and I must live cautiously. I must not be in the streets where problems or accidents may happen, and I must stay away from places and things with negative influences. I must not go into hospitals or into cemeteries. I must dress completely in white for three months,[15] not take any drugs (except, of course, the three Cuban favorites: sugar, caffeine, and nicotine), and not go out into the dangers of the night. I must stay inside the realm of tranquility.

On the eighth day, January 27, 1992, I walked through the streets of Havana dressed in white, and many people stared at me. While walking past a bus stop or a construction site, occasionally someone would cross their arms and say "santo," saluting me. They recognized me as part of something, whereas before I made ocha I was deemed an *aleyo* (a stranger). One elderly lady at the store, a worker, was very kind and asked me if I felt good in my reincarnation. A middle-aged Afro-Cuban woman eyed me coolly. When our eyes met, I winked, and she crossed her arms and nodded. I did the same, and she left.

Presentation to the Aña Drums

I arrived early at Hans's house, where my presentation took place. In a back room, Rubén had already set up a throne for his Oshún. Because Oshún was not yet "seated" (placed on her altar/throne), I was allowed to photograph the yellow, gold, and green cloth that adorned the setting. Later, miniature batá orishas and cakes were placed on the throne along with Oshún, and Rubén's Eleguá was placed at the foot of Oshún. Many santeros and babalawos attended, and I was guided to salute most of them. Many in my ocha family were there, as well as several other new friends. The *bataleros* (those who play the batá orishas) started the ceremony with an *oro seco* (a orishamed sequence without singing accompaniment) in the altar room for Oshún.

Along with the two other iyawós to be presented, I was put into temporary seclusion in a side room. According to the santeros, we were "castigated" or "in penitence" for the day, another hardship the iyawó must endure. We were to be presented before the main ceremony for Oshún started and then sent back to our room, unable to participate in the rest of the ceremony. In a presentation, the ritually oldest iyawó must go first, the youngest last. Thus, the Balogún was first, his "twin" in ocha next, and I came last.[16]

Madrina came to dress me in the room of the castigated iyawós. I wore the satin red-and-white outfit of Shangó, a cowrie-covered brocade crown on my head, an ax of cedar wood in one hand, a skirt of palm leaves around the waist, and a live rooster tied over my right shoulder. I was given a plate with two whole coconuts, two candles, and a specific number of pesos for the derechos of the singer, the batá players, and my padrino. Carrying the plate in both hands, I was instructed to look down at the plate as I was led to the orishas, where a wide-open circle of santeros left a space for me to fill with dance.

As was the custom for the padrino in this ceremony, Rubén stood by the orishas and watched as Ogún Deí and another santera led me around the open circle. Rattling the bell for Obatalá, the singer, Pedro Saavedra, chanted and led me slowly forward and backward, forward and backward, about eight steps each, in front of the batá orishas.[17] While looking at the plate, I felt the presence of several santeras dancing behind me. I was motioned to put the plate down in front of the *iyá* (mother orisha). The rooster was given to the orishamers, and I lay prone, my head over the plate as instructed. A song began, and madrina turned my head so that my left ear rested on the coconuts. My head was turned again and the right ear placed on the *cocos*. I got up and was led to run and dance within a tight circle of dancing santeras. Led to the batá, I put my forehead to the wood and kissed each orisha, starting with the iyá. As I did this, each orisha sounded, sending vibrations deep into my brain. Then everyone dispersed, and I faced the orishas alone as a song for Shangó started. The batá rhythms were very complex, and I was nervous. I kicked to the slap of hands on skin, reaching to the sky to motion pulling thunder bolts from the clouds, injecting the fire and electricity into my groin. Santeras danced behind me—my thunder ax rising and falling, cutting swathes through the sky, and shouts of ¡Kawo-Kabiosile! (Welcome Your Majesty!) rang out from the santeros.[18] The music rose, with all hoping that I would be mounted. After a couple of songs, the music stopped, and I was led back into the room, made to sit quietly until the *tambor* (batá orisha event) was over.

After the presentation, the *toque* (rhythm) for Oshún began. The tambor was held because an *ahijada* (goddaughter) of Rubén had an obligation to give his Oshún a batá party, and this was it. A set of consecrated orishas known as "Los Tambores de Jesús Pérez" was used by the bataleros.[19] Rubén was soon mounted by Oshún, and cries of triumphant laughter were heard over slaps of hands on the batás. Oshún was taken to the throne room to salute her altar, eat honey, and be dressed. Later she came directly to the room where we, the iyawós, were sequestered. Oshún looked at me menacingly, hands on hips, and I was told by santeros to prostrate myself before her. I saluted Oshún, whose eyes bulged and body swayed coquettishly. She was fierce and jealous. Oshún said I must never forget who made my head for Shangó, and no matter where I go in the world, I must never forget that Oshún loves and protects me—it is she who gives me everything. Later Oshún counseled the other iyawós and many of the santeros present. Many people followed Oshún as she danced, hoping to receive a message or blessings.

The Today Show?

At that moment, an NBC TV crew arrives. They are in Cuba to report on the Special Period for the *Today* show. Eager to report about Santería, when they see a huge crowd of neighbors in the street looking through the windows and doors of the ceremonial space, the crew begins filming from the streets and tries to enter the packed room. When the santeros see the cameras, they begin to dodge them, disrupting the ceremony. Finally, Okantomí sternly tells the crew to stop filming. Being in ritual seclusion in a back room, I know nothing of this occurrence, but a friend guides the crew to where I sit.

The interviewer, who had met Rubén the day before, asks to speak to Rubén, thinking he will grant her permission to film. I try to explain that Rubén is "unavailable," that he is mounted by the goddess of love, and that the crew has arrived too late. Ceremonies with sacred batá music were not to be taped under any circumstances. To do so is considered a *falta de respeto* (lack of respect) to the orishas and spiritually dangerous for the crew. Thus, the crew blunders back to the ceremony with all their equipment. Their bright Hawaiian shirts and shorts convey US fantasies of exotic tropical climates. They are nervous but they try to look friendly as they scan the ceremony for newsworthy items. Shrieks are heard, and soon Ogún Deí is led past the crew, body trembling and contorting, into the altar room. One of the crew members comes up to me, extending his hand to greet me. I cross my arms in the iyawó's customary salute and explain that I can't shake hands, nor can I leave the room, but I hope that they enjoy watching the ceremony.

To see the film crew invade a ritual space made me embarrassed for my compatriots and sad for their insensitivity. I recognize how important it is to be respectful of both the practice and its specialists if one is to operate within another culture. When the NBC crew realized there wasn't a story for them, they soon left.

Just then, Oshún (who had mounted Rubén) came out—spinning, laughing, and taunting. Seeing Rubén's madrina of Palo Monte, Oshún stopped still. The orisha saluted this elder by lying on her side with a queenly, almost arrogant air, while coquettishly fanning herself. Tension arose in the exchange as the orisha delayed in completing the homage, turning this gesture of respect into a coy performance, as if to say, "I bow before you, my elder, who has endowed me with ashé, but all present should recognize that what I have received from you has made me Baaaad!" She then turned to the other elbow to complete the ritual salute, hugged the elder, and went on to counsel others. Soon after, Okantomí's daughter Gisela was mounted by Oshún and led back to the altar, body quivering, head jerking as her hands tried to hold her head steady.

The next morning, I passed an elderly Afro-Cuban woman on a walk, dressed all in white lace, wearing *collares* (beaded necklaces) and bracelets for Orula, Obatalá, and Yemayá (she is a priestess of Yemayá). She is an iyawó. In her hand was a chunk of white cascarilla, and as she walked, she sprinkled the powder over her head to cool and bless it. While we saluted each other, she blessed me by praying for my health, and I asked the same for her. Then a few minutes later I walked past a hospital and heard a voice call out: "¡Iyawó!" Replying with the correct response, "¿Awó?," I turned to see an elderly woman salute me, as I did her, and say: "santo."[20] There is a loving dynamic between Santería practitioners in Havana, where I, a newborn child, am greeted by my elders, as they let me know they are surrounding me and will protect and bless me.

Conclusions

My encounters with Cuban culture—since meeting Juan Boza in 1987 until my reentry into Cuban society as an iyawó and a year later as santero—have given me deeper insight into processes of transculturation, or "give and take" between cultural traditions, as well as how heritage becomes a resource in the process of migration. It struck me that Boza was initiated in the United States. While he came from a family of orthodox practitioners and went to ritual specialists to protect him on his journey before leaving through the Mariel port, he felt no reason to make ocha until confronted with the challenges of exile. I learned that Juan's experience was consistent with Lucumí tradition, because over the years, many elder Cubans told me they were initiated to an orisha to protect themselves from mortal danger, often after medical doctors were not able to heal them.

The practice of Lucumí by Cuban immigrants in the United States shows an alternative to the assimilation of US mainstream values. In fact, it seems that some Cuban communities are being transformed by an increase in ocha practice. A dramatic example of this transformation was broadcast nationally in the 1991 Supreme Court ruling in favor of animal sacrifice.[21] This type of transculturation has increased the practice of ocha by non-Cubans throughout the Cuban diaspora, including Puerto Rico, many US cities, Mexico, Venezuela, Colombia, Spain, Italy, and beyond.

Examples of transculturation were abundant during my preparation for and initiation into ocha, when elders directed me to acknowledge and seek the blessings of the Catholic Church and to utilize Espiritismo practices, Ifá, as well as multiple forms of divination. As I passed through the requirements of each tradition, I was instructed to respect each for the help it might offer me and to treat each as a specific category; that is, there was no confusion about which tradition was which. "Somos junto pero no revuelto"—we are together but not mixed up, as the Cuban saying goes.

My experience taught me the value of oral history toward grasping the continuity of tradition. I became poignantly aware of this while being led by madrina around the plaza after leaving the throne. As we walked past the stalls that had been empty of produce for over thirty years, madrina told me how the presentation of the iyawó to the market was performed before the Revolution because although a crucial part of this ceremony had been absent for over a generation, it remained part of the oral history. Comprehending the power of oral tradition in Cuba opened my ears to how unofficial oral narratives serve to challenge state narratives. For example, elders in my Havana Lucumí community began to spontaneously narrate their knowledge of the role of African-derived initiation systems in the Cuban Wars of Independence (1868–1898) and in the personal lives of Cuban political leaders throughout the twentieth century, which then became the core of my doctoral dissertation.[22] Pioneering transatlantic scholar and Ifá initiate Pierre Verger once said that his method was not to ask questions when interacting with an initiation community, but instead to participate and listen.[23] This was my experience too, as Lucumí elders began to narrate these histories without my asking them.[24] I was grateful for their tutelage but also realized that they were using me to document their perspectives on how their ancestors contributed meaningfully to the process of building a Cuban national heritage.

6

Finding Home in the River

MORGAN M. PAGE

"Eleguá says, 'You've found what you've been looking for. Stop looking,'" the diviner told me. While it would be easy to stop looking elsewhere for the spiritual growth I'd been seeking, it would have been impossible for me to stop looking at all—from the cowrie shells on the straw mat between us and the extravagant pink-haired diviner himself, to the tantalizing glimpse of beads and fabrics I could see through the slightly ajar door beside us. This priest of Yemayá's house was an exercise in maximalism, with no surface left barren, no object without interest, a dizzying array of colors and textures everywhere I turned. When I had shown up at eight o'clock that morning, having taken an overnight Greyhound bus from Toronto to Detroit, I don't know what exactly I had been expecting, but the sensory overload was unlike anything I'd ever experienced. I could neither look away nor keep my eye trained on any one detail for long.

It was a post on LiveJournal that had propelled me across the border and landed me on his doorstep. A now forgotten relic of the pre-Facebook internet landscape, LiveJournal was where I'd spent most of my teenage years, writing about my feelings and exploring subcultures that caught my attention. One of the people I'd been following on the platform, who today I know as my godsister, Nandi, had posted that she was worried about her *padrino* (godfather) in Santería, who'd been in ill health for a while, and put out a call for someone to go check in on him. Nandi would have done it herself, but she was living in the mountains in Colorado at the time. Her padrino lived in Detroit, and in a fit of hubris that only a twenty-one-year-old can have, I volunteered to make the six-hour bus journey to go knock on that door myself. It was May 2008.

But if Afolabí, the six-foot-five "Judío Tatuado" (Tattooed Jew, a nickname Cubans in the religion had given him in the 1990s) who answered the door was a bit unusual, with gauged ears, a goatee, and a fresh set of acrylic nails, it has to be said that I was not exactly your typical twenty-one-year-old myself. I'd spent the previous decade transitioning between genders, from an openly gender-nonconforming child to a post-op trans-sexual woman. That transition had not been a smooth one, occurring across years of physical violence and threats, being kicked out of high school, and problematic substance use. But reflecting on it nearly two decades later, my transition was also one of the things that fed my growing interest in spirituality. For me, to be trans is to know, on some level, that there is more to this world than the flesh. Transness is itself a form of spiritual awareness. And to decide to change that flesh because of this awareness, is that not magic in action, the manifestation of prayer?

A sense of spirituality has always been a key component of my life. Born and, for the most part, raised in Canada on the traditional territories of the Haudenosaunee, my parents were a glamorous Welsh immigrant and a Canadian comedian who had first met while acting in a theater production. The two shared not only their obsession with performance but also their lifelong interests in psychicism, eventually starting a short-lived psychic group with some of their friends.

After she experienced a profound precognitive dream about a landslide, which came to pass as a child, my mom had filled her library with the collected works of Lebanese spiritual philosopher Kahlil Gibran, subsequently discredited "Tibetan Buddhist" T. Lobsang Rampa, American clairvoyant Edgar Cayce, and dozens of books on Welsh folklore. As an adult, I can now recognize the heavy influence of both Spiritualism and Theosophy on her personal beliefs, as she often explained the unifying truth of all religions: "God lives in many mansions." My mother taught herself how to read both playing cards and tarot cards, as well as a working understanding of palmistry and tea-leaf reading.

By the time they had children, my parents had both largely stopped practicing these forms of spirituality. Just as she later would be about my transition, my mother was conflicted about her spiritual gifts. On the one hand, she took great pleasure in telling stories about her encounters with ghosts and divination, but on the other, when pressed about why she no longer did these things, she would defer to Christianity. The story she told went like this: She had got deeply into bibliomancy—the practice of opening the Bible at random and using the first line your eye lands upon to answer a given question—and one day, her finger had landed directly upon a passage that expressly forbade the practice of divination. Terrified, she slammed the Bible shut and gave up all her metaphysical inquiries.

While my parents regularly regaled my brother and me with tales of ESP and even began taking us to a Spiritualist church from time to time, my own forays into spirituality became much too occult too quickly for them. If we weren't arguing over my gender, we were arguing over witchcraft. Inspired both by my parents' stories and the explosion of 1990s witch media, particularly the film *The Craft* (1996), I secretly bought myself a deck of tarot cards and various books on witchcraft. As a nine-year-old, I began casting little spells—half on boys I wanted to have crushes on me, and the other half on a sort of vague idea of "becoming pretty," which I would later realize was about changing gender.

As I got a little older, I tried to attend some public Wiccan ceremonies and quickly realized it did little for me. While I connected deeply to the idea of a divine feminine, the intentional focus on ritual as theatrical psychodrama left me cold. The experience sent me searching for something else. I read books on Hinduism and Buddhism, Satanism and Sufism, anything I could find at the library or on one of my clandestine trips to the local occult shop.

Then, two things happened. The first was deciding to medically transition. Suddenly I had to grapple with what it meant, on a spiritual level, to be trans. The Christianity of the '90s had set itself up as the primary cultural antagonist against LGBT people, and the few strands that didn't had little room for mystic investigation. Wicca and Western occultism seemed founded on the idea of a male-female polarity, which my very body increasingly refuted. And although I could find minor mentions of gender-variant people like the *hijra* and deities like the half-male, half-female Sri Ardhanarishvara in Hinduism, there was no clear path to conversion for an outsider.

Equally impactful was the disintegration of my family. My parents split up, I fell out with my father, and just a few years later my grandmother and mother both suddenly died in short succession. Out of nowhere, I found myself living on my own as an eighteen-year-old transsexual with almost no one in my life. These unexpected deaths fueled an interest in ancestor worship. Before I'd even heard of a *bóveda*, the ancestor shrine of Cuban Espiritismo, I had set one up in my room.

An online friend heard that I was trying to find some kind of spirituality that had room for LGBT people, and she recommended I check out a book called *Queering Creole Spiritual Traditions* (2004) by Randy P. Conner and David Hatfield Sparks. The newly released book contained a series of interviews with various practitioners of Afro-diasporic religions. I'd heard about Haitian Voodoo before and thought it would make for interesting reading, so I picked up a copy. But it wasn't Voodoo that grabbed me when I started reading; instead, it was a description of the orisha Yemayá by one of her priests that I couldn't get over. The words didn't matter. What struck me so forcefully was how he was talking about her as a person who was an active part of his life. In all my years reading about various forms of religion and spirituality, I'd never heard someone so casually discuss a deity as a living force in their everyday life with such conviction, someone who you not only could talk to but who would talk back.

Though the orisha presented in this book were fascinating, I thought, *What could the orisha possibly want with a white Canadian vegetarian transsexual?* Although at age nineteen I had little understanding of identity politics, I could feel their shape, and I worried that attempting to get involved in the religion could be invasive or unwelcome. And although I had no problem in theory with animal sacrifice, I was a vegetarian who, much like my mother, was sensitive about animal suffering. I remember thinking that I wouldn't be able to handle seeing the sacrifice, much less take part. And so, despite how strongly I felt about the orisha, for a year or so I put it aside and tried to move on with my life.

But the orisha, evidently, had other ideas. Narratives of religious conversion in Afro-diasporic religions, particularly Lucumí, tend to follow one of three streams: 1) a health or other crisis leads to divination and *ebó* (offerings); 2) a friend or family member converts, leading to divination and ebó; or 3) the orisha are chasing me. Mine seemed like the third variety. Everywhere I went, there they were. Toronto is not a major center of orisha worship, yet after reading that book, a different side to the city opened to me that I had never noticed before. At the back of dusty knick-knack shops, I'd find myself standing in front of a small selection of orisha candles. Walking down the street, my eyes could catch the glint of beads just below the collar of someone passing by. Once I knew how to look, my eyes never shut again. Without thinking about what I was doing, a corner of my room slowly started to accumulate objects—first a pretty mirror, then a yellow bowl I began filling with change, peacock feathers from the market, and, finally, a novena candle for Oshún.

Before marking my head, Afolabí asked if I had any idea which orisha might claim ownership of me. I knew almost nothing about the religion and probably could have only named five or six orisha with any confidence if pressed. I thought it over while he smiled at me, knowing exactly how clueless I was. "Well," I hedged. I thought about what an impression the description of Yemayá had made on me at first. "I guess Yemayá. Or maybe Oyá."

Most priests I know today are hesitant to mark people's heads, as I am now too. Better for the person to be sure this is the path they intend to walk and that this is the godparent they need to walk it with before pulling down the orisha to the mat. Ideally, as a head marking is only supposed to happen once, if the person leaves the godparent, this can cause confusion for their future godparent. Can they trust the previous marking? Can they even be sure a marking occurred if they don't know or can't contact the original diviner? I've heard some elders discuss, too, how orisha can fight over a head, and if the person takes too much time between the marking and initiation, a different orisha may assert itself over the person's head. Lucumí history is full of whispered stories about initiations gone wrong, where the *iyawó* (new initiate, literally "junior bride of the orisha") gets mounted by a different orisha midway through, causing great scandal. Afolabí, though a highly skilled and reputable priest, took a different stance: he just loved finding out.

Despite my total lack of inkling one way or another, I can see all these years later from the notes that it took Afolabí only a single ask to mark my orisha. Oshún is the orisha of the river, the embodiment of femininity, the much-beloved and often feared deity of all the things that make life worth living: sex, money, dance, and power. Commonly mischaracterized as the coquette, Afolabí would teach me to respect her as the mother of survival—a woman who, despite impossible adversity, always manages to find a way to thrive in this world. In one *pataki* (myth), Obatalá sets out to kill all male children in retaliation for Ogún's rape of Yembo, and out of a mother's love, Oshún dresses her baby Ideu (Idowu, the child born after twins) as a girl to save his life. To this day, some priests sew a skirt for the boy doll that is received with Ideu. I learned later that my gender surgery, two years previous, had occurred on the feast day of Caridad del Cobre, the saint syncretized with Oshún in Cuba—she had been with me all along.

From that moment on, Afolabí and I were inseparable. Famous for his phone calls, Afolabí spent several nights a week on the phone with me for upward of four hours at a time, my sporadic minimum-wage work back then barely managing to pay off the resulting mountains of long-distance phone call bills each month. Every few weeks, I would hop on a bus and head back to Michigan to stay for a week. It was not just religion that we shared; we both loved 1970s radical groups (especially the hilarious Symbionese Liberation Army and their poster girl, Patty Hearst), queer cinema and politics, and the kitsch of female camp icons. He became not just my padrino but also my political and artistic mentor.

Before long, he gave me *elekes,* the reception of the bead necklaces of the orisha. And shortly thereafter, I underwent the ceremony Warriors, the initiation in which one receives the consecrated orisha Eleguá, Ogún, Oshosí, and Osun. The ceremony took place on the weekend of his initiation anniversary, and as luck would have it, his close friend Ode Lenu flew in to help him celebrate it. Tall, British, and butch, Ode Lenu cut an unmistakable impression when she walked into the room. She stood in as my secondary godparent, the *ojubona,* for the ceremony, a particularly appropriate choice given that she is a priest of the somewhat rare orisha Oshosí herself.

Months later, in his purple living room, Afolabí and I were chatting, as usual, about all things. I asked him to give me a reading, and as he was setting up he casually mentioned that whenever he was ready, I could probably pull together the money for my initiation as a priest. He sighed and pointed at the open door to his orisha room and said, "Don't go giving them any ideas!" When the Odu or divination sign Ejiogbe Meji fell on the mat that night, he sighed again and turned to my godbrother Sean to whisper something in his ear. Sean got up and disappeared out of the room. He came back with two things: first, a mass-produced book on *dilogún* (sixteen cowrie shell) divination that was a source of much controversy; and second, a large white *mazo* (beaded sash) for Obatalá. Afolabí asked me to count the shells for myself while he flipped through the book. He laid out the page in front of me and told me to read it out loud because he didn't think I'd believe him if I didn't see it for myself. "You must make *ocha* [initiate as a priest]. You are a slave to the orisha."

"You know," he said, "in the old days, when this sign fell, they wouldn't even let you leave the house. They'd call your family and have them bring over everything needed for your ocha and do it as soon as possible. That's how serious this Odu is!"

Preparing for Initiations

It had only been a year, and now the orisha wanted my head. "Do not pass go, do not collect two hundred dollars," Afolabí laughed. Things moved quickly. To defer the urgency of the Odu, I received Olókun, the ambiguously gendered orisha of the depths of the sea. Olókun, being the foundation of the world, is thought to provide stability to people in this situation who are supposed to immediately make ocha but need time to prepare.

Somehow, despite often having so little money I could barely afford to eat, even going a whole month without buying food once, the money for my initiation poured in. All the riches in this world eventually end up in Olókun's domain at the bottom of the sea, it is said. In a few months, I went back down to Michigan with a fat envelope to put in front of Afolabí's Yemayá. And while I collected the clothes, the tools, and the pots for my future orisha, Afolabí set out to plan the weeklong ceremony.

While my being white and a vegetarian (outside of ceremony) hadn't yet proven to be much of a problem, we quickly ran into a wall. In 2009, years before the so-called Transgender Tipping Point would launch my community into the global spotlight, it was still very controversial to initiate trans people in the Lucumí religion. Elders differed on how it should be handled. Some said that any trans person who had had surgery would automatically be made to Obatalá Alagema—the road/aspect of Obatalá associated with the chameleon, who they said would accept "disfigured" bodies. Others said they could be crowned the orisha to whom they were marked; after all, why would an orisha claim a head if they didn't actually want it? But almost all seemed to agree on one thing: that trans people had to be initiated as our birth sex, with some even going so far as to say we would have to live as our birth sex for the entire *iyaworaje*—the traditional year in which the priest wears only white clothing following our initiation ceremony.

The idea of detransitioning, even for just a year, was unthinkable to me. Transitioning had saved me from suicide; it had been a hard-won struggle medically, legally, and socially. To reverse it all would have not only erased everything about who I was as a person; to say it plainly, it would have killed me. It was not an option. Though I couldn't have imagined walking away from the religion, I knew I could not deny who I was in order to continue with it.

Afolabí was no stranger to this issue. His best friend as a teenager was an African American trans woman named Grace. It was Grace, in fact, who had originally piqued his curiosity about Afro-diasporic religions. Her family members were all "Hoodoo ladies," and he told me many stories about the roots they worked on people, including a particularly dramatic, and possibly embellished, tale of "live things in you," the practice of magically inserting live insects or snakes into people's bodies—in this instance the body of an abusive husband. When Afolabí eventually entered Lucumí, he brought Grace with him. She became HIV positive, which rapidly progressed into

AIDS in the mid-1990s, and Afolabí gave her Olókun to save her life. His decision to honor her humanity by letting her dress as a woman during the ceremony caused a schism for many years with his *madrina* (godmother), but he remained firm that it was the right decision, one that resulted in four more healthy, happy years of her life before she died suddenly in her sleep.

He struggled to find an *Oriaté* (master of ceremonies) who would initiate me as a woman. To hear him tell it, doors were constantly slammed in his face. While this was certainly true some of the time, I now know that his declining health was also a source of people's hesitancy to work with him. Afolabí had been having grand mal seizures the entire time we knew each other. I often spent half of each trip taking him to the hospital, fighting with homophobic nurses who openly discriminated against him, and trying to figure out what could be done to help. Some priests I spoke to later told me that they were afraid that if they helped him do my ocha, the physical and spiritual exertion might kill him.

In November 2009, Afolabí's father called to let me know that he had passed in the night. Apparently, he'd had a severe seizure. Though we had only been in each other's lives for a year and a half, it was and remains an immense loss. Afolabí had been my padrino, my mentor, my dear friend, and, truly, my family, *ibayé tonú*.[1]

Fullfilling Promises Made

In the months that followed Afolabí's death, I despaired at ever finding another *ilé* (orisha house or religious family) and fulfilling my promise to Oshún. I had found Afolabí practically by accident, and though I now knew a small handful of priests, I had no clue where to look for a new godparent. His initiated godchildren grieved for him in Michigan, and it seemed almost intrusive for me to bother them. I collected my ocha money—missing half, perhaps spent in advance by Afolabí—and returned to Toronto. Months went by, and as they did, Olókun went on remaking the foundations of my life. I had entered the religion as a high school dropout, and through Olókun's influence managed to get into a college program. And Olókun, too, helped me land a student placement that, miraculously, turned into a full-time job at a major LGBT organization in Canada.

That spring, I got an unexpected phone call with a familiar British voice at the other end of the line. Ode Lenu, whom I had only met the one time at my Warriors ceremony, asked if I still intended to make ocha. We talked a bit about the issue of gendered clothing, and I could hear her weighing it

Figure 6.1. Morgan's initiation anniversary throne. Photograph by Morgan Page, 2015.

up in her head across the line. Finally, she told me, "Listen, in a few months I'm crowning a trans guy, and I'd be open to make you two as twins if you still want to be crowned. What do you think?"

It was September 2010 when I arrived in Los Angeles. Waiting at the airport for me was Paul, the trans guy who would be initiated to Yemayá alongside me, who drove me back to the house where the initiation was going to take place. Much like the first time I'd set foot in Afolabí's house, it was overwhelming—the only person I knew was Ode Lenu, and we'd barely spoken. Suddenly, I was surrounded by people dressed in white—a mixture of Ode Lenu's ilé, then based mainly in San Francisco and Portland, and the family of the prolific Mexican American priestess in whose home we would conduct the week of ceremonies. I barely had the time to get my bearings over the next two days before I had a sheet thrown over me and was knocking on the door to ocha.

It has now been ten years since my initiation as a priestess of Oshún Ibú Aña in the Lucumí religion. So much has changed—for me, for trans people broadly, and for the religion. I now live in London, where I work as a writer, historian, and activist. I even have a few godchildren of my own. Trans people have become a global topic of both conversation and consternation, resulting in a wonderful array of positive media representations on one hand and an increasingly polarized culture war on the other. And our once-secretive Lucumí religion has, for mostly better and only occasionally worse, entered pop culture through the iconography of Beyoncé and other stars.

Through these changes, I've observed the same arguments over trans initiations being hashed out across the private online groups where priests discuss ritual matters. Often cloaked in the passive-aggressive language of "en mi casa" (in my house), some priests remain stalwart in their claims that trans people must be initiated in our birth sex if we are to be initiated at all. But more and more, a younger generation of priests in the United States and abroad challenges the legitimacy of this idea. Practitioners' increased access to academic texts about early colonial Yorùbá practices has revealed that gender nonconformity not only existed prior to the influx of Islam and Christianity but was deeply tied into the priesthoods of certain orisha.[2] Transphobia is unequivocally a colonial import that was enforced through the Spanish and Portuguese Inquisitions—one of many examples includes the Spanish burning to death an "African transvestite" in 1585.[3] *Travestis* and *transexuais* remain to this day strongly represented in Lucumí's Brazilian sister religions Candomblé and Umbanda, many of whom are initiated to Oxum (Oshún) or her androgynous child Logun-Edé.

For my part, I am hesitant to enter the fray, but my own experience is crystal clear. Throughout the past decade, through dozens of readings, *itás*, orishaming, and other ceremonies in Los Angeles, Oakland, Philadelphia, Detroit, Toronto, and even here in England, I have never once been told by an orisha that there was anything wrong with my initiation, my gender, or the modest dresses I wear to ceremonies. In fact, quite the opposite has happened. Through Paul and me, my madrina opened the floodgates in our ilé. Since we were made, nearly a dozen other trans people have been initiated in our multiracial and heavily queer house. We now have enough priests that when the time comes for a trans initiate to be stripped in ceremony, we can let the trans priests take care of it ourselves. There are, for me, additional layers of love and care in our ilé because we know we're something a little different. My madrina's decision to respect the people who come to her as they are has not been without criticism, but her courage and resolve on this issue have earned her respect in the eyes of many; frequently, she is now consulted by priests considering initiating trans godchildren.

Though we were certainly not the first to do it, this ilé has become a sort of beacon in the debate over trans initiations, brought up in conversations online as proof that the sky won't fall if we respect people for who they are. At a orishaming a few years ago, a respected elder was mounted by their orisha. The orisha brought us in close and told everyone how proud he was of our ilé, that it was a positive and necessary revolution, that this orisha in fact had brought all these odd people together for a reason. We all knew exactly what the orisha meant.

Activism, Forging Alliances, and Building Community

The cultural conversation around race has also evolved over the past ten years, in no small part due to the seismic influence of the Black Lives Matter movement that sprang up in response to the ongoing epidemic of police violence against Black and Brown people in America. Identity politics are at the forefront of many people's minds, and with them, questions around the stakes of cultural mixing.

Cultural appropriation is a hot topic among my generation, pushing us to critically interrogate the ways in which white people participate in, absorb, and most often exploit the cultures of others over whom we have systemic power and violent dominance. My introduction to the concept came, like many Canadian settlers, through Indigenous communities pushing back against the commercialization of traditional crafts and the rise of "plastic shamans"—non-Indigenous cultural outsiders who sell "native" ceremonies, such as sweat lodges, to other non-Indigenous people for a profit without any relationship to Indigenous communities. These types of cultural theft are distinguished from respectful outsiders being invited into practices—for example, pow-wows open to the public, to which my parents frequently brought my brother and me as children.

Though I did not have words to fully articulate these conversations as a twenty-year-old high school dropout when I first became aware of Lucumí, as I said earlier, I could sort of see the shape of them stirring beneath the water. Reckoning with my whiteness seemed imperative if I was to have any kind of healthy involvement, so I started reading books by bell hooks and Angela Davis to educate myself about racism, Blackness, and white supremacy. Afolabí provided me with more resources, in part through our shared love of '70s radical groups like the Black Panthers and the Young Lords. To this day, my madrina has remained a constant source of critical reflection on the role race plays in the religion. This political education, a lifelong work in progress with many mistakes along the way, has been essential to my growth within the religion and as a human being.

We know today that there are currently people of all racial and cultural backgrounds in Lucumí, as it has spread not only across the United States but also throughout Mexico, Venezuela, Spain, and, most recently, Japan.

But is it cultural appropriation for people without African ancestry to practice Lucumí? This is a question I have been asking myself for years. To find
an answer, I turned to the traditional Lucumí method for adjudicating issues of religious orthodoxy: examining history. The Lucumí religion as we
know it today coalesced in the mid-nineteenth century in Cuba, following
the destruction of the Òyó Empire in the 1830s and the resulting mass im-
portation of enslaved Yorùbá people into Cuba. The religion became organized through the *cabildo* system—Catholic mutual aid societies that separated different African ethnic groups, in theory quelling the cross-ethnic
solidarity needed for Haitian-style slave revolutions while in practice allowing ethnic groups to maintain their distinct religious cultures on the island.

One of the issues the cabildos had to contend with was a growing community of Creole-born people, many of whom had mixed ancestry—whether
that be between multiple African ethnic groups or across races. This may be
what prompted the shift toward the marking of the head orisha, a practice
that seems to have had little point in precolonial Yorùbáland where one was
simply born into the worship by family or by the town of a particular deity.

White, Chinese, and Filipino Cubans entered Afro-Cuban religious
groups by at least the 1850s with the enigmatic Abakuá leading the way.[4] By
the end of the nineteenth century, cabildo records show the Lucumí following suit, such as the legendary Cabildo Africano Lucumí, whose 1901 membership register lists the *blanco* Bonifacio Valdés, a prominent *babalawo*.[5]
Despite, or even perhaps because of, negative press coverage of Afro-Cuban
religions at the turn of the twentieth century, this influx of white and other
non-Afrodescendiente Cubans continued to expand, including, eventually,
the respected *babalorisha* Rigoberto Rodríguez (Oshún Yemí). While inter-
racial marriage also likely played a role in this shift, it is not inconceivable
that some elders may have strategically formed alliances of ritual kinship
with well-positioned white Cubans who could provide a certain level of
protection for the cabildos through their racial privilege and class clout.

When the Lucumí diaspora began reaching American shores in New
York and Miami in the late 1950s, the main determining factor of whether
one could be involved was the ability to speak Spanish. African Americans
faced difficulty in becoming involved with the Cuban and Puerto Rican
Lucumí ilés of that period due to the language barrier as well as racial ten-
sions.[6] One of the first priests to break this cultural and racial divide was
Asuncion "Sunta" Serrano, Osaunko, an Afro-Puerto Rican priestess of
Obatalá remembered fondly in New York for her trailblazing work initiating Black Americans through Oseijiman Adefunmi's Yorùbá Temple in

East Harlem. Adefunmi, born Walter King, was the first Black American initiated in the religion and founded the Yorùbá Temple to bring together Black Nationalist politics and African-derived religion, later spinning off into the orisha-Voodoo movement of Oyotunji Village. In 1962, Serrano also famously initiated the first white American in the religion: Judith Gleason, Oyalola.

Judith Gleason (1929–2012) wrote some of the first nonacademic English-language books on orisha religion, including *Oyá: In Praise of an African Goddess* (1987) and the lightly fictionalized retelling of her entry into the religion, *Santería, Bronx* (1975). While I am certain she probably caused something of a stir, even the staunchly Black Nationalist Adefunmi is quoted as saying, in 1966, "There is no room for racism in our religion. If the religion is valid for Blacks, it applies to whites as well. We teach that when an Afro-American has self-respect, he has no need to fear or hate the white man."[7]

Following Gleason's initiation, a steady stream of white Americans and Europeans, among other non-Black people, have been initiated into the religion. It's worth examining these white people. One wave of white initiates seems to coincide with the worst years of the AIDS epidemic in the late 1980s and early 1990s. LGBT people have always been disproportionately involved in the religion, to the point of affiliation with Lucumí inferring possible homosexuality in popular Cuban society. The mass death experience of the AIDS crisis drove many gay men, including white gay men, into the religion as they sought ways to protect their health and spiritually process the relentless onslaught of loss. Though neither ever said as much to me, reflecting on it, I think this may account in part for Afolabí's own conversion to the religion in the late 1980s and perhaps similarly influenced my madrina's conversion in the mid-1990s.

The history is clear that people of various racial and cultural backgrounds have been involved in the religion from its early days, and some of the most respected priests—such as those at the preeminent Cabildo Africano Lucumí—are responsible for their initiations. We then must ask, why would they decide to do that? A cynical answer I have occasionally seen lobbed about is greed, although setting aside the complex later development of "*ocha* tourism,"[8] this is hard to reconcile with priests like Serrano who have such spotless reputations. Elders I have spoken to emphasize that following their orisha's will—as mandated in divination—is that a priest is not permitted to turn away anyone who comes to them seeking the religion. This is explained that the orisha themselves may be guiding the seeker to the person for help and they may become part of the ilé or religious family. More significantly, divination is a constant in the religion, particularly within the initiation itself, and the approval of the orisha and *egun* (ancestors) must be obtained at each step along the way for initiations to move forward.

The danger of cultural appropriation and theft is real, and I understand when people, particularly those outside the religion as is most often the case, are suspicious of the intentions of white and other non-Black people entering Lucumí. For those of us who follow the legitimate traditional routes of divination and initiation, becoming active members *within* the community and under the aegis of our elders, I think this process is more accurately understood as religious conversion. Appropriation, within the Lucumí frame, refers instead to the illegitimate "*fakería*" of people without proper initiation, training, and *licencia* purporting to conduct divinations or initiations *outside* the community, bilking people out of money while pretending to be Lucumí—a sadly frequent phenomenon in the age of social media from frauds of all races. Still, I believe it especially behooves white and other non-Black as well as non-Cuban practitioners to tread lightly, to engage in the work of undoing racism within ourselves, to join ourselves politically with the movements for racial justice, and to remain critically reflective about how and when we take up space as representatives of this increasingly globalized religion to outsiders.

Several years ago, I attended an Aña (a formal orishaming ceremony). Oshún came down in one of her priests—a Mexican American woman— and came over to my elder godsister and me—both white women crowned to Oshún. The river deity took both of our hands and told us at length in Spanish about how she wanted to "speak all the languages of the world." We both interpreted this to mean that Oshún intended the orisha religion to spread across the globe. The orisha have their own plans, and we're all just along for the ride, I realized. A river that is flowing cannot be stopped.

Reflections in and on the River

This past December, after hours of backbreaking, sweaty ceremony work, I sat at a table that was delicately dressed half in blue and half in yellow. Fine china sparkled in front of me, and around the table sat my Madrina, Ode Lenu, my initiatory twin, Paul, my younger godsister, and many of my elders—white, Black, Cuban, and Mexican. A priestess of Oshún served the table while each person in turn gave a short speech about the ceremony

Figure 6.2. Morgan, Odofemí, and her orisha throne. Photograph by Morgan Page, 2015.

my godsister and I had gone through that day. We had received the knife—also called *cuchillo, obé,* or *pinaldo*—a singularly Lucumí ceremony with no known Yorùbá equivalent. This ceremony confers not only the permission to perform sacrifice but also a certain level of independence as a priest. For many, it is the culmination of years of study and apprenticeship and represents a step into or toward elderhood, thus the reason we get to sit around the "big kids' table."

When it came time for me to deliver my own speech, much to my utter embarrassment I started crying. Tears of gratitude for the *ashé* that Oshún has given me but equally, gratitude that this religion has returned to me what I lost many years ago: a home and a family. Having nearly all my blood relatives pass in rapid succession as a young person, my godfamily has become the only living family I've got. My madrina, my ojubona Eshú Okán Ladé, and my twin are now the most important people in my life. I might not ever fully understand all the reasons Oshún brought a white Canadian transsexual vegetarian to this religion, but I think giving me family was a big part of it. As the divination Odu Ejiogbe Meji says, "a head will find its home," and somehow this dazzling, arduous, and politically fraught Afro-Cuban religion is where I've found mine. *Moforibale Oshún.*

7

How I Came to the Tradition

SUE KUCKLICK-ARENCIBIA

Outside Las Tunas, Cuba, I was standing in an outdoor bathroom with a cracked wooden seat, surrounded by coffee sack curtains, the sunlight illuminating a rusty enameled bowl filled with yellow flowers and herbs torn to pieces in water by *padrino* (my initiatory godfather), the fragrance was minty, floral, and herbaceous, my dry clothes hung on a nail. Pouring the water over myself, I scrubbed the mixture onto my skin and brushed the herbs off while praying for good health. The afternoon heat dried me quickly, and I dressed and returned to the yard with my husband, brother-in-law, padrino, and his wife.

I grew up in a suburb outside of Cleveland, Ohio. My recent ancestors came to the Americas from England, Scotland, Wales, Ireland, Germany, East Prussia, and Congo. I have a grandfather several generations back who was of the Choanoke people in what is now North Carolina. My mother grew up in South Carolina and moved here after marrying my father, an Air Force sergeant, a few weeks after her high school graduation. My paternal grandparents had moved to the area in the 1920s and opened a radio repair shop that expanded into appliances, furniture, and dry goods. It was the kind of town where the elders referred to houses by the names of the families who used to own them. The old folks told of various locations around town like the sandstone cave on the river with a tunnel that led to a basement that was used to hide people on the Underground Railroad. The girls who lived in the house said the tunnel was cemented over, so the story had to be true. The little history the town has with the Underground Railroad didn't mean the town was any less racist than the small southern city where my mother grew up; they just hid it a little better. I am old enough to remember the Jim Crow laws, with segregated drinking fountains and schools. I'm not surprised that my family down there didn't talk about their entire ancestry.

My mother's side of the family has deep roots in Protestant Christianity: Methodist, Baptist, and Presbyterian and generations of deacons and preachers. Even further back there were Quakers, but that didn't get past the move from Virginia. In our small town there was a Protestant church and a Roman Catholic church. My mother was active in the Protestant church and made us attend, but my father didn't really care one way or another. Being active in a church or the Masons cemented one's place in the community. I really had to attend church when I visited family down south; my cousin would make me go. The services lasted the entire morning and then some. I was accustomed to Sunday school and being out in an hour or two. I didn't like church; the lack of female representation in the higher ranks, the racist missionaries, and the rigid thinking bothered me. I did like singing in the choir, asking pointed questions, and pulling extra meanings out of the verses.

I went to college for a few years and worked in the family business. In the mid-1970s, a friend from university invited me on a trip to Florida and Mexico. We met someone selling his artwork; he learned we were sleeping in our truck and he insisted we stay at his home in Coconut Grove, Florida. We got a whole room to ourselves. There were other people staying there too. The refrigerator was stocked with expensive snacks, and it was a party every day. The fellow who rented the house was something of a hustler and sold jewelry and artwork on consignment. One night he showed us a necklace a Cuban goldsmith had made of twigs of gold inset with diamonds kept in a box lined with black velvet. The effect was as if one was looking into the starry night sky.

My friend and I went to Mexico, and we were even driven to the airport. When we returned to Florida just two weeks later, the phones were disconnected, and our friend had taken off for New Jersey. He hadn't paid for that necklace, and the housemates said the goldsmith had hired a Santería priest to set things right. Every vehicle had become inoperable, the grocery store cut off the credit, and the landlady was demanding the overdue rent. A Spiritualist came over to try to help, against the advice of her own guides, and was seriously injured in a car accident on the way home. My friend was dismayed to learn that our friend had never mailed his checks and credit card receipts from the art show. My friend knew there were plenty of expensive items still in the house he could potentially take to make up for the loss.

I woke in the middle of the night to a presence swirling and flying around the room. She said clearly that the spiritual work was done and that we were safe if we stole nothing from the house. I told my friend the next morning, and he looked at me strangely. I wondered what this Santería thing was and how it transformed people's lives so quickly and dramatically.

I returned to Cleveland and my regular retail work life. My family sold the store to the employees and my parents retired. I met a guy in the grocery store who was starting a metaphysical study group, and I said, "Well, why not?" We studied astrology and wrote papers about the history, philosophy, and religions of ancient cultures. Part of the curriculum was studying the Chinese martial arts of Shuai Chiao and T'ai Chi Ch'uan with a doctoral student from Taiwan, Weng Chi-Hsiu. He went by the name Daniel. He studied with Grandmaster Ch'ang Tung-Sheng in the police academy in Taipei, Taiwan. Daniel founded an academy in Cleveland with students from other schools and invited his teacher to visit the United States. Professor Ch'ang was in his seventies and was one of the few surviving old masters, sort of like the ones depicted in the movies we saw at the Hippodrome Theater on Saturday afternoons. There were warring schools just like in the movies too. He adopted our school as his own, and we became part of his lineage of students. He also has a lineage of disciples. The disciples learned different material, but he taught us that too. Later he adopted my friend Margaret Newman and me as his granddaughters. We didn't speak Chinese and he didn't speak English, but we'd call him in Taiwan, drive to Columbus, or fly somewhere just to see him.

The metaphysical study group regrouped when the teacher moved out of town to attend college in New York. We began studying with another already established group. We studied a lot of subjects, including astrology, Carlos Castañeda, Gurdjieff, and, eventually, divination. I was assigned geomancy. I had no idea what that was. Why couldn't I have a subject that I was interested in like the I Ching or tarot? I went to the White Collection at the Cleveland Public Library where we spent days surrounded by piles of books. That room even had its own fragrance of ancient paper. Back then we were allowed to browse the stacks of this invaluable collection, which had been amassed as a private collection by a man named John G. White. I found a few books on geomancy, one from the 1800s and others more recent. I looked through the bibliographies, and one word came up over and over: Ifá. I found 'Wándé Abímbọlá's book about the Ifá divination corpus and started reading it there,[1] sitting at the wooden table. The room disappeared as I read about this religious, spiritual, and cultural tradition. I found my path and my aim that day. I was going to learn as much as I could about Ifá and orisha. I sent a check to Oxford University Press in Nigeria and got a copy of the book by return post.

The metaphysical group decided to make a trip to New Jersey to see our friend and teacher, but one by one people canceled, leaving only my friend Margaret and me. We got there late in the evening, and our friend Al said, "I have someone I want you to meet. He's a real babalawo from Africa!" First, we met his friend Mimi, who had introduced Al to the Lucumí community in New York City. She is a priest of Yemayá, and we started learning that people worshipped the orisha there in New York and had been doing so for a very long time. We later had dinner with the *babalawo* (an Ifá priest) at a Brazilian restaurant. His name was Afolabí Epega, *ibayé tonú*. After dinner, Al drove through Manhattan in a rainstorm; Fola leaned over from the front seat, teaching us Yorùbá cosmology and divination basics while I took notes on scrap paper. The next day, Margaret and I got our first Ifá divination. I even remember the sign, Odu Ifá, that came that day thirty-five or so years ago, and the orisha Oshún spoke as she would in reading after reading. Margaret's reading said that if she were male, the reading would have stopped and she would have been initiated to Ifá on the spot, but women didn't get initiated into Ifá. She got angry about that and didn't think that was fair. In retrospect, I didn't realize how serious that reading was regarding her well-being; she was soon living with an illness that shortened her life.

Margaret worried incessantly about the sacrifice prescribed by the divination. A few months later, Fola visited Cleveland to conduct divination for other members of the group. He told each person which orisha guided their lives and "ruled their head." No one had any idea what that meant or what to do about it, so we started reading everything we could find. What was available then were academic works or trade sensationalist paperbacks written by those with superficial knowledge of the religion (unfortunately, they became very popular). Fola returned later that year to initiate the leader of the group to Eshú, orisha of the crossroads, and later initiated other members of the group. I did not receive any orisha from him. When I visited him in New York, he gave me a set of *obi abata* (divination instruments) made by a Lucumí babalawo with a cowrie shell on a coconut shell backing. He instructed me how to use them for divination.

The books we had read didn't include important information, although I didn't learn that until later in my journey. Initiations to orisha are not done by a single priest. The religion is practiced in a community in which people specialize in different tasks; the community is an extended family, and one-to-one teaching by godparents who take responsibility for the growth and guidance of the godchild is paramount. Important transitional ceremonies are done in person.

The interactions in the group became increasingly toxic and involved sexual boundary violations. I understand now that improperly done spiritual work can have terrible consequences going far beyond the individual. I separated myself from the group voluntarily. My years-long friendships were gone. Even though Margaret and I were roommates and coworkers, that too ended. I was not a part of the community for years.

I have been very fortunate indeed to meet Lucumí priests in Cleveland who were connected to houses of orisha worship in New York City and who have been ethical and upright and excellent teachers. Thank you to my first teacher in Lucumí, Baba Ibi, ibayé tonú, and his family, Baba Oloye, Iyá Adetutu, Magdalena and Ivia, ibayé tonú, who always welcomed everyone into their home. Thanks, also, to Baba David Coleman and my *oyubona* (second orisha godparent), Barbara Barrett, Oshúnnikantomi. Some of us also had the assistance of Yeye Luisah Teish, who was living in Oakland, California, and was on the lecture circuit. She helped a few of us regain our trust and power as women in the tradition. My padrino, Manny Urquiola, and his wife, Marisol Sánchez, who is a priestess of Yemayá priest, have welcomed me to their *ilé* orisha (orisha house or family).

Those years went by. I was working two jobs and attending a master's program in counseling. I was feeling out of sorts and a classmate said I sounded depressed. I was, and it wasn't the first time. I headed to one of two *botánicas* (Afro-Atlantic religious goods store) in town. I told the woman at the counter I needed help, and she said something about tarot cards. I told her, "You know what I mean." She made a show of looking through a notebook for a phone number she knew well. Soon I was on my way to a house on the west side of Cleveland with an iron bathtub with a statue of Mary inside it half-buried in the front yard. An irritable man came outside to greet me. He warmed up quickly when he learned I was there to get some help. I became a part of the routine of the house soon after getting a reading. A set of *collares,* the sacred necklaces linking me to his house and the Lucumí tradition, followed a set of spiritual baths. Later I received warriors and Olókun from Marcos. Marcos was from Camagüey, Cuba, and was initiated to Yemayá. He never told us who initiated him in Camagüey. He told us he went to live with his madrina at an early age and worked for her and that she eventually initiated him. There was a language barrier between us, and he relied on his girlfriend and another godchild to translate. I didn't speak Spanish then. He introduced us to Magdalena. He didn't appear to work the religion with anyone locally, and if he brought someone from out of town to work with him, he didn't tell us. I didn't know that was a problem then; he was isolated from the rest of the community, and looking back, these were some potential signposts of how things would develop.

I went to get a reading from a well-known diviner in Chicago whom I heard about on an AOL group, with Marcos's blessings. I got some very good advice about what occurred in the past, the damage it did, and how to fix it. The diviner told me who he knew and trusted locally to help with the work needed to break the cycle. I saw Marcos on the street a month or two later, and he accused me of being a liar. He was upset that I had work done by someone else and had distanced myself from the chaotic situation developing in the house. I learned later from another godchild that the chaos was nothing new, and other godchildren had left en masse in the past. We shared and compared notes about how everyone had received divination consultations and was instructed to pay for work and rituals around the same time there was an appearance of an outdoor pool, a backyard shed, or new living room furniture.

I had called one of the women who was recommended, a priest of Oyá who lived about an hour's drive away. She drove up to Cleveland and helped me complete the recommended work. She invited me to the anniversary of her initiation in her home. When I arrived, it was a beautiful July day and people dressed in white clothes were out in the yard socializing. I was greeted warmly. A orishamer came up from Atlanta with his father, Baba Medahochi, ibayé tonú, from Milwaukee, who had been initiated for Shangó for thirty-four years and for Ifá. He was well known as a scholar and for his deep studies of metaphysics. Obatalá possessed one of his priests during the orishaming and said I needed to get initiated, while Iyá Aboyade took careful notes. She said that it was best to take notes because invariably one would forget part of what was said. Obatalá indicated that Baba Medahochi should be my godfather and that Iyá Aboyade should be my godmother. I was advised to begin buying new white clothes and the other things I needed for the initiation and the novitiate period following it, which requires the person to dress in white throughout. By the end of September 1996, all the arrangements were complete, and a small group of orisha priests, some from the metaphysical group, gathered to work my initiation for Oshún. The wind blew hard around the house the night I entered the *igbodu* (the room where the initiation takes place), and even as I am writing, there are

Figure 7.1. Sue Kucklick-Arencibia, Oshúnmilaya. 2016.

strong gusts of wind that cut the electricity. I felt anxious and happy at the same time. I heard a lot of activity downstairs and had no idea what was going on, which was the case for the several days that the ceremony entails. I was given the name Oshúnmilaya, which means Oshún, wife of Orunmila, who owns the divination system of Ifá.

I was now an *iyawó*, a "junior bride" or new initiate in the tradition. I wore white and kept my head covered daily and ate my meals from my own plate with my own spoon and cup. I quickly learned to keep track of my cup and plate at events because unheeding people would put our things away in a cupboard. I was home by sunset if I wasn't working. I found that I was much more sensitive to other people's energy and learned to use caution in my interactions. I stayed on my *estera* (straw mat) on the floor often and took baths with *efún* (white chalk used to dispel negativity). All the while, my job took me inside jails, courtrooms, and hospitals, all considered liminal areas that can unbalance the iyawó's delicate spiritual energy. I also worked an evening security job in a theater. One night, the Balé Folclórico da Bahia from Brazil was there. They were facing a language barrier with no translator, but we were able to communicate through the language of our religion. Another evening, a orishamer walked in and saw me dressed in white and hollered out, "I have a sister here!" He began singing to Oshún, and I reminded him I had to work. Was I a perfect iyawó? Not at all. Did I learn why the many rules to protect the iyawó are enforced? Yes, I did.

Practitioners were beginning to coalesce into the Usenet newsgroup alt. religion and other online mailing lists and discussion boards. Incredible rudeness occurred in flame wars, but friendships and new associations were being made, and the way information was transmitted about the religion changed. No longer was information access solely the province of pulp journalists, academics, and oral transmission from mouth to ear. Academia was changing too; participant observers recounting history gave way to initiates telling our story.

In 1999, an alt newsgroup for the orisha tradition led to groups of orisha practitioners from around the United States converging upon an academic conference called "Yorùbá Tradition in the 21st Century." The conference was held at Florida International University and was the brainchild of scholars Jacob K. Olupona and Terry Rey. A Brazilian woman who was a Candomblé priest was a coordinator and was hired as a temporary worker. Maria de Oxalá, ibayé tonú, ensured that the online orisha community knew about the event and made sure we were able to arrange lodging and transportation to the conference site. I have a photo of the bus that took the participants to the site, and in it are most of the published authors who were initiates in the orisha tradition. We listened to presentations and panels from scholars from all over the world. Afternoons and evenings were spent with new friends talking about everything having to do with orisha. We had never had an opportunity like this to just meet face to face with people outside our spiritual houses.

In July 2004, a group of friends and I traveled to Santiago de Cuba for the Festival del Caribe. My ojubona Barbara Barrett and I presented a paper about the mind, body, and spirit connection and how we utilized this in our professional lives as a nurse and a counselor. It was published in the *Del Caribe* journal. We wondered if we'd be accepted as practitioners by the Cubans and tried to stay invisible on the sidelines. Part of the activities for the festival then involved inviting various religious groups to educate the attendees about their practices and perform music and dance. Vodou followers came from their town in the mountains, a dance troupe came from Matanzas, and one year a Kumina group came from Jamaica. People around town opened their homes for Palo and *espiritista* (Spiritist/ medium) ceremonies. The government wanted these events to be folkloric presentations, but real ceremonies were taking place in homes, rural areas, and Casa del Caribe on Calle 8. We found it by following the sound of the orishas. One evening an iroko tree was being planted in the courtyard of Casa del Caribe. The officiants, who included the late Palo Mayombe priest Tata Vicente Portuondo, called for all the initiates to step forward and participate by contributing their *ashé* (ritual energy, life force) to the ceremony.

They looked right at us. We were welcomed as orisha initiates, so far from home, and invited to work with them. For the first time, I felt in my heart that I was accepted as a part of a larger spiritual community. The experience of being in a community where orisha worship was an everyday part of life changed my perceptions of the tradition. I no longer felt isolated and marginalized. Children came up to us on the street, and adults were surprised to see people from the United States wearing the necklaces identifying us as Lucumí.

A lot was happening in Cleveland. My ojubona was asked to be a part of a PBS series called *This Far by Faith,* a documentary about African Americans and religion. A film crew arrived in Cleveland during an orisha initiation for Obatalá. The protocol was explained in detail about what they could and couldn't record. The whole crew remained entirely respectful throughout the filming. The project encountered difficulties in postproduction, and the finished work was a severely pruned version of what the original creators had proposed.

Our small community in Cleveland continued to grow. Our proximity to a farming community helped, as did the presence of an African community. We were able to make a short drive to get the animals required for *ebọ* (sacrifice). The local store specializing in Puerto Rican and Mexican food expanded their inventory to African foods, which meant we no longer drove to Chicago to get basics like palm oil and kola nuts. We learned to cook African foods for the orisha like *akará,* bean fritters made from black-eyed peas. Baba 'Wándé Abímbọlá, came to Cleveland and taught classes and looked after us spiritually. During my iyawó year, I was able to get my *Ise'fá* (one hand of Ifá initiation) from him.

My godmother Iyá Aboyade moved to Chicago after a series of stressful events that had begun before my initiation. She moved to the South Side of Chicago, where she'd lived a few years before with her ex-husband. She, her mother, and her three younger children shared a small house off 93rd and Halstead Street. She tried to reunite with spiritual associates from the past, but many rejected her orisha initiation because Lucumí protocols were not followed. Some did accept her as a priest of orisha, but it wasn't an easy process. I was still an iyawó when she moved. My initiation was done in a similar way, and I felt limited as to what I could do spiritually for people. I have avoided being anyone's godparent because I did not receive as part of my initiation the full complement of consecrated orisha shrines/vessels (Oshún, Obatalá, Shangó, Yemayá, and sometimes Oyá) as is given in the

Lucumí system. We both had Lucumí priests who worked at our initiations and received the one orisha that ruled our heads. I kept practicing divination with the Obi Abata I was given, and I kept many notes, which turned into a book over the years. I sometimes did readings for people, following Fola's instructions, and they were accurate.

I made another trip to Cuba, but this time I went alone. I made another presentation, and this one was about the growth of the orisha tradition on the internet. At that time, people in Cuba outside the government had no access to the internet and barely had access to email. I showed them how communication was changing in the community. The practitioners there were surprised and weren't certain that the increased communication regarding the tradition was a good thing. I met Julian Mateo Tornes, who oversaw the programming at Casa del Caribe II under Joel James Figuerola, who had his office at Casa I. Casa II operated as an art gallery and presentation space and had a patio yard on the side with a bar that opened for events. Each room in the old colonial house, located in the Vista Alegre neighborhood, was dedicated to a different tradition in the Afro-Cuban traditions practiced in Santiago de Cuba. The front room hosted various artists. Another room was set up as a working space for Espiritismo *cruzado* ("crossed Spiritism," Spiritism that contains elements of Lucumí worship), and another was typical of the room an orisha worshipper would have in their home, with a cabinet that held the *soperas* (lidded vessels) containing the orisha and their embroidered *pañuelos* (large squares of cloth in the colors of the orishas). Farther back, Abelardo Duarte, who was initiated in Lucumí and Palo, created a space for Palo Mayombe with a straw hut and signs of the *nkisi* (his Palo spirit/deity) painted in bold flourishes on the walls. Julian became a dear friend and thought my Obi Abata book was important; thus, he translated it into Spanish. He advocated with Ediciones Oriental to have it published in Cuba, but after he passed away, I wasn't sure what happened to the project—until Baba Willie Ramos sent me a message, saying, "Hey! I didn't know you were published!" Julian also translated *Ifá Will Mend Our Broken World* (1997) by Baba 'Wándé Abímbólá into Spanish.

I met by husband-to-be during a presentation where he and a friend were taking advantage of being mobile to see some presentations in which they were interested. He was born into a family of espiritistas in Santiago de Cuba. He spent most of his life in the Cuban military and was a great tour guide. He has taken me to every historical feature of eastern Cuba and into areas where few tourists have an opportunity to venture. He was initiated as a priest of the orisha Shangó a few years after we met. We often visit his padrino in Palma Soriano, where he presides over a large house of worship. His entire home is a shrine. The orisha pots sit in the front room, and just past the small kitchen, a wooden shelf holds the multiple Eleguás (orisha of the crossroads) of many of his godchildren. The next room is a larger space where he holds ceremonies for Espiritismo cruzado and the igbodu for orisha initiations. It's the largest room in the house and can comfortably seat fifteen people in a circle. The backyard is an open area filled with the plants needed for spiritual practices and has chickens, ducks, and doves. All the way in the back is a small house made of wood slats and a corrugated metal roof. A pair of palm trees are growing through the roof, and sun shines through the slats. This is the home of his Palo nkisi, some of which are housed in metal cauldrons and stand taller than a person.

On the day of the presentation, a mother and her son were visiting for her son to become *ngueyo* (a new pine—an initiatory title in Palo), which in the Palo tradition is the term for "a new initiate." The son had gotten into some trouble living in Florida, and the mother hoped this would help keep him away from troublesome influences. Other families were there waiting have their children "scratched," the term used for a ritual process in Palo initiation that is the first ceremony performed for the person. For some families this seemed to be like a Christian baptism, which is done for protection and their children's success. I asked padrino how many people he had scratched, and he said more than a thousand. He also had many orisha godchildren in different parts of the world. His godchildren in the neighborhood helped with the ceremonies and helped his wife in the kitchen. Later in the evening, the Palo orishaming brought godchildren and neighbors to sing and dance until it got late. The next day, padrino took me on a walk showing me all the places in town where the sacred herbs like *vervaina, atiponlá,* and *peregún* grew. We picked up palm fruits for an offering to his spirits. Not all the herbs can be found in town, and he goes to *el monte* (the wilderness, or forest) to find what he needs.

Padrino isn't my direct godfather, even though I have spiritual things he has given me like an eleke for an orisha and an *mpaka* (a consecrated Palo emblem). However, I respect him as a godfather—as I do the people who conducted my initiation and from whom I've learned various aspects of the traditions of which I am a part as an initiate, as well as the espiritistas with whom I've worked. I appreciate and honor the time and energy they take to continue these traditions through their work. I share what I've learned to the degree that I can and even try to make sure knowledge seekers receive good information and avoid the rampant frauds. I try to help them understand that the magic in these traditions happens face to face, and the knowledge and wisdom occur within the hand-to-hand, mouth-to-ear transformation of sweat, stone, blood, herbs, trust, and love.

8

Practicing Ifá in Tokyo

Yoshiaki Koshikawa

I was born in 1952, shortly after World War II, in an old fishing town called Choshi, Chiba, located about twenty-five miles from Tokyo. Growing up, most of the people in my community were of modest means, and both of my parents worked as elementary school teachers. Unlike in urban centers where space is at a premium, the tradition of large families was maintained for farmers in my prefecture; however, in the 1950s, many nonfarming nuclear families like mine were also increasing. Another tradition that is also maintained widely in Chiba is that most households have both Buddhist and Shinto altars, as we had in our house. As I will explore here, it is a form of sharing or syncretism of Shinto and Buddhist religions maintained in Japan.

My mother was a reverent, strict, and beautiful person, and if she had had received *awofaka* (a foundational Ifá initiation) and had her guardian orisha divined in the Afro-Cuban tradition, she would have been a child of the lofty and wise Obatalá. My father, on the other hand, was hardly like my mother in character; he was practical and diplomatic in his approach to life. To my mind, he could have been a child of the thunder god Shangó. My father was a music teacher, and our house was filled daily with the sounds of different melodies either on records or from my father's practicing. During the war, he had been held captive for two years in Siberia as a prisoner of war. It's not hard to imagine just how much that may have impacted him for the rest of his life. In his spare time, he composed music or always kept busy working on something, anything—he didn't know how to rest at all. Observing him going about his pursuits, I got the impression that he didn't want to waste a moment of his life, that he was trying to pack in as much as he could, and perhaps that he lived with the feeling that he could die at any moment. He lived happily in that manner until he was well over ninety years old.

So too was I confronted with mortality at the early age of eighteen, when one of my high school friends died in a tragic accident. Later, when I viewed his calm face in the bed of his house where he was laid so that we could pay our respects, I came to realize the ephemeral nature and fragility of human life. However, the spirit of my friend has lived on inside of me ever since. I call this feeling of closeness "the vitality of the dead," inspired by an imaginative passage from Harry Mathews's novel *Cigarettes* (1987) that the souls of the dead enter through the attractive holes of the living.[1] Later I will elaborate on this unique notion of the dead, citing another case I experienced in Havana.

My First Encounters with Afro-Cuban Religions

My initial visit to Cuba happened in 2008, after I had finished writing a book in Japanese called *Tōgarashi no Chiisana Tabi: Bōdā Bungakuron* (2006, *The Short Journey of a Red Hot Chili Pepper: Border Culture Theory*) and a book that explored poetry and other forms of expression on the US-Mexico border culture, *Gitā wo Daita Wataridori: Chikānoshi Raisan* (2007, *A Migratory Bird with a Guitar: In Praise of Chicano Poetry*). Over the course of a decade working along the US-Mexico border areas, I learned firsthand how the existence of popular forms of veneration of Our Lady of Guadalupe of the Catholic Church provided spiritual support to a multitude of working-class people in Mexico and in the Mexican American diaspora. Although the sacred beliefs and practices of the Indigenous people were obliterated by Spanish conquerors and whose gods and sacred sites had been syncretized with Catholic saints and usurped by the Christian doctrine, many of their beliefs remain and thrive. Many revere Our Lady of Guadalupe as Tonantzin (Nahuatl for "Our Sacred Mother"); she continues to be called as such, and she had become one of my guardians during this work. In doing so, I formed my own personal form of devotion to Lupe, and I didn't feel the need to convert to Catholicism.

On my first visit to Cuba in 2008, I spent two weeks in Havana. I had traveled to Cuba on my own and had spent those initial days visiting the various tourist sites that you would find in any guidebook to Cuba. I explored mostly by foot to better acquaint myself with the geography and sights of this magnificent capital city. Part of my wanderings included being on the lookout for signs of Afro-Cuban rituals and ceremonies as I roamed the streets of Old Havana, venerable Vedado, and other Havana neighborhoods. But I wasn't successful, and I wasn't satisfied with the Afro-Cuban religious content in the museums I encountered in Regla and Guanabacoa, two suburban towns across the bay from Havana. Neither was I interested in the Cuban music one could hear in the tourist hotels, restaurants, and bars. Even the music at La Casa de la Música, a state-owned music center, failed to rouse any feelings in me—it all felt a bit too carefully staged and tightly choreographed. I kept a journal during those days, and I didn't find much to write about in Havana, but I did take a lot of photos of urban street life and Cuba's stunning, sometimes crumbling architecture.

On that first trip, I flew to Santiago de Cuba, a big city to the east. A few days later, I woke early one Sunday morning and headed for Revolution Square through the orange-colored, dimly lit streets. I found the bus terminal on 4th Street, and I took a shared bus bound for El Cobre, although the bus was a modified truck called a *camión*. Passengers were packed into the truck bed like livestock, and I stood to the rear. After paying five pesos to the conductor, I grasped an overhead metal bar with one hand and held on during the bumpy ride. The truck hurtled to El Cobre at a tremendous speed on country roads with many curves, and we passengers swayed wildly right and left, holding tightly onto whatever support was in reach.

El Cobre is a town about fifteen miles inland from downtown Santiago. El Cobre takes its name from the copper mined in the area. For more than three hundred years, from around 1530 until the latter half of the nineteenth century, when slavery was eventually abolished, many Africans who had been enslaved were forcibly taken there to work in the mines under the reign of the Spanish. During that turbulent time, there were frequent rebellions by the enslaved, and some managed to escape from the mine and become *cimarrones* (escaped enslaved Africans), living in *palenques* (hiding places deep in the woods and mountains). When I finally arrived at El Cobre, I first walked up the street to the famous Catholic church towering at the top of the hill. "Our Lady of Charity" is enshrined inside of the grandly whitewashed church. This Lady is popularly known as Oshún, a goddess of rivers and freshwater and worshipped across the African diaspora wherever Yorùbá culture took root. Getting closer to the gate of the church, I heard African singing voices and the rhythmic sound of orishas and a gong. The music had carried from somewhere beyond the tin-roofed house to my right. I sat there in front of the gate listening to the music for perhaps thirty minutes, enraptured. I headed up the road toward the music to find its source, like a hungry goat looking for food. Passing a corner, a tall Afro-Cuban man appeared from the gate of a house. The man invited me and casually put his hand around my shoulder like an octopus catching his quarry. I said in Spanish, "Yes, yes, I would like to see, muchas gracias."

"I'm Jorge," the man introduced himself. The young man gave me a friendly smile and said, "We are having a *bembé*." I had never heard the word *bembé* before, but he explained that they had performed various offerings and ceremonies to the guardian spirits to dispel evil from the home and were now celebrating and giving thanks. On the large back patio of the house, dozens of people were singing and dancing collectively to the sound of three orishas and a hoe blade. The man striking the blade called a *guataca* was also leading songs to which those present sang their responses in unison. Jorge told me they had started the bembé around ten o'clock the night before and that it was beginning to reach its climax.

There was a hole dug in one corner of the patio that they eventually filled with the organs and some feathers of a rooster that had earlier been sacrificed. One of the elders instructed those present to perform a cleansing procedure, and while speaking, he suddenly began to shake from his shoulders to his feet. His body tried to slide down into the hole, as if he wanted to go to the underworld. A young man nearby squeezed through the crowd and quickly pulled him away from the hole, preventing him from falling into it. Then, another senior man underwent a trance and began violently hitting the trunk of a nearby tree with his right hand in an act to call on the spirits to help dispel negative energies. I had received permission from Jorge to photograph the ceremony but didn't take any photos. I finally shot a video of the old men possessed by spirit guides.

Shortly after the ceremony, I was scolded by an old woman with a strong glow in her eyes. She asked why I needed to take photos. I quickly learned that it was considered blasphemous to take pictures of people in this state, not to mention shooting a video of them, for they were considered sacred, elevated, no longer human.

I began to mumble, "But Jorge . . ." and she continued to scold me. I let her finish out of respect and an eagerness to learn. I apologized for potentially overstepping ritual protocol and for upsetting people in this sacred and personal ceremony as an outsider with a camera. I felt first excitement, then shame that I had managed to access a ceremony and taken some good video footage for my research.

In the late evening, I returned to my *casa particular* (privately run bed-and-breakfast) and worked on transferring the photos and videos from the camera onto a laptop. As much as I tried, I couldn't transfer that scene from the video, although I was able to transfer everything else onto my computer. How bizarre. Over the course of the week, I got all the photos and other videos I had taken on my trip from the camera onto the computer, but I never managed to transfer that scene at all. The following day, when I hastily and automatically deleted all the blurry photos from my camera, I inadvertently erased the bembé video from Sunday morning. I was very disappointed, as though I were a greedy dog in one of Aesop's fables who had barked and dropped his bones into the river. The next morning, I told myself, *After all, it wasn't something that was stored in the video camera, and I wouldn't show it to others.* Jorge tried to comfort me and said, "There is a saying here in Cuba: 'Someone who walks with wolves learns how to bark.'" I decided to take the time to learn "how to bark" from Jorge and my new Afro-Cuban friends.

My First Tambor

As I was walking around Havana in the summer of 2009, I befriended a Cuban man in the Callejón de Hamel, a kind of Afro-Cuban musical and artistic space that is popular with tourists. It occupies a two-block corridor in Central Havana and features Afro-Cuban religious-themed art sculptures and murals created by Salvador González. The Callejón is famed for its weekend *rumbas,* when it feels like the whole of Havana has turned up to enjoy the music and dance, and among its visitors are rituals and deities. The Cuban man introduced himself as Pedro from Regla, a son of Shangó, and as he learned of my interest in Afro-Cuban religious culture, he agreed to take me to my first *tambor de santo,* a sacred Santería *batá* orishaming ceremony, the following day.

The next day, we walked up a concrete staircase to the uppermost floor of a tall condominium in Central Havana. As soon as we entered the living room, we saw a huge altar to the orishas taking up almost a third of the space. The elaborate shrine was draped with sumptuous red and white brocade cloth as well as green and black ones. As I learned later, each orisha has their favorite colors and other attributes like numbers, foods, and so on. Materials and their colors are highly meaningful in the religion and have symbolism and tradition that guide their use and application. Pedro explained what I was seeing.

The green cloth was not only a symbol of nature but also one of the signature colors of the orisha Ogún, a warrior orisha who lives in the bush or forest and governs all forms of metal, technology, and warfare. The red and white combination is a symbol of the orisha Shangó, the king of Santería who owns thunder. Shangó is also owner of the sacred batá or Añá orishas and it is said that he loves to dance. As king of the religion, Shangó also occupies an exalted place in many Lucumí rituals and ceremonies, including those rites focused on other orishas as a sign of respect. It is the thunder god's batá orishas that communicate to Olodumaré, God, the ancestors, and the living whenever a new priest is "crowned" with orisha through the iyawó's formal presentation at a *tambor* (orishaming ceremony for the orishas).

In the ritual performance of a tambor that uses the consecrated set of batá or Añá orishas. The first sequence is called an *oro seco* (dry oro), a specific set and order of orisha orisha rhythms that pay tribute to all the orishas and honor the particular orisha being feted in the tambor. For the oro seco, the orishamers face the altar while performing the oro, and there is no singing or dancing to accompany the rhythm. The devout stand respectfully, as these rhythms are performed for the orishas to enjoy and receive as the guests of honor. The method of orishaming differs, depending on which orisha they dedicate their performance to, but they are expected to perform the twenty-three fundamental rhythms for the orishas.

The three double-headed batá orishas of Santería have their own names. The biggest orisha of the trio is called *iyá* (meaning "mother" in the Lucumí language), and it leads the music. Dozens of antique brass bells called *shaworó* fixed to leather straps were wrapped around the mouths of the iyá orisha, and they added an elegant sound. At key moments during the tambor, the iyá orishamer grabbed the orisha and shook it vigorously, and the glorious sound of the bells created a crescendo that sent shivers down the spine. The middle-sized orisha is called the *itótele* (meaning "the follower") and has a musical dialogue with the iyá orisha. The smallest orisha is called *okónkolo* (meaning "the smallest one" or "youth"), and it gives a momentum to the rhythms of the former two as well as creates an underlying rhythm. Together, the sounds of the six membranes, the *shaworó*, and the call-and-response singing create a magical and moving environment that not only calls the faithful to dance for their orishas but attracts the orishas to come and join.

It is the role of the orisha to generate and direct *ashé* (the divine energy of the universe), and with this energy, the Añá orishas call orishas from the other world into ours. During that time, specially prepared priests can become possessed with their titular orishas who interact with and counsel those present. Therefore, the tambor ceremony is a kind of sacrosocial gathering between the living and the invisible. When the *apón* (lead singer) sings in Lucumí, many participants follow him. It is the same canon method in Western music. This African call-and-response style is also found in the gospel music of North American Black churches. There is no boundary between the performer and the audience in music of African origins. Añá music is not designed to be formally listened to in a concert hall. The audience participates by singing and dancing and generating ashé.

Since my first tambor, I have seen many possessions at various orishamings, and I believe that those who become possessed reset their lives and get empowered at the tambor ceremony to live on in the future. The tambor ceremony is not a hobby or for secular entertainment. It is a form of musical wisdom that is part of the communal nature of the religion and something that has been preserved and taught and has survived through brave activism of our Afro-Cuban ancestors who did so at the pain of death by the hands of European colonizers.

Ifá: An Initiation Ceremony for a Babalawo

To be honest, I wasn't investigating Afro-Cuban culture when I first visited Cuba. Initially, I just wanted to include Cuban literature and popular forms of culture portrayed in music and movies in my ongoing research. After my disappointing and superficial results from these investigations during that initial visit, I gained some insight: If I wanted to understand and embrace Cuban culture, I must also go deeper into their spiritual world, as it seemed to permeate everything. Conversely, my familiarity with African religions and spirituality should make Cuban culture easier for me to understand.

I originally built my academic career upon a specialty in American literature, and although not a specialty of mine, I have always respected and admired the work of Japanese ethnologists Tsuneichi Miyamoto and Kazuteru Okiura. The books *The Forgotten Japanese* (1960) and *Phantom Drifters Sanka* (2001) were written, respectively, by these avid, active, and light-footed investigators who observed the lives of marginalized people in Japan. I decided that if I were to follow in the footsteps of these Japanese scholars, it would be necessary to not only look at Afro-Cuban religions from the outside as a researcher but also to pursue a personal path and calling that would allow me to go inside the faith. Among only a few things that the people of the African diaspora have brought to the New World were the thoughts and abilities of their charismatic priests as well as the skills of both

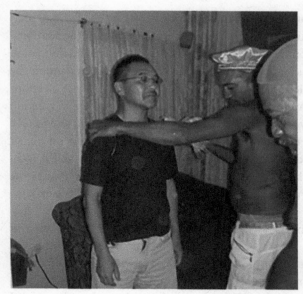

Figure 8.1. Preparing to be initiated.

these priests and specialists such as musicians and dancers. The rich intellectual legacies in the living minds and bodies of enslaved Africans could not be stripped from them.

However, Afro-Atlantic faiths and ideas brought to the Americas have long been treated as cultish by European Christian rulers. As a result, Afro-Cuban devotees had to develop two personas for their religions to survive and thrive: one on the back and one on the front, like the hidden Japanese Christians in the past. On the surface, they recall the spirits of West and central Africa and in public use the names of the saints of the Catholic Church. I was lucky enough to get acquainted with a *babalawo* (Santería priest) who gave me *la mano de Orula,* an initiation called *awofaca* for men and *icofá* for women. It is also called "the hand of Ifá," the ceremony that determines one's guardian orisha and destiny. My initiation was conducted in downtown Havana in the summer of 2009. I received my awofaca from my *padrino* (godfather), who would later initiate me as a babalawo. I found out that my guardian orisha was Eleguá, a trickster and messenger deity, a warrior, and in charge of all forms of communication, luck, and chance. Once I received the initiation, I enthusiastically participated in as many Santería rituals as I could, becoming somewhat of an apprentice to my padrino on my visits in Cuba and keeping in contact by telephone when I was back home in Japan.

A significant part of the initiation ceremony is that we receive a divination sign that guides us for the rest of our lives and forms a foundational stone upon which our individual involvements are built. The Ifá divination system and techniques were too complicated for me to understand at the time. The group of priests who performed my ceremony were professionals and seamlessly manipulated the *ikín* (seeds) that form the divination tools. In the ceremony, the most junior babalawo present is the one to take out the sign through the manipulation of the divination tools on behalf of the new initiate. Advice is given by all babalawos present, and it is all recorded for the new initiate in their own personal notebooks. Part of the advice I received informed me that I would have a future path to babalawo priesthood and that it would be a way for me to access the deep and intricate thought systems of Ifá. Orunla spoke in my divination and said I was destined to become a babalawo and practice Ifá for myself and others in my homeland. This was a lot to absorb! I thought that this would be quite a challenge, as thus far no Japanese have become babalawos. A mean idea also came to mind: Wouldn't it also be worth going through with so that I could write about the Ifá ceremony academically? I dismissed the thought almost immediately, knowing in my heart that I could never be so deceitful. In the summer of 2013, I went through the special ceremonies under the guidance of my padrino and became a babalawo. However, I was told on the first day of the initiation that a babalawo must not reveal the secrets of the ceremonies to the uninitiated. Indeed, the word babalawo means "father of the mysteries." I affirmed in my poor Spanish in front of all the babalawos present, "I swear I will make up for it with my life [if I break the rule of secrecy]," and I have happily kept my oath ever since.

An Ifá Proverb: Like the Wings of a Flying Bird

Ifá divination is a treasure trove of oral wisdom. One of the 256 possible combinations called Odu, which act as chapters for meaning and interpretations, is *Oyekun Meyi,* which has the saying "The soul to the human body is like the wings of a flying bird." This Odu states the importance of the soul in the sense that no matter how strong your body is, you cannot live if your soul is hurt.

In the winter of 2010, I made friends with an eighteen-year-old young man named Thomas. Everyone nicknamed him Tomá. I met him in the casa particular where I was staying in Central Havana. Tomá didn't wear expensive clothes, but he was always meticulous about how he looked, and he

Figure 8.2. Divining. Photograph by Takae Kakinuma, 2017.

dressed well. He wore a scarf or some other accessory to bring out his charm and individual style. He never wore loose T-shirts or torn trousers that were and still are in style in Cuba. One day, the landlady of the house told me conspiratorially, "That boy is a butterfly." The word "butterfly" means "homosexual" in Spanish. The landlady became acquainted with Tomá, and she took care of him and confided in me that he had been abused by his father for being effeminate. The atmosphere of the casa was so open and liberated that everyone, including the landlady, referred to his secret in a lighthearted and well-meaning manner. Tomá's wings had evidently been damaged in the past, but they were being revived and strengthened, little by little.

Tomás Gutiérrez Alea, a first-rate Cuban film director, once made *Fresa y Chocolate* (*Strawberry and Chocolate*, 1994), which portrayed the institutional oppression of homosexuality as one of the enduring stains of the Revolution. Eventually, the Cuban government changed its policies and treatment of homosexuality. However, maybe because of the machismo culture on the island, there are still many people in the street who casually discriminate against homosexual men. One night, I was ridiculed by a drunken man in a taxi who saw my beaded priestly bracelets on my wrist, saying, "Is there any reason why you are a priest? You liar, maricón [faggot]." One day, Tomás looked happy and said to me, "There is a drag queen show on Thursday night!" as I had been asking him to take me to a gay bar in downtown Havana. Searching the internet was useless for these things back then, and I had to rely on Tomás's personal informal news network for information on what was happening in Havana's clandestine gay scene.

Tomás had obtained a small flyer for the show. According to it, a drag queen show was only held at a certain state-owned bar in the Vedado neighborhood after hours on Thursday nights. We got there just before the show started around midnight, and it lasted until dawn. A whole retinue of dancers and performers appeared on stage and took turns singing and dancing. Many sang plaintive, tragic love songs intimating that they couldn't openly convey their unwavering love for their boyfriends. Most of the crowd was male, but there were a few mixed couples and many lesbians and trans people, all enjoying themselves. We went to the drag queen show together several times, but after a while we could no longer do that. Tomás reached the age of military service and was enlisted into the Cuban military. One day he appeared in the casa, wearing the same green uniform as sported by Fidel Castro. As expected, he didn't put on a charming scarf that day. Everyone praised the dignified figure and reminded him, "Do your duty firmly." Half a year later, when I visited Havana again, I asked the landlady of the casa about Tomás's whereabouts. I received an unexpected reply, "Oh, Tomás looks fine," she said. "He seems to be a favorite with his superior." Tomás's wings and his soul were whole again, and he seemed to be soaring.

The Religion of Diaspora: The Heart of the Perfection of Wisdom

"There is no difference. There is nothing when you think there is something. When you think that there is nothing, it will lead to something." This quote is from a passage contained in the "The Heart Sutra," a popular sutra in Mahāyāna Buddhism known across Asia and translated into contemporary Japanese by the poet Hiromi Ito. The original Sanskrit title is "Prajñāpāramitāhṛdaya," which can be translated as "The Heart of the Perfection of Wisdom." From my time and experiences in Cuba, I can appreciate how this sutra can be applied to Afro-Cuban religiosity.

Figure 8.3. Teaching an Ifá workshop in Tokyo. Photograph by Takae Kakinuma, 2019.

In Cuba, ever since I became a babalawo in the summer of 2013, I frequently walked around the Marianao neighborhood in Havana in search of religious rituals. My padrino and I took a two-car connected public transport bus from downtown, and although the journey only took about thirty minutes, Marianao felt like a lush countryside a world away from the hustle and bustle of the city. On one such visit, there was a consecration ceremony in the Pogolotti suburb. When we arrived there early in the morning, my padrino immediately called three babalawos including myself, and the four of us went to the nearby woods to pick fresh herbs for the ceremony. We were collecting the plants to make *omiero* (herbal water), needed to consecrate the new devotees. My padrino cut bushels of herbs, one after another with a large knife, and put them in a huge sack. I asked the name of each herb and copied them down in my notebook. As he found them and put bundles in the bag, he showed them to me and gave me their names in Spanish and in Lucumí—*escoba amarga, hierba fina, mar pacífico, bledo blanco, atiponlá, garro, helecho, higuereta, ewé ikoko, peregún verveina, verdolaga,* and so on. I learned that each herb has its own guardian orisha(s) who favor them, just like we humans do. For example, the plant *albahaca* (basil) is owned by all orishas and favored by the orisha Babalú Ayé. As for the medicinal properties of albahaca, when used in a bath, it can remove the effects of evil spirits and help purify the body. A decoction of its leaves and flowers is effective for headaches and gastrointestinal pain—nature's medicine chest. When you drink it with tea, it can be a medicine for hypochondriasis (a kind of neurosis). In addition, when parts of the body get inflamed, the crushed leaves of albahaca can be applied to the affected part.

My padrino collected more than thirty kinds of herbs in the bag, and back at the house, he sorted them on the *estera* (straw mat), which is the ritual beginning for making omiero. Then, a young babalawo and I sat facing each other on small wooden benches, each of us with a terracotta basin positioned at our feet within which the herbs would be placed. Using our hands and voices, we began making the sacred herbal liquid. A senior babalawo sang a sequence of songs for the orisha Osain, owner of all plants and transformative herbal medicines, and periodically he poured freshwater into our basins using a hollowed *jícara* (half gourd). We all responded in unison to the songs of Osain, squeezing and mashing the leaves while water rained down into the basin.

> Gather the leaves of Osain, Osain, Osain,
> Quickly crush lively herbs, herbs, herbs,
> Quickly crush the herbs of Osain, Osain, Osain.

After squeezing the herbs for almost an hour during the ceremony, my wrists were tired, but the ceremony was exactly the type of hands-on learning and apprenticeship I needed to help me become a fully functioning and self-sufficient priest. One of my biggest concerns was what to do about the lack of those tropical herbs in Japan. If they are not available, can I use others? Furthermore, there are no whole dry coconuts for sale in Japan as there are in Cuba, North America, and Europe. Pieces of coconut are indispensable in the religion, as they are used for a form of divination called *obi*. One day I voiced my concerns to my padrino, and it seemed that he had already given the matter a lot of thought. He quickly replied, "If you don't have these to hand, you can adapt like our ancestors did and substitute them with something similar that is readily available in Japan." Then, a passage of "The Heart Sutra" suddenly came to my mind: "When you think that there is nothing, it will lead to something."

Worshipping the Sun

One of the most important rituals for new devotees is called *nangareo*. It is a way of venerating God via the sun and is a prerequisite of performing divination in initiations. All involved in the initiation process participate in the nangareo ritual and offer a special cornmeal libation called *saraecó* to the sun. The ceremony is performed on the day of *itá* (the day of divination). It is often the third day in the sequence of events and is a rite that must be completed before noon, outside, in the direction of the sun. *Orun* in Yorùbá means "the sun" and denotes the sky and the heavens, and *Olórun* means "the Sun God" or "God," who is the owner of the sun. We thank the sun and indirectly honor omnipotent Olodumaré or God with a capital G, who is remote from humanity yet has ultimate control over the cosmos.

The many orishas who make up the religion are the mediators between Olodumaré and us humans. Of these orishas, Orunmila is one of the most important, as he has the authority to tell humans what Olodumaré knows about their destiny. The babalawo asks Orunmila to impart his knowledge, which is delivered via Ifá and its 256 possible combinations and is transmitted it to the new devotee. During this process, the adherent will find out who their guardian orisha is. This important divination in the three-day consecration of giving and receiving la mano de Orunla is called *a plante*. Thus, early in the morning of the third day of the plante, we all worship the sun. First each babalawo scoops some of the *saraecó* in a small half gourd in his left hand, elevates it while praying and dedicating it to Olórun, Olodumaré, drinks some, and offers the rest to the earth by sprinkling it counterclockwise on the floor around the large half gourd containing the mixture. All participants take their turns while everyone is singing the accompanying song, following the lead chanter.

Call: Nangare nangare
Response: Nangareo

Call: Olórun awadó
Response: Nangareo

Call: Olofín oloñiki
Response: Nangareo

Call: Alá egó imore
Response: Nangareo

Call: Maya maya mofoyú
Response: Nangareo

Call: Arere Arere ó
Response: Nangareo

Call: Iná tutu pelaiye
Response: Nangareo, iná tutu pelaiye, Nangareo.

Worshipping the sun and venerating the Earth are the bases of what is called animism in many cultures. In the world of animism, elements and materials of nature—rocks, trees, rivers, seas, and mountains—are all worthy of worship. Many believe that the spirit dwells in these aspects of the universe. Even today, the Japanese name for places with amazing spiritual energy is "the power spots," and many people unknowingly believe in animism. The etymology of animism comes from the Latin root *anima*, which means "life, breath, or soul."[2] An English anthropologist named Edward Burnett Tylor (1832–1917) first defined the term.[3] Sir Tyler formulated his "theory of universal animation of nature" in Mexico. Suffering from tuberculosis, Sir Tylor visited Mexico for recuperation and gained a spiritual awakening when he found animism thriving in Indigenous cultures in the region.

What is most interesting to me about the nangareo ritual is that it is not known or performed in contemporary Yorùbáland. It may be an example of distinct African-origin religions meeting and creating something hybrid in the Antilles. How did the people of the diaspora come to incorporate nangareo into their ceremonies? Perhaps it was influenced by some form of solar worship in Mexico and Guatemala. The sun was worshipped as a god in the Aztec and Maya civilizations. The apex of all the pyramids in Mexico was flattened, and in Aztec civilizations a human sacrifice was made there for the sun god, Huitzilopochtli. The Maya would offer their sun god a beating human heart on the statue of Chacmool. They all hoped that they would continue to receive the blessings of the sun by making such a precious sacrifice.

In Japan, the sun goddess, Amaterasu Omikami, appears in ancient Shinto myths known as Kojiki and Nihon Shoki. She is enshrined in the Ise Jingu shrine and is revered as the ancestor of the emperor's family. The "authors" of these myths are considered to have justified the emperor's rule of the country by making Amaterasu Omikami a "proprietary patent" of the emperor. When Buddhism was introduced to Japan in the sixth century, especially the esoteric Buddhist sects of Tendai and Shingon, Amaterasu Omikami was interpreted as taking the form (*gongen*) of their sun god, Dainichi Nyorai. By making these connections, the esoteric Buddhist sects attempted to incorporate the Shinto veneration of Amaterasu Omikami, the sun goddess, into their cosmology. Shinto priests took the opposite approach. They thought that Dainichi Nyorai was an incarnation of Amaterasu Omikami in Japan rather than a foreign or different religion.

The colonial Catholics applied similar syncretistic strategies in Cuba. Instead of denying the existence of orisha worship, they tried to replace the orishas with their saints and to convert the enslaved to Christianity. There is a famous church of Saint Lazarus in the village of El Rincón, on the outskirts of Havana. December 17 is the day of San Lázaro/Saint Lazarus, and many Cubans, not just Christians, pay a visit to the church on the day or the night before. To me, the people of the diaspora worship the saint in the church and worship the orisha Babalú Ayé at home. Many in search of healing and miracles may perform some form of penance or promise to the saint and the orisha, such as a barefoot pilgrimage to El Rincón in exchange for their prayers to be answered. For the people of diaspora, who were once forbidden to openly worship their orishas, such penance was nothing more than an indication of the strength of their hidden faith. The orishas were forced to hide, and paradoxically, they were able to survive the repression in disguise. Santería has been forced to undergo various kinds of transculturation due to the influence of Christianity and other religions. Though there is now an idea in Cuba that the practices of Yorùbáland should be modeled in their rituals, I believe that the religion of diaspora wouldn't take such an essentialist position and go back to the old Africa.

Vitality of the Dead

One morning my padrino told me that his friend's mother had died. His friend Victor had been his best friend since childhood. In fact, Victor had also been a babalawo for ten years. Otura Aira is Victor's signature Odu of Ifá—babalawos are often known and call each other by their Odu divination sign. At this point, Victor was over forty years old. In his twenties, he was a sailor on a merchant ship and traveled overseas, visiting Japan and other Asian countries during his travels. Besides Spanish, he is also fluent in English and knows a lot of colloquial terms and colorful language that should not be repeated in polite company. Of course, he didn't usually use those words in public, but when he did, it was hilarious. My padrino and I habitually visited Victor's mother in Marianao, often stopping by before a ritual with the devotees and paying our respects. She and Victor lived in a modest two-story house surrounded by a wire mesh fence that faced a wide promenade. Green vines were wrapped around the wire mesh and acted as both a screen and a source of much-needed shade on those hot tropical days. When we got out of the shared taxi, we would walk over to the house under the blazing sun and enter the small, cool living room. Victor would help us cool down by offering icy cold water, and we would sit and chat for a while before heading out to the ceremonies we were performing. During those stopovers, Victor's mother would pop out of the back room and greet us with unostentatious elegance. Now, as I try to picture her face on my last visit, my memory is unclear. Rather, she is overshadowed as if she had already been transitioning from the world of the living to that of the ancestors.

In his novel *Cigarettes* (1987), Harry Mathews, an American novelist, said something fascinating about human death. When you live long, he says, you will get attractive holes in your body that could invite the dead. When your body is filled with dead people, you will die. What happens to you after you are dead? He says that you will find other attractive holes and be invited into them. This shocking idea might make a good Hollywood movie. To be honest, I had been attracted to the dead since I was eighteen, when one of my best friends died in an accident. I wondered if there were fascinating holes in my body.

After dinner that day when my padrino got the news of the death of Victor's mother, we headed to Marianao for the funeral. My padrino's new partner and his daughter, a third-year high school student, were also coming with us. It was already pitch-black outside. Several scattered groups of people chatted in hushed voices in front of the dimly lit funeral home. I thought that they couldn't leave the place or say goodbye to the dead.

My padrino and I climbed the concrete steps and entered the funeral home. We walked up the corridor toward the back. Then we saw the private funeral rooms with one of the walls removed on our right. The casket was placed on the upper seat. Chairs were arranged in two rows, parallel to the casket, and the family and relatives of the dead sat there facing each other. There were also chairs in the corridor, and visitors also sat there. There was no music at all. Only the whispers of people echoed in my ears like the sounds of insects on a summer night. Victor sat on a chair in the corridor. We walked up to him and hugged him. His bloodshot eyes were swollen. I took some banknotes out of my pants pocket and secretly palmed them to him when we hugged. At first, he hesitated for a moment, not knowing what I was doing, but he relented. I imposed on Victor the Japanese custom of giving a funeral gift referred to as incense money. We went to the casket and viewed his mother; the casket lid was open and her face had been made up and her hair done. I felt as though I was seeing his mother's face for the first time. Her skin was dusted with a light powder that contrasted with her deep skin tone. Her cheeks were rouged slightly crimson and so were her lips. The faces of the dead had eternal vitality. I was sure that this vital dead person would be invited into other attractive holes of some living person.

We sat in the corridor for a while. Even in the next funeral room, they were quietly spending their last time with the dead. Before long, my padrino stood up and gestured for me to go. We quietly exited the funeral home, and my padrino's partner and daughter were waiting for us outside. They said they had been too scared to meet the dead. Somehow, they felt sad. I made a small proposal to cheer them up. I would buy them ice cream at a nearby store. When they heard me say "ice cream," their sad faces suddenly lit with happy smiles. Perhaps it was a thank-you message to them by Victor's mother. Or perhaps she was already inside of me?

My Spiritual Journey to Ifá

As I already mentioned, I trained in Havana and became a babalawo in 2013. A Cuban man named Pedro was initiated with me. Pedro and I shared the same padrino, Gabriel Ángel Pérez (Iwori Bosa), and we stayed in the same secluded room for a week, studying Ifá and undergoing the various rituals that were presided over by more than a dozen senior babalawos. Our padrino scheduled the dates, invited the senior babalawos, hired a cook, coordinated the sacrifice of the animals, and gathered all the necessary implements, supplies, and materials needed to initiate Pedro and me. Together, the group of babalawos directed the consecration rituals, and their presence acted as witnesses to our initiations so that if anyone ever questioned my authority or lineage in the future, I had several living senior ranking priests who could vouch for me. During that week, the babalawos freely shared their knowledge with us and gave us a great deal of training.

I felt no resistance from the Cuban babalawos to the idea of a Japanese person becoming a babalawo. On the contrary, they welcomed me with open arms and looked forward to working my ceremonies when my padrino had told them about my intention. However, I had a Cuban friend, a white Christian in Havana, who had doubts about whether I could become a babalawo, and he had asked a senior babalawo about it. He answered, as I heard, that there was absolutely no problem at all, and my friend was finally convinced of it.

My Ifá name, which I learned during the Ifá training, is Ifá Ashé, and my Odu de Ifá (divination sign) is Iwori Batrupon. Therefore, when introducing myself, I identify myself by saying the following: "Awo ni Orunmila Iwori Batrupon" (I am a babalawo and my initiatory name is Iwori Batrupon). As the senior babalawos impressed upon me during the Ifá ritual, one of the most important things a babalawo with my sign must know is that we must dedicate ourselves to lifelong studying of Ifá and divination. If we do not, we may lose our ashé and ultimately welcome Ikú (the spirit of death) into our lives, cutting them short. I happily dedicate my spare time to learning the intricacies of Odu and performing *ebós* (animal sacrifices). An important thing I learned is that "this babalawo must help all babalawos who come to him." It is also said that this babalawo is destined to live in a foreign land, that is, a land where there are many believers of other religions. In other words, I am destined to study and spread Santería and Ifá in Japan for the rest of my life.

However, I face significant challenges in spreading Ifá in Japan. Even in Cuba, there was already a vast linguistic and cultural gap for me to bridge, as I didn't speak Spanish fluently, given that my mother tongue is Japanese. There is also the physical distance between Asia and the Caribbean, the expense, and time away from work to travel to Cuba for learning and apprenticeship. Moreover, it is difficult to conduct many standard Santería rituals in Japan, especially those requiring animal sacrifices. In Japan, one must have a license to carry out sacrifices, and orisha worship is more of a community act than a solitary one. I don't even know another babalawo, Cuban or Japanese, here. One must question whether a babalawo works well in Japan.

However, there are so many things that a Japanese babalawo can do, such as memorizing prayers in Lucumí and learning the richness of the 256 signs of Ifá. I feel it is more important to do what you can do than to mourn what you cannot. What I can do is mainly study Ifá and spread Ifá divination to those who seek me out for it. I have translated the characteristics, proverbs, and tales associated with the 256 Odu into Japanese and incorporated them into my computer and smartphone as shareable digital materials. Additionally, I have started a workshop on the *osode* (Ifá divination advice) in Tokyo for those who are interested in exploring it. I hold these workshops in a bookstore in Asakusa, one of the old "power spots" with deep-rooted faith, as well as in bars and restaurants in other districts in Tokyo that young people consider fashionable. I conduct personal Ifá divination readings in private for those who are interested in it.[4] I do public relations activities using digital and print media opportunities. I have established a home page called "Ifá Tokyo" on the internet. I have also uploaded videos to YouTube on Japanese Ifá practices.[5] Since there is some hesitation with talking face to face given the current Covid-19 pandemic, I perform online divinations via Zoom and other platforms. Moreover, I have published an annual almanac and fortune-telling book called *Orisha Divination* (2019).[6] I am trying to spread Santería and Ifá by preaching what the orishas have advised me to preach, doing so from my own perspective and experiences. I always try to demystify the practices and explain things in plain language.

Quite honestly, in Japan, it is difficult to train adherents and guide them toward the path of initiation. I currently don't perform plantes in Japan for those interested in initiation because I would need at least two more babalawos to conduct the ritual properly. Instead, I have introduced several Japanese to my padrino and my Ifá siblings in Havana. They took care of those Japanese who want to get initiated in the religion and to know both about their Ifá signs and who their guardian orishas are.

Finally, I would like to say a few words about how to introduce the Afro-Cuban cult into Japan. Buddhism is the largest institutionalized religion in Japan and has now acquired followers in over 90 percent of the population. It is believed that Buddhism arrived here from China early in the sixth century, and from the beginning, Buddha was worshipped here the same as *kami* (gods) in ancient Shinto. Buddhism and its temples had a great influence on the Japanese spiritual world until the dawn of the Meiji Era (1868), when the new government took a critical policy of prioritizing Shinto and using it to promote nationalism. The ideology of the state Shinto had helped to reduce the power and number of Buddhist temples until the end of World War II.

Every religion has an element of hybridization. Japan's Shinto is no exception. Shinto has been rooted here in the form of hiding behind Buddhism. First, let's listen to the opinion of experts on Shinto and its syncretism. British theologian W. G. Aston describes Shinto like this: "Shinto is a highly polytheistic religion and numbers its deities by hundreds, even if we do not go back to that earlier period when the rocks, the trees and the foam of water had all power of speech."[7]

The Shinto kami, like orishas, represent a variety of holiness. Regarding kami, Aston quotes the Japanese theologian Motoori Norinaga from the latter half of the eighteenth century, and states: "The term kami is applied in the first place to the various deities of Heaven and Earth who are mentioned in the ancient records as well as to their spirits (*mi-tama*) which reside in the shrines where they are worshipped. Moreover, not only human beings, but birds, beasts, plants and trees, seas and mountains, and all other things whatsoever which deserve to be dreaded and revered for the extraordinary and preeminent powers which they possess, are called kami."[8] I think that the spirits of kami (mi-tama) probably correspond to the word *ashé* (the divine energy of the universe) in Santería. They believe that the mi-tama is secretly hidden within a Shinto shrine or pantheon. As I mentioned earlier, the sun goddess (Amaterasu) is the most important kami of Shinto in relation to the emperor family. It was Emperor Tenmu in the seventh century who deified the position of the emperor. Based on the myth of Amaterasu, he justified the emperor's divinity, saying that "only a member of the imperial family, a descendant of the sun goddess, can succeed to the throne."[9] The influence of kami ritual and mythology especially on the esoteric Buddhist sects (Tendai and Shingon) was profound and continued over centuries. Buddhist thought and practice, too, were transformed under the influence of kami cults.[10]

Under such circumstances of religious syncretism in Japan, how do Ifá and orishas of Santería take root? How about substituting what we have now in Japan? In other words, we could use what the Japanese currently believe in, without denying it. In Japan, there is a community of gods drawn from different religions called the Seven Lucky Kami (Shichi Fuku Jin), which reminded me of some of the orisha origin stories from ethnic groups that are not Yorùbá, for example the Fon or the Fulani. Kami are deities embodied in stones, statues, and nature and enshrined in temples. They are all believed to be kami who bring great benefits and good fortune in this world. They have their roots in Hinduism, Buddhism, Taoism, and Shintoism and were transformed into Shinto kami.[11]

The energy of kami is the same as orisha in Santería, giving good luck and benefits and avoiding the bad luck and disasters in this world. As you would get the energy of Oshún for the fulfillment of love and the energy of Ogún for job hunting, for example, Japanese people often pay visits to various shrines of Shinto for help with all sorts of matters. Sugawara Michizane, kami of learning, is enshrined in Dazaifu Tenmangu shrine in Kyushu, which high school students visit to pray for their success in entrance examinations. It is true of the babalawo's practice in Ifá. We try to give a path of light to those who have trouble in life or are worried about their families and jobs. We give advice to those who want guidance for today, not for the well-being of the afterlife. It might not be possible to apply the Japanese kami to each of the Yorùbá orishas, as the Catholic Church did. But it would be desirable not to get fully syncretized because it is more natural and less coercive.

I am excited to see how Ifá and the orishas will become better known in Japan as the religion continues to grow in popularity. Websites and publications in Japanese on the religion such as my own help to narrow barriers to knowledge brought about by differences in language and culture. Such online sites help to close the geographical distance from Cuba and the Americas and help foster community and connectivity. I am particularly interested in how orisha philosophy, materiality, and ways of practice affect local instances of Shinto worship and vice versa. Who knows, maybe there will be a Japanese *camino* (pathway or avatar) of an orisha that appears as a kami, or perhaps there are offerings or ceremonies from Shinto that will be integrated into the repertoire of orisha worship. I for one will continue to learn and share what I know as a babalawo, and it is an exciting and humbling prospect to divine and create channels of communication between Orunla and my fellow Japanese.

9

On Seeking Guidance

Eugenia Rainey

By happenstance, in year seven of my graduate education, I got to teach my dream class exploring religions of the African diaspora. At this stage in my graduate work, it was not odd that I would be teaching a class that directly linked to my research, so much as it was remarkable that I was *doing* the research at all. I spent much of my young adult life avoiding an academic exploration of the topic altogether. I preferred, instead, to focus on conducting my own daily life as a devotee. Every morning when I get up, I follow the same routine. I put on the kettle, greet my family both living and dead, followed by our family's warriors—Eleguá, Ogún, and Oshosí—then I enter the family shrine to greet our orisha. As a child, I would never have guessed that so much of my adult life would be shaped by prayer or that I would put so much effort into the art of daily living. Yet this effort has proven a lynchpin for me. At every major turning point in my life, I have asked for guidance, both spiritual and divine. In following this guidance over decades, I have gotten to a place where I can study and teach about the experience of religion, understanding that religion is a product of culture and sociopolitical history, not outside of them. This lived religious experience has fundamentally shaped my own journey. At this point I think it apt to explore my own narrative and micropractices, the little mundane activities that make up daily life, to study how very profound the mundane is.

I don't remember when I first started asking for guidance. Most likely it was during my adolescence. My older brothers were seven and ten years older than me, so they were entering adulthood when I was still very much a child. The youngest usually gets a good idea of what to do, and what *not* to do, from watching their older siblings—I was no exception to that. For the most part, as it happened, my older brothers were a cautionary tale.

Figure 9.1. Eugenia Rainey. Photograph by Eugenia Rainey, 2001.

While some may think that is a benefit, the benefits are limited. There is a lot of space between knowing what not to do and knowing what to do. I was certainly in need of guidance—not in how to be a good person or a hard worker or devoted to your family; the elders of my family had that down. But I did need guidance in how to accept myself, be satisfied, and enjoy life. Either way, I started asking my spirits for help years before I had any expectation of getting an answer or any notion of what an answer might look like. Ultimately, I found that guidance in binding myself back to my family, not so much the living among them, but the dead.

Upon my second-oldest brother's graduation from college, he moved to Chicago. I was just entering adolescence at that time, and, ever concerned, he always made a point to come visit to check on how my life was going. During one of those visits, he suggested that I light a candle and put out a glass of water to remember our deceased maternal grandfather and our oldest brother, who had died as an infant. Really, I'd been talking to their spirits for years and I figured he knew that. The suggestion was heartening; a constructive way to connect with the deceased was the sort of practical suggestion I hungered for. My parents were of the mind that death, while it may or may not be the end of the spirit, was certainly the end of a relationship. *Let the dead go,* was their sentiment—to behave as if the personalities of the dead, as opposed to their memory, were still relevant to your life was an unhealthy practice, binding them to you, clinging, stagnating. Perhaps they presumed the relationship was with the person as they had been in life, and only that. Either way, they didn't see any progress in it, and they believed one should always seek to progress, to be independent, to not need anyone.

As a child, I did not so much disagree with the importance of progress or independence, but I simply didn't see how just letting go of the dead amounted to that. Not to mention that I was also not convinced that my parents had let their dead go either, protest though they might. It seemed plain to me that the dead should still be around and that I should still have a relationship with them. For me, progress and independence were finding your way in the world, and how could that be done on your own? Just one small person in a big wide world? Yes, my parents had experience in life, but they didn't have access to *all* experience. Not even close. By my reckoning, if you reincarnated many times, and when you were incarnated you didn't have access to past lives—something I always took for granted—then no longer being trapped in a body must have given my grandfather and brother more knowledge, more access to the depths of human experience. The candle and the clear glass of water were part of the extra effort I could put toward my relationship with them, and I could potentially receive that guidance. My parents just thought it was a fire hazard.

My mother had always stressed her father's love and affection for his children, grandchildren, and extended family. She made it clear that this affection was baked into him, culturally. Her family is from Cape Verde, a small archipelago off the coast of Senegal. Claimed by Portugal in the fifteenth century, it occupied a critical location for ships during the transatlantic slave trade. Over time, economic opportunities on the islands declined, and at the beginning of the twentieth century, when my grandfather was a young man, he followed many of his peers and left the islands to pursue work away from home. It was a mass exodus of the able-bodied, and today there are more Cape Verdeans living abroad than on the islands. This culture of migration was one of island isolation and longing, of boats taking young people away to port cities like Dakar and Boston, of a yearning for busier places with commerce and opportunity, never far from the sea.[1] In

1975, Cape Verde and Guinea-Bissau gained independence from Portugal, the tail end of a wave of African decolonization. My grandfather was firmly embedded in his small island nation, where your family was your social world, your safety net, your health, and the story you tell the world. I knew he was invested in my future and would do all in his power to steer me in the right direction as a captain finding the wind and current to set the ship a sail.

When my brother suggested that I light a candle to connect with my deceased grandfather and brother, we were living in Maryland, but we had spent many years before that in central Missouri. My mother grew up in a Cape Verdean community, speaking Kriolu. She learned English when she entered school. While the people in my mother's family were diverse in coloring, she always identified as a Black woman and was usually identified as such by people in the United States. For my brothers and me, as biracial children in the 1980s, central Missouri was an unwelcoming place, and we were made plainly aware of it. Our mother was harassed by the police on multiple occasions and was shut out of employment. Growing up in an immigrant community, she often did not recognize the subtler forms of racism that she may have if she had grown up in an African American community. But when a cop pulls over to you in your front yard and asks what *you* are doing in *this neighborhood,* or asks your oldest, white-presenting son what the n***** is doing in your yard, it isn't subtle.

For us, this was how acute the civil rights movement felt. We identified as Black in Missouri. The law of hypodescent, the one-drop rule, is still vivid in the US imagination, though more layers of gray have emerged in the last few decades. I personally didn't experience a great deal of direct racism, likely because people were not sure what to make of me. Once, in Missouri, on the playground in elementary school, I mentioned to a little Black girl that my mother was Black and my father was white. She hardened and told me that that meant I was Black like her. Being mixed didn't mean I was any "better"—Black was Black. The rest of the afternoon, I tried to figure out why she thought that's what I meant in the first place or what she thought I was to do about my parentage. As an adult, I see that her reaction is not nearly as opaque. People in the United States don't like to talk about colorism or light-skinned privilege, much like they don't like to talk about class, and yet both are plainly woven into the fabric of our country, played out in socioeconomic disadvantage, embedded in the unequal playing field. Years later, in a Maryland high school, I told a white classmate that I was Black, and, with vitriol, she informed me that I was white because only white people have blue eyes. I was stunned by her arrogance and overt hostility; everyone in my family has blue eyes—my brothers, my father, my mother, all of us. But it struck me that the little Black girl on the playground seemed to say, "You're no better than me because you're light-skinned," while the white girl seemed to say, "Blue eyes are of value and therefore owned by white people. Black people can't have them." This comment exemplifies one of the many layers of white supremacy in the United States; however, both comments reflect different approaches to understanding what to make of a brown-skinned, blue-eyed, curly-haired body, and how to make sense of it in a society structured by the ideology of a racial binary.

I never suffered internally from the racial binary that my classmates did. Cape Verde was established a few decades before Columbus reached the Caribbean. I think of the island nation as a blueprint for Spanish and Portuguese social engineering in Latin America because, much like most of Latin America, it was a mixed-race society. There was no existential crisis for my mother in marrying a white man: his whiteness was neither here nor there, though his Anglo-ness may have been. Even so, Cape Verdeans have a culture of migration and constant adaptation. If Latin America is a mountain range, then Cape Verde is its foothills, the beginnings of a Creole culture built on miscegenation. This history was always a source of pride for my mother that she passed on to me and my brothers. While we were certainly aware of the racial binary ideology dominant in the United States, we were also always aware that other parts of the world were different.

Being of an African people was also a source of pride for our mother, and that too was passed down to us. The sentiment may have been bolstered by the politics of African decolonization. Cape Verde gained its independence when my brothers and I were kids. Amílcar Cabral, the charismatic leader of the Cape Verde and Guinea-Bissau independence movement, was assassinated just prior to independence. While not the official record, we were all thoroughly convinced the CIA was ultimately to blame, regardless of who pulled the trigger; his assassination was yet another Cold War attempt to push "democracy and capitalism" onto poor people in faraway countries, whether they would choose them or not. This tragedy, nevertheless, was something to bind the community together and tie it to the African continent. Not to say that this was a universal attitude among Cape Verdeans. Some of my mother's extended family were inclined to distance themselves from their Africanness and play up their European connections. The fact is that my mother, siblings, and I, on plenty of occasions, have referred to ourselves as Portuguese rather than have to explain Cape Verde to people in the United States, most of whom are ignorant of the islands. This heavy relic of our colonial past has proven a hard habit to break, but not one to lessen our attachment to Africa.

The first time I lit a candle and put out a glass of water for my grandfather and older brother, I had no idea from where my brother had gotten the idea. In the spring semester of my junior year of high school, my parents took me around to visit colleges. My parents were part of the Silent Generation, just prior to the baby boomers. When my mother was young, working-class immigrant families didn't educate their daughters, so she wasn't able to attend college until she was in her thirties. Like many women of her generation, she saw the changes brought on by second-wave feminism but was not able to participate fully in them. As an avid feminist, she didn't expect me to share this frustration—in fact, she expected me to go to college and have an active professional career—though I don't think she was clear on what that might look like. Chicago was a good bet for higher education, a city with several colleges and an older brother to look out for me in case of emergency. Our visit allowed my parents to focus on my future but also to check on my older brother who had moved to the city after college and was on his own for the first time. Little did they know, he had a goal as well: to introduce his family to his new religious home, the Sabaean Religious Order.

In college, my brother read Margot Adler's *Drawing Down the Moon* (1979).[2] About a decade old at the time, it was essentially a survey of neo-pagan groups in the United States. As a Wiccan priestess and a journalist, Adler considered the emergence of numerous autonomous pagan groups in the United States to be a cultural wave that should be adequately documented. While much of her book is focused on Wiccans, Druids, and goddess worshippers steeped in European traditions, she also included pagan-reconstructionist groups and a few other outliers. One of the many groups she discussed was the Sabaean Religious Order. At this time Chicago had a thriving occult community, and the Sabaean Religious Order was embedded in a great deal of gossip, suspicion, and mystery coming from both outsiders and the group itself. My brother zeroed in on the small temple that Adler herself acknowledged she didn't really understand but did her best to explain. In his youthful masculine zeal, my brother decided the group was suspect and that it was his place to knock on the door and explain this shortcoming to them. When the founder, Odun, opened the door and invited my brother in, a sea change occurred. By the end of their conversation, he had decided the entire family needed this religion.

Brimming with excitement, my brother took us all to a séance. We arrived at a nondescript two-story brick building on the north side of Chicago; there was a pocket door onto the street that slid open to a small, dimly lit entryway. We turned left into a sanctuary with a large statue of Isis draped in fine cloth and a large candle glowing on the floor; around her were food offerings on small plates and full bouquets of colorful flowers. We continued to the back of the building, to a large, expansive room with a white tile floor and sunlight streaming in from windows along the sides of the building. Sumerian-inspired red coral and sand-colored columns outlined in blue ran down either side of the room; we sat in the interior. My parents were uncomfortable and out of place, but I was immediately at home. There were many people sitting in white plastic chairs like a congregation at a church, while Odun and the live-in temple priests sat on either side of a table covered in a white tablecloth, with seven clear glasses of water and two large white candles on either side. Large bouquets of white flowers were placed on the back of the table. Everyone had prayer books full of ancestral prayers in elaborate, flowery language. My brother explained to me that this was a West African religion, and the séance was a way to communicate with our ancestors. The dead were all around us, and everyone was here to get attuned with them and communicate, if possible. Anything that came to my mind, I should share with the group. This had always been my understanding of the world, but I'd never known anyone to acknowledge it in anything other than an intellectual way—never with action. According to Elizabeth Pérez,[3] *misas* (what Odun called Spiritist séances)[4] can serve to activate history and give it a presence in the lives of people in attendance. In effect, misas give ancestors a means to participate in our lives.

My brother sat on one side of me—I could feel his excitement—and my parents on the other side were a two-person fortress. It was in this moment that I also had my first experience with the common doubt that faces mediums, the uncertainty of determining what is a message from spirits and what is our own imagination. For the most part, it is a matter of trial and error. Suddenly, my grandfather appeared to me and asked me to greet everyone in the room for him. I made excuses to say nothing, to keep quiet as a newcomer, to not interrupt; after all, it was such an innocuous message, and so mundane. What was it supposed to mean to anyone? Nevertheless, he kept waiting, until finally I spoke up. "My grandfather is here. He says hello to everyone." Once I'd announced his presence and greeting, he spoke directly to me, saying, "This is you."

This was the answer to the question I had not articulated: "Who am I?" Yet it is a classic human question and one that the baby boomer generation has spent much of its time seeking out, according to Wade Clark Roof.[5] While I am not of that generation, most of the people sitting in that room were. Who am I? My brothers and I had grown up deeply embedded in the ideas and sentiment of the civil rights era and second-wave feminism. We cared about equality first and foremost. In this space, my primary concern was to be a full version of myself, with the understanding that in doing so I was better positioned to make possible a world where all people could do so. For me that full version of myself was yet to be discovered, but I had a clear notion that to realize it, I needed to figure out what the flow of the cosmos was so that I could flow with it, not against it. But the cosmos is a vast and mysterious thing, and the flow isn't so easily grasped, especially for those of us with only two eyes able to see in only one direction: ahead. Clearly, I would need the help that I'd been asking of my spirits. The idea that ancestors as historical actors could help me actualize my present and, by extension, my future, was not so much a major shift in my outlook as the proper prescription to clarify my vision.[6] In that moment, my grand-father needed me to prove that I was listening, listening for real, before he would give the message he had for me. In that moment, he waited for me to acknowledge him, overcome my shyness and doubt; in that moment, I managed to pass the test to receive what I'd been awaiting.

During that trip, we also visited the University of Chicago. I instantly felt at home, once again, amid the Gothic gray stone buildings surrounding the lush green quad, the buildings covered in ivy and the imposing doorways: those doors made you feel like what lay beyond them was timeless. As we drove away from the campus, my grandfather appeared to me again and said, "This is where you need to be." I told him that I would need his help to make it happen, and, in short, he granted me that help. The theme of the personal journey, prominent among baby boomers, is the throughline here. While I was born after the baby boom, it is probably no surprise that this theme still resonates with me. It is also evidence of all the time I have spent socializing with people older than me. That fall, I moved into a dorm on campus and started attending séances and temple rituals regularly. I don't remember what I told my roommate and other college friends about what I was up to. On the outside it may have appeared that I had an active social

Figure 9.2. Odun. Photograph by Robert Boldt, 2001.

life, but really, I was just very intent on fully following through on the agreement I had with my grandfather. He helped me get to this place so that I could be my full self, so it was my responsibility to not slack off but to learn about this religious experience as best I could. This meant that throughout college, I socialized as much with baby boomers at the temple as I did with my peers in the dorm.

I spent most of those years at religious rituals in the kitchen. The center of the temple was much like the center of a home. All the rituals that took place in the sanctuary relied on work done in the kitchen: cooking, cleaning, preparing, and staging. As Pérez points out, the conversations had in the process of food preparation for religious ritual provide structure to religious life and serve as models for making sense of your own life.[7] Yes, kitchen work is humble, but it builds "bit by bit," seeping into you, making the religious experience gained from it stabilizing and profound.[8] If I wasn't studying on campus, I was across town sweeping floors, plucking chickens, earnestly meditating at a séance, or assisting with stage management for one of Odun's elaborate seasonal festivals. I spent plenty of time with my brother but rarely at his apartment. Sometimes I barely knew where he was living.

I went through my own initiations as well, receiving my necklaces, warriors, and Olókun. I had my head read. Odun's house was very active. Lots

of people were initiated into the priesthood; Odun staged elaborate seasonal festivals and extravagant orishas. He had been active in the pagan community since the 1960s. His mother was a medium, kept a *botánica* (religious goods store), and read tarot cards. Although she was not initiated into
Lucumí, she was from a Basque family that immigrated to Cuba and was
connected to the Lucumí community through Spiritism. As an adult, Odun
had studied with priests of the Egyptian mysteries, Masonry, and various
other neopagan and occult groups. After his mother's death, he maintained
her store and her gatherings and expanded these efforts, hosting pagan
events as well. By the mid-1970s, he had soured on the pagan community,
citing its lack of lineage; they could produce no solid line linking them to
the past, a quality that Adler and others in the community had often noted.
Longing for some structure and authority, he returned, so to speak, to the
community that he had grown up in, keeping the philosophy, ascetics, and
some of the rituals that he had been cultivating in the pagan community for
years. Lucumí is one of multiple Afro-diasporic religious traditions and has
a direct lineage to the Yorùbá through the transatlantic slave trade. When
Adler met Odun, he was an *iyawó* (new initiate) in *la regla de ocha*,[9] with a
shaved head and wearing white as all new initiates do; he had just taken the
name Odun, the sacred name given to him in Lucumí. As a young man, he
had trained in set design focusing on operas and the ballet, a talent he used
to create extraordinary *ilés* (sacred space)[10] for initiations and orishas,[11] and
to stage elaborate seasonal festivals complete with dramatic ritual, operatic
dance choreography, and festive feasting.

Mystic traditions are often sought out by generations in search of a more
authentic spiritual expression than that offered by institutionalized religions.[12] For me, having grown up in the Unitarian Church, where religion
was more of an intellectual exercise, this attention to action and the power
of theater was a dramatic—pun intended—change. Oddly enough, even
though I was actively involved with religious activity and academic activity,
I never brought the two together. I did not do any research on the religion. I
didn't explore. I didn't critique. None of that mattered to me. It was my spirits I expected to guide me, and I did not want to second-guess them based
on a book. Perhaps I needed a constructive space away from academia. All
my professors wrote books. I respected them, but book knowledge is something distinct from hands-on knowledge. Also, Odun always expressed a
suspicion of intellectuals, although he, and many others, considered him
one. In his mind, intellectuals didn't "do" anything but lounge around reading and hypothesizing about those who did. His critiques conjured images

Figure 9.3. An orisha throne to Obatalá created by Odun with two of Odun's godchildren. Photograph by Robert Boldt, 1998.

of academics sitting with religious experts, sipping coffee, and asking important questions, then coming to lofty deductions about the motivations of the people mopping floors—if they considered them at all. In fairness, Odun's impressions, while hyperbolic, were not removed from reality, as much of traditional Western scholarship at the time was focused on the commentary of "experts" in order to reveal the essentialized "truth" of a given subject. My search for meaning in the tradition of Western philosophy led to conducting extensive research into religious ritual,[13] and Lucumí was enticing because of its impenetrable secrecy and long-fought-for survival through the brutalities of slavery and colonialism. I feel honored to be a part of this long legacy.

When I first began attending Odun's temple regularly, the understanding I came away with, from my brother and the people I met, was that you learn by doing. Books gave a false sense of security. Many of the people who wrote them either hadn't done the work or didn't even realize that much of what they'd been told was untrue. This was in large part due to their presumption that asking questions, as opposed to *doing*, was how you learned. Odun's temple was not the only place where the tension between book knowledge and hands-on knowledge flared. As George Brandon points out, accusations of inauthenticity in religious dialogues often hinge on the accused relying on books for knowledge when she or he has no sweat equity in a religious house.[14] The test of sensory knowledge-gathering is often used simultaneously to prove a sincere desire to learn or a deeply held overall devotion, both highly valued character traits. In part, this highlights the knowledge that comes of raw labor, often performed by poor people unable to access education, knowledge that the "Western philosophical tradition" has historically dismissed.[15] It's funny, because one of my daughters is a philosophy major, and she and her peers often comment that you can always identify a philosopher who never did their own laundry. In Odun's temple, you didn't trust religious information given about Lucumí from someone who didn't know how to pluck a chicken.

I took this to heart during my time in Odun's temple. I directed my effort toward religious knowledge through building sweat equity that I believed would illustrate my credibility as a sincere religious actor. My intellectual effort was spent on getting through college, where I studied India, learned about Hinduism and anthropology, and basically kept my religious and intellectual lives separate. While it may sound like I dismissed book learning, I didn't. I enjoyed others' book learning on the topic, but I didn't have time to engage in my own. Also, I feared getting into the middle of disagreements between practitioners and academics and being expected to pick sides. For me, keeping the two worlds separate was the most tolerable space to navigate.

It was a long journey from Odun's temple to the present. In 2000, the temple moved from Chicago to New Orleans—myself, my husband, and our children along with it. Still, it would be over ten years more before I began pursuing graduate work. In 2005, Odun passed, and with him his temple. Ultimately, it proved a singular vision that was not sustainable. The "line" that Odun so admired in Lucumí, the religious lineage, proved critical as my husband and I sought out a new home. We eventually were introduced to one by Odun's eldest godchild and our longtime friend. It was the house I'd been looking for, that of the Obá Oriaté (ritual expert)[16] who had performed my own initiation years before.

By February 2007, we found ourselves in Miami walking into a new ilé. Upon opening the door, we were met by a reflection of ourselves in a wall-sized mirror set behind an elevated, life-size statue of Santa Bárbara with a glass candle lit on the floor.[17] The statue was surrounded by a set of warriors and Shangó's wooden vessel (batea). It was the first time that I had walked into a Lucumí house outside of Odun's ilé, and I knew that I was in the right place at the right time. Had I been met with a Catholic saint towering over me when I walked into Odun's temple fifteen years before, I would have walked out. The full version of myself that I was seeking was not possible through Christianity. You might wonder about my relationship to Catholicism. I really had none, outside of its place in history and the overall wider society. My mother had grown up in the Catholic Church and grown disenchanted with it, but she never expressed hostility toward it. I had no personal experience with the Catholic Church, nor any interest in it. Christianity, for me, was the schoolyard variety. Whenever the topic of religion came up, if I was asked about my own, I'd tell the other children that I was Unitarian. Inevitably, they had never heard of it. The discussion of religion caused as much of an existential crisis among my childhood peers as the discussion of race. Completely unmoored by an unfamiliar religion, they would definitely inform me that I was going to hell. Whatever rhetoric my classmates were enmeshed in I can only shudder to guess, but the mindless exclusivity and intolerance of it was a turn-off from the schoolyard on.

Most Cuban santeros that I know consider themselves Catholic, many referring to Lucumí as an expression of Catholicism. What this means to a given practitioner varies greatly: I've met some who go to church infrequently out of respect and loyalty to their egun (ancestors), others who proudly proclaim themselves believers in Jesus, and many in between. Still, most have a comfort level with the Catholic Church that I do not share and Odun never supported. This relationship with the Catholic Church has been part of an ideological divide between Cuban communities and some African American communities of orisha worship who disavow the Catholic trappings of Cuban traditional practice.[18] The Catholic trappings of Cuban practice were also a source of tension for Odun, who was concerned solely with the passed-down Yorùbá body of ritual knowledge that is Lucumí practice, upon which he layered the ascetics and noncompeting ritual of the ancient classical world. For the latter he had no formal authority to answer to, while for the former he bowed to the Lucumí hierarchy, most especially his godfather, the elder who "made" him. My Obá Oriaté was also an elder in the community, and I was comforted by his years of experience and traditional approach, even if I didn't fully engage with the Catholic elements of it. He was also very supportive of book learning in conjunction with hands-on learning, and at that point I had begun to hunger for the book learning and intellectual space that I had been skirting for over a decade and a half.

Once we joined the ilé run by the Obá Oriaté and his wife, we were able to continue our journey with a solid connection to Lucumí. A few years later, I came to the realization that the answer to the question that had dogged me since my college graduation was right in front of me. I knew that I wanted to return to graduate school, but for years I debated what project to explore. As an undergraduate I had worked in an office full of graduate students, and I recognized that much of their dedication and drive were the result of a clarity of purpose. Those who lacked that clarity wallowed, unable to complete their dissertations. I was convinced that entering graduate school without a clear vision and purpose would be a waste. My time studying South Asia had been rewarding, but I did not see a practical way to return to it. I considered a few different projects along the way, but they fizzled. Finally, I realized that I had been working toward graduate study in Lucumí in my everyday devotions for decades and that ultimately it was the topic from which I would benefit the most and could contribute the most to as well. But I didn't want to make that decision without that clarity of purpose that came from clear guidance of my new Lucumí community. So, while in Miami, I sat down with my Obá Oriaté on the mat to ask, once again, for guidance concerning what direction I should take in my life. In this instance the message was clear, much as my maternal grandfather's message had been, but this message in divination came with an adamant fist pounding: "Yes," the orishas say. "This is you."

10

Finding My Place in the Lucumí Tradition as an African American Woman

TERRI-DAWN GONZÁLEZ

My Childhood and Family

I am an African American woman who was born and raised in Los Angeles, California. I am the product of an idyllic two-parent middle-class home. Both of my parents attained a postsecondary education, my father held a master's degree in business administration, and my parents owned multiple modestly successful small businesses. I attended some of the best public schools on the affluent west side of Los Angeles at a time when California public schools were still respected nationally. I was fortunate to secure a coveted spot in a limited and selective school integration program. I was required to read the various works of classical Greek, Roman, English, and American literature that were foundational to the "Western canon" as it was understood in the United States. I also received "assignments" from my father to read works of African American literature as well as works regarding African American history and the civil rights movement. My childhood social circle consisted of my younger sister and children with diverse cultural but similar socioeconomic backgrounds as compared with ours.

I have always been an avid reader of nonfiction as well as of fiction. As a child, my favorite activities were riding my bicycle and reading. I also watched entirely too much television, and I spent Saturday mornings watching classic films at a nearby cinema. Reading was a form of adventure for me; it was my passport to other historical periods and far-flung places, as well as providing me with a peek into other cultures. I have always fantasized about my ancestors, what their lives may have been like, and what their beliefs may have been. It is often said in our tradition that one simply cannot "learn the religion" from books. This alludes to the fact that Afro-diasporic religions are oral traditions in which knowledge is passed from elder priests to younger initiates via word of mouth and embodied experiential instruction. Those truths notwithstanding, I believe that books and written knowledge are essential to the holistic development of a priest of these traditions in modern Western societies because they provide necessary insights into the history and the cosmology of our traditions, as well as insights into how the religion is practiced in other branches, that may otherwise be inaccessible. Well-researched and accurate books have always made up an important part of my world, and they have always served me well.

My Religious and Cultural Backgrounds

I did not grow up within the Lucumí religious community. My parents were members of a Calvinist Protestant church, which our family attended each Sunday. However, my father had grown up Catholic in southeastern Louisiana, and, for some reason, I was also sent to attend mass at a Roman Catholic church each week with an older cousin. My parents were nominally Christian: they were more ethical than religious, and our home was always welcome to an extended community of family and friends of diverse backgrounds and beliefs.

Although the media often depict African Americans as a homogeneous group, the African American community of the city of Los Angeles during my youth was a rich tapestry of cultural diversity and American regional diversity. Los Angeles was the destination for tens of thousands of Roman Catholic Louisiana Afro-Creoles during the tail end of the Second Great Migration from the southern United States during World War II; the city was home to numerous African American Catholic churches, Creole restaurants, and Creole neighborhood markets where seafood, meats, and imported spices specific to Louisiana were sold. During the mid-twentieth century, Los Angeles was also the terminus point of many African Americans from the Midwest, the Gulf Coast, the Mississippi Delta, and the Southwest. These groups arrived in waves, and they were culturally distinct with their own foods, colloquial speech, and modes of worship. Even when I was a young Black child, my perception of my own African American group was one that included equal parts of commonality and diversity.

How I "Discovered" the Tradition

My parents were middle-aged at the time of my birth, and my father was significantly older than my mother. I grew up within the bosom of a family that my father had carefully curated from distant relatives and related families with origins in the same rural Louisiana parish where he had been born. I had "cousins" who were as much as twenty years my senior, and one of them, Dr. Lance Williams, played a pivotal role in my first exposure to Afro-diasporic spirituality. As a teenager in the Fairfax district of Los Angeles, I often spent time at the home of this "cool older cousin," who held a doctorate from the University of California at Los Angeles. His wife, Sydney, holds an MS in public health administration from the California State University, and she was an administrator with the Veterans Administration. Sydney's father was an important African American photographer of the twentieth century. She was beautiful and cultured, but unpretentious and approachable. Lance and Sydney's home was always filled with music, books, discussions, laughter, and love. The very walls were shelves filled with records of rare music and books, and I could listen to and read whatever I liked! Lance's library included books about Afro-diaspora musical traditions and spirituality.

Through the books I discovered in Lance's library, I learned that the cultural retentions of the African diaspora were an extension of the religions and spirituality of our West African and central African ancestors. Another important influence and source of exposure to Afro-diasporic spirituality during my youth was the mother of one of my dearest girlhood friends. Jean Hubbard Boone is an actress, jazz vocalist, and world traveler who exposed me to the music, fine art, culture, and spirituality of northeastern Brazil. The more I was exposed to Afro-diasporic spiritual traditions and their root cultures on the African continent, the more connected I felt to my own ancestors, and the more driven I was to learn more. I began to scour the independent African American bookstores of Los Angeles in search of more information. Although my own ancestral heritage was likely more connected to Vodou, I was especially drawn to the religious systems established by the enslaved Yorùbá people in colonial Cuba and Brazil. I felt a deep connection to those people whose ancestors had shared an experience like that of my own ancestors. My search and connection were never about running away from Christ or Christianity. I was aware of the involvement of the Roman Catholic Church in the transatlantic slave trade, just as I was aware of the colonial Christian justifications for the enslavement of Africans. However, on a personal level, I did not feel antipathy toward Christianity or Christ. I simply had a burning desire to connect with the *orishas* (deities), with the forces of nature, and with my own ancestors. My search was an adventure in and of itself, and by the time I was around seventeen years old, I declared to myself, "When I am an independent adult, I will pursue this as my spiritual path."

In the late 1980s, I moved to New Orleans to attend Xavier University. I was in the bosom of my father's family and, as if in a dream, living upon the soil that my ancestors had tread. In addition to school and the typical undergraduate social activities, I spent a lot of my time exploring the city. I walked the French Quarter and the historic Downtown and Uptown neighborhoods. I explored my school library, the Tulane University Library, the Historic New Orleans Collection, the St. Louis Cathedral, and the Cabildo. Most of my spending money went to books, and I spent many hours at the Book Star on Decatur Street next to the River Walk shopping mall. I also spent an inordinate amount of time at the old F&F Botánica on Broad Street, investigating every inch of the store and furtively asking questions of the late owner, Mr. Félix Figueroa.

How My Head Found Its Home

One summer, while I was at home in Los Angeles on vacation from school, I went out for cocktails with a group of my childhood and high school friends. After the last call, a few of us returned to my parents' house to dip our feet in the pool and catch up during the quiet hours of the early morning. It was at that time that I noticed my friend Ricardo was wearing *elekes* (the beaded necklaces representing the orishas and extending protection from the godparents' orishas to the wearer). When I asked him about the necklaces, he responded, "You *know* my mom is Cuban!" Certainly, I knew that his mother was Cuban, but it had never occurred to me that Ricardo's mother was a practicing *santera* (an initiated priestess of the Afro-Cuban Yorùbá faith), *palera* (an initiated priestess of the Afro-Cuban Bantu religion), and *espiritista* (a practitioner of the Afro-Cuban branch of Kardecian Spiritism). This lovely lady, Mrs. Thompson, whose home I had visited with other kids as a teen to pick up my friend for outings, was an *iyalorisha* (an elder priestess who initiates other priests). Could this really be happening? Could I have known a practitioner of my desired faith all along?

Afro-diaspora religions are initiatory, hierarchical, and secretive. The secretive nature of these faiths has diminished somewhat, but this was almost thirty years ago. Discrimination was a real danger in those days. That was prior to the *Church of the Lucumí Babalú Ayé v. the City of Hialeah* case, in which the United States Supreme Court ruled to protect the religious right of our community to perform ritual animal sacrifice. Practitioners were in danger of legal prosecutions for practicing their religious rites; they were also in danger of harassment by law enforcement, antagonism from their neighbors, and even in danger of losing their employment and livelihoods.

When I first became involved in the religion, it was a complicated and often dodgy process to identify a legitimate Ilé Oshá (religious house of worship). Even today, identifying a religious home is not always a linear process. At that time, most of the *botánicas* (Afro-Caribbean religious supply stores) in the greater Los Angeles area were connected to the Mexican and Central American spiritual practices known as *brujería* (witchcraft) and *curanderismo* (Latin American folk healing traditions), as opposed to the Afro-Cuban Santería (a commonly used misnomer for Afro-Cuban Yorùbá Lucumí religion) community I was seeking. These religious supply shops were usually located in dangerous parts of the city. This was during the crack and gang epidemics in Los Angeles, and I was a single young woman exploring areas of town where I had never been. Some of these shops had been the sites of crimes related to sexual abuse and fraud. Even within the legitimate community, as an English-speaking non-Latina, I would have been suspect. Unlike South Florida and the East Coast, where Caribbean Latinos and thriving African American Lucumí communities abound, the tradition was established in Southern California primarily by non-Black Cubans initiating Mexican Americans and Central Americans. Anti-Blackness was, and continues to be, an issue within Latino communities. I had studied Spanish in school and at university, and I was orally conversant and literate in the Spanish language, but I was certainly not fully fluent, and I was clearly an *aleyo* (outsider/foreigner). Learning that my friend's mother was a religious elder in the tradition I was seeking to enter was a tremendous blessing that cannot be overstated.

I arranged to receive a reading (divination session) from Mrs. Thompson at her home. She was gracious, kind, insightful, and stunningly accurate in her assessments during my reading with her. It was the first spiritual reading I had ever received, and although I had been studying books about the religion for years, it was hard to comprehend that someone could see so many personal things about me with such accuracy. Mrs. Thompson prescribed some cleansing practices for me that ultimately proved to be highly efficacious. She asked me if I had informed my parents about my interest in the religion, and she informed me that I should not become involved in the religion until after I had completed my undergraduate studies. I returned to college in New Orleans at the end of that summer, and I kept in touch with Mrs. Thompson until I returned home to live in Los Angeles after my father suffered multiple strokes. The year after my return, I received elekes (the ceremony of receiving a set of necklaces beaded for the orishas that places the recipient under the protection of the godparent's orishas) in Mrs. Thompson's *ilé* (religious house/temple). Two years later, I traveled with her to Cuba to be fully ordained as a priestess of Oshún (riverine deity of love and procreation) at the ilé of her older cousin, the prolific and formidable iyalorisha Gladys Ela Prieto, Olufándeyí, my *ojubona* (secondary godmother).

Growing up within an Afro-Creole family, with older parents and deep southern roots, prepared me well for entry into the Lucumí community. The initiatory religions of West Africa, western central Africa, and their diasporas are rigidly hierarchical. These are ancient traditions in which our elders are not only the repositories of tremendous knowledge and spiritual power (*ashé*); they are also the closest living beings to the revered and venerated ancestors (*egun*). As priestesses and priests (*olorisha*), they are the living representatives and manifestations of the orishas themselves. Our elders, though human and imbued with human faults and failings, possess a spark of divinity that increases with age. Alejandrina Herrera-Thompson, iyalorisha Oshún Ibú Koromí, was not only my religious sponsor and iyalorisha. *Madrina*, as I affectionately addressed her, was a mother to me in every sense of the word. She gave birth to me as an olorisha, my orishas were born from her orishas, she was my teacher, and she was my best friend.

Over the twenty-four years of our godparent-godchild relationship, my love, respect, and gratitude for her only grew deeper. She was my religious and secular mentor and adviser, and she was a living example of the qualities I hope to one day exhibit as a human being and as an iyalorisha. Madrina's influence on my life and my character was just as significant as those of my own mother who raised me, whom I love and admire with all my heart. Her late husband was a second father to me, and her two sons are my brothers. She expanded my family and my heart with every priest and priestess she ordained. Madrina passed away in December 2019, at the age of eighty-six, and not one day passes during which I do not thank her for my crown. I cannot imagine what my life would have been without her presence and influence.

Development and Practice

My years of development, training, and experience as an olorisha have involved a great deal of study, rote memorization, and reading about the history, cosmology, and culture of the tradition. The weekend manual labor in the *igbodu* (sacred ceremonial space) is an ongoing aspect of the olorisha's life. Although I had been ordained in Cuba, which can create challenges to learning opportunities here in the States, my godmother had been a long-standing member of the Cuban exile community in Los Angeles, so she was well known and well regarded. Being her *omo orisha* (spiritual child) afforded me the opportunity to work and to learn. I was also fortunate to meet elders like the late Clayton D. Keck Jr. (Afolabí) and the Lucumí Obá Oriaté (ritual specialist) and historian Baba Miguel "Willie" Ramos (Ilarí Obá), who were generous with me. Spanish-language studies from middle school through two years of undergraduate Spanish instruction at my Catholic university in New Orleans, with a priest who prepared clergy for work in Latin America, by no means prepared me for the rapid-fire Afro-Cuban Spanish that is common within the Lucumí community—but it nonetheless served me well. One recommendation I make to all non-Latinos entering the Afro-Cuban religions is to study Spanish. Take some classes. Many of the gaps in knowledge and communication are language gaps, and they can be avoided or at least mitigated with some effort.

In 2001, I met an Afro-Cuban American priest of Obatalá (arch divinity of wisdom and creator of the human form), who was eleven years my senior and almost twenty-five years my senior as an olorisha, Félix González (Oshá L'ashé). We were married in 2004, and we were blessed with two healthy sons in 2009 and 2011. Then, in 2012, my husband succumbed to cancer, and although our time together in this life was shorter than I would have liked, it was a beautiful and fruitful learning and loving experience for me. Félix was a competent *babalorisha* (orisha priest who has ordained others), *tata Nkisi* (priest of Afro-Cuban Bantu religion), *dilogún* (Yorùbá cowry shell) diviner, esoteric herbalist, beadworker, ritual orishamer, and orisha tool artisan. He was a loving and devoted husband, father, son, and brother; and he was a wonderful teacher, from whom I learned a great deal regarding orisha, Egun, Afro-Cuban culture, and life. During our eight years of marriage, I learned about the miraculous plants that our ancestors had used to heal for thousands of years. My husband had learned from his own mother, an iyalorisha of sixty-six years, regarding the esoteric and medicinal properties of our sacred plants; and he generously shared with me some of his knowledge regarding the propagation, the medicinal use, and the ritual use of plants in accordance with Afro-Cuban culture and spirituality. I also had the honor to serve as *ofeyisitá* (recorder of divination sessions) when my husband and my mother-in-law conducted dilogún readings (sixteen cowry shell divination) for their godchildren and clients, which provided me with valuable insights into the nature and the power of Odu (the living entities that are the spiritual manifestations of our sacred divination patterns).

The years immediately following the death of my husband were years I devoted to the nurturing of my young sons. It was a time of introspection for me, as well as a time during which I cultivated relationships with my adult stepdaughter and with my younger siblings in the religion, who have been a source of love and support. What remained consistent in my life were my relationships with my orishas, with my elders, with my religious family and community, and my continued religious studies through books, online classes, and in-person classes and lectures conducted by ritual specialists and scholars. In addition to my own madrina, I have been fortunate to have had access to elders such as Baba Felipe García-Villamil (Ogun Deí), his late wife Iyá Valeria García (Oyá Sholá), and their family, as well as my dear friends and mentors, the late *oluwo* (a title given to a *babalawo* that notes that they were first initiated as an olorisha) Baba Craig Ramos and Baba Michael Bejarano, who have each been a uniquely prolific fount of knowledge and support for me in unique ways.

Building a Religious Family

As olorishas, times of tribulation can call us to question our destiny as healers, as leaders, and as teachers; but as we say in the Lucumí tradition, "el itá nunca cae en el piso." This phrase translates to "itá never falls to the ground," meaning our *itá* (priesthood life divination) does not falter. One way or another, with time, what has been predicted shall come to pass. On the third day of the weeklong Lucumí priesthood ordination process, each *iyawó* (newly ordained novice priestess or priest) receives a lengthy divination session that essentially provides that individual with an esoteric roadmap of their future life. This includes instructions regarding the ethical fulfillment of the destiny that this individual soul selected in Orun (the heavenly realm) prior to their incarnation into this life. The itá includes prescriptions and proscriptions to ensure the success of each priestess or priest. Each individual olorisha has their own destined path to follow, with their own unique objectives to accomplish. This is never an easy road, and we are often required to overcome character flaws, to learn unpleasant lessons, and to overcome seemingly insurmountable obstacles. I spent many years avoiding the role of iyalorisha, out of a fear of the deep emotional attachments and the attendant emotional vulnerabilities that role often brings. The loss of my husband was traumatic for me, and I saw the numerous disappointments my own godmother had experienced as the result of ingratitude and the lack of consideration from godchildren; but my madrina had made it clear to me that being an olorisha meant that my life and choices would no longer be my own. This is a path of facing one's fears and personal feelings of inadequacy. My religious upbringing was strict and traditional, though my madrina relaxed a great deal over the years with my younger siblings. After a rough start, I am now clear on the fact that my parenting or teaching style is traditional, with high standards. I am not everyone's cup of tea, which requires me to be very honest and transparent regarding my leadership style as well as my expectations. It also requires moving slowly into relationships with prospective godchildren.

Allowing myself to step onto the path of becoming an iyalorisha (also styled as *iyalocha,* elder priestess who initiates others) involved the understanding that I have a responsibility to share with others all that was given to me. It is the same approach I take with the sons I brought forth into this world from my own womb. I have a responsibility to mold my *ahijados* (godchildren) in the same way that my madrina molded me. I have a responsibility to guide *aleyos* (outsiders) into this culture in a manner that will foster respect. I can be a lifelong learner, because this culture is about learning forever, while still being a teacher. I am opinionated, which is something that rubbed off on me from my Afro-Cuban elders (including my late husband and in-laws). Conversely, I understand the importance of being willing and able to revise my opinions and positions as I continue to learn and grow and as I am exposed to information that I did not previously possess. Coming to the realization and accepting the fact that I don't have to be perfect to be an *iyá* (mother) was a huge step for me.

As I find myself more frequently perceived as an elder and as a teacher, it has become clear that I have an obligation to place an emphasis on *respect for the culture that gave birth to this spirituality.* Those of us who come to these traditions as outsiders and converts have a deep responsibility to attain a level of understanding of the culture we are entering, and those who grew up within the culture have a responsibility to uphold it. We in the West are the products of heterogeneous societies that valorize individuality, personal freedoms, and nonconformity. Entitlement is embedded within our mentality. However, orisha worship is the product of a communal, homogeneous, ethnocentric society that is hierarchical. Many of the values, cognitive patterns, and ways of interacting that are normal within a modern Western society are simply not in alignment with an ancient African tradition. One of the first concepts that was repeatedly stated to me by my elders when I entered the tradition was that as my involvement in and understanding of the tradition deepened, I would experience a paradigm shift.

Orisha worship is systematic, initiatory, communal, and hierarchical. Its *fundamento* (foundation) consists of *reglas* (rules and regulations), *awo* (secret, sacred knowledge), and *licencia* (ritual authority and authorization), among other things. It is an intact system of worship that is an unbroken chain thousands of years old. It is orthodox and structured. It is neither random nor eclectic. Its structure and orthodoxy were established and maintained at great personal cost by *alagba-lagba* (revered elders), mandated and guided by the orisha (deities) themselves.

To me, orisha worship is not about picking and choosing. It is an initiatory system, with a priesthood that has existed in the diaspora for hundreds of years and in West Africa for thousands of years. Priests are entrusted with sacred and social responsibilities, which include providing guidance and information to others regarding the tradition. All priests who have been trained by their own elders have a requirement to assume this leadership role in some capacity, including those of us who may not always feel comfortable with that role.

Of late, I am seeing a lot of people entering the tradition who make no effort to understand it. I see an astounding exhibition of entitlement, and I see "elders" who have become more accommodationists than priests and teachers. Orisha worship is not an ideological *safe space*. I honor my own elders, who gave me so very much, by upholding the tradition and the culture they shared with me. To be ordained is to be physically and spiritually joined with the deity, to function and to be recognized as a member of an ancient community of priests, and to be the recipient of a profound set of responsibilities.

Pivotal Experiences and Valuable Lessons

On a deeply personal level, I have had to overcome my feelings of impostor syndrome, which was something that my godmother as well as the late Iyá Valeria García (Oyá Sholá) were instrumental in helping me do. Those

Figure 10.1. Portrait of Terri-Dawn González. Photograph by Gail Oliver, 2019.

of us who are conscientious and meticulous tend to be overly critical of ourselves, and in life we will always encounter negative human beings who wish to see us fail. Although the Lucumí tradition has become virtually universal, being practiced by people of every race and cultural background within modern pluralistic societies, converts who were not born into the tradition often find themselves in a place where they are forced to make a position for themselves.

Some people will always attempt to relegate those who entered the tradition as cultural outsiders to the position of permanent "others." African Americans and other non-Latinos as well as non-Cuban Latinos in these traditions must develop a strong sense of self and of faith. This is just as true for non-Africans practicing *eṣin òrìṣà ibile* (Yorùbá religion practiced today in West Africa). It is essential that we understand that it is the deities themselves who grant us our place within these traditions, through divination, possession, and the various ways that they communicate. If it is one's destiny to become an olorisha, then that is what they will become. However, that does not make us entitled to anything, and it certainly does not obviate our responsibility to understand and to uphold the tradition. Knowledge of the history of this tradition can be a tremendous defensive weapon as well as a tool for building bridges.

Figure 10.2. Terri-Dawn with her *madrina*. Photograph by Félix T. González Jr., 2019.

Like so many who have overcome hardships in life, my madrina was a woman of tremendous faith. Just like my parents, she constantly reminded me of my value, of my worthiness, and of the gifts that I have a responsibility to share with others. She was a remarkable spiritualist (medium), a formidable woman, and someone who possessed prodigious personal magnetism and charisma. The faith that I have learned to have in my own *ashé* (creative life force energy/grace) has as its foundation the tremendous ashé imparted to me by my exceptional madrina, her belief in me, and my faith in the sacred words of the orisha themselves as imparted to me in itá.

Integrating the Lucumí Tradition into Meaningful Work

My educational background and work history are in the areas of political science, public policy research, finance, and business, but in 2018 I began a small business that represents my passion and allows me to engage in work that I find meaningful on a personal and spiritual level. My madrina had always encouraged me to study and to work with the sacred plants of our tradition, specifically because it is the area of expertise of my primary spiritual guide, who is also an ancestral spirit that walks with me. While I was always interested in the sacred plants of our tradition, the formal study of those plants seemed an overwhelming endeavor to me. There are thousands of plants within our system. However, my marriage to an herbalist and propagator of these plants changed that. Living with someone who was growing these plants all around our home and who was utilizing them in religious works daily made it much more accessible.

Knowledge of nature and the harmonious interaction with the natural world to access divine power (ashé) are cornerstones of this tradition, as are concepts of ritual, spiritual, and physical cleanliness and purity. Practitioners of Afro-Cuban orisha worship have a mandate to maintain their bodies and their environments in a state of physical and ritual purity. One of the first and most basic forms of spiritual self-care and maintenance in support of this cleanliness about which religious neophytes receive instruction is the ritual cleansing of their bodies and surroundings with powerful plants and other sacred elements that pertain to the deities they worship and the spiritual entities with which they work.

Spiritual baths, floor washes, anointing oils, condition soaps, and esoteric powders confected from the sacred herbs of our ancestors are all integral aspects of Afro-Caribbean culture that are held in common with African American cultural practices that were preserved in the southern United States. A spiritual bath is an ancient cleansing ritual that combines the therapeutic and esoteric properties of water with the use of sacred plants, herbs, roots, barks, minerals, oils, and other natural ingredients to dispel negativity, produce a desired positive outcome, promote healing, and bring us into alignment with our higher purpose or destiny. This restorative practice is an integral part of the holistic healing modalities of many cultures. For centuries, the practitioners of African traditional religions and Afro-diaspora religions have employed the use of medicinal, ethnobotanical, magico-religious, and aromatherapeutic herbs to assure their physical, spiritual, and emotional health and well-being.

In the Afro-Cuban religious systems, we utilize the spiritual bath (*baño espiritual, ebó misí,* or *ebó ewé ní l'ara*—forms of ritual or purificatory baths) to remove destructive, negative, and unclean spiritual influences. These lustral baths are composed of specific plants, medicinal herbs, roots, barks, and other elements that work in unison to restore spiritual equilibrium and alignment. We believe that each plant possesses a specific ashé. Often a plant's ashé is in alignment with that of a specific orisha/*lwa*/*nkisi* (deity), spirit guide, natural element, or Odu (divination pattern); and the plant's ashé can be activated by the priestess or priest to act as a conduit to manifest the ashé of the orisha or the divination pattern to bring about a positive outcome for the individual using the bath. There is a long history of African American Hoodoo and New Orleans Afro-Creole Voodoo practitioners utilizing many of the same herbs that are employed in Afro-Caribbean religious rituals. Our ancestors brought their powerful knowledge of medicinal and magical plants with them to the Americas, learned about the plants native to the Western Hemisphere from Native Americans, and passed down the knowledge of their use so that we might heal ourselves of negative spiritual influences and achieve the positive outcomes we desire for ourselves and our children.

I was trained in the confection of these esoteric herbal preparations by my madrina and by my late husband. I was absolutely enchanted by this work from the beginning. The study of the esoteric and medicinal properties of our sacred plants, as well as their propagation, will absolutely be an area of continuously humbling lifelong study for me. I do not refer to myself as an herbalist because I am neither an *osainista*, an *olosain*, nor an *onishegun*, which are specialized priests who undergo specific rituals and several decades of direct and formal apprenticeship within their priesthoods. I am, however, an iyalorisha who has a solid ashé and the ritual license to work with and study our sacred plants. This work is meaningful, challenging, and deeply rewarding to me in a personal way, and I have been the recipient of teachings from the spiritual plane as well as from the physical. My madrina, my *muerta* (primary spiritual guide), my ancestors, my late husband, my mother-in-law María-Antonia Hernández (Oshún Koyímí), and my dear religious brother oluwo Luís Marín (Orilana Èṣùdina Edeniyi Akinwale) have all taught me and have all shared generously with me. There have been too many others to name here, but it is true that I have been the beneficiary of great generosity from many in this regard. I believe deeply in this work, as it is my passion, and while my public business only commenced in 2018, I have been engaged in this work for more than twenty-five years.

With my company, Spiritual Bath Tea, LLC, I have found a way to offer the fruits of my passion. My herbal spiritual bath products are all created by hand, organic, and produced in accordance with the orthodoxy of my religious tradition. I sell my preparations on my website at SpiritualBathTea .com and at select spirituality and personal empowerment events in the greater Los Angeles area. My passion for creating these baths and oils led me to create an in-person seminar here in Los Angeles that developed into a series of classes recorded on video that will together comprise a complete seminar of approximately twenty hours. I have also taught a rudimentary class regarding the tradition. These teaching projects have been extremely successful endeavors; I have received positive feedback from the participants, and they have been incredible ongoing learning experiences for me. Creating this content has taken me out of my comfort zone, and it has forced me to step out into the public eye in a way that I have never previously done.

There is a Yorùbá proverb (*owe*) that says, "It is bit by bit that we eat the head of the rat." Among the Yorùbá, *eku* (bush rat) is a prized delicacy and a valuable source of protein. The most valued part of the eku is its head, which contains many tiny and sharp bones. Although it is highly coveted and delicious, one must partake of this delicacy with great care and patience to avoid harm. This proverb cautions us to engage in our every endeavor with attentiveness and patience. We eat the rat's head both because it is a delicacy and because we do not engage in waste, but this act requires great care and patience. Eku is sacred to every branch of orisha worship because its head represents the wisdom of Ifá (body of divination knowledge, orisha of divination) and the orisha, which absolutely must be attained incrementally over time. The paradigm shifts from our blinkered Western worldview to the more profound perception of the natural and spiritual world that our ancestors possessed happens incrementally. My path has not been an easy one, and it was never promised to be easy, but I have not strayed from my path of learning and sharing. I will always strive to honor this practice, the orisha, my ancestors, and my impeccable iyalorisha by walking my path with integrity.

11

Beading Spirit

Lessons Learned on Healing and Community in Lucumí

Belia Mayeno Saavedra

I grew up in a very mixed family—here come all my parentheses: mixed race (Japanese and Ashkenazi Jewish mom, Indigenous-descended Xicano dad, Chinese American stepfather); mixed class (low income/street economy, working class, and middle class); mixed religion (cultural Jewishness with the occasional Passover or Hanukkah, Soto Zen Buddhism, Catholicism mixed with Mexican *curanderismo,* and my agnostic stepfather's dad was the first Asian American bishop elected in the United Methodist Church). My parents were teenagers when I was born, and they turned to their parents and siblings to help care for my sister and me. I moved through many different cultural contexts, ways of relating, and, let's be honest, trauma survival strategies as I grew up. But somehow it was never disorienting.

That was mostly because I always felt loved, no matter what family space I was in, even if the adults and their choices didn't always make sense to me. But besides enduring love, there was another set of twining throughlines: beading and Spirit. No matter what family unit I was with, I was always beading something and feeling the company of Spirit. And I was very lucky that my family always encouraged both, even when I didn't always make sense to them.

When I was bullied in middle school, I went to the public library and checked out all the witchcraft and *brujería* books I could find. I learned about calling good spirits to keep me company when I didn't have a lot of friends. I beaded protective amulets to stay safe, even though sometimes the white kids threw garbage at me during lunch. My maternal grandmoth-

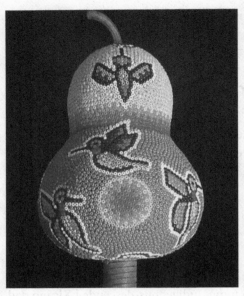

Figure 11.1. Gourd rattle made by the author Belia Mayeno Saavedra to honor *egun* (ancestors), in the bead inlay in beeswax and pine resin style of the Wixarika people of Jalisco and Nayarit, Mexico. Photograph by Belia Mayeno Saavedra, 2009.

er noticed these tendencies in me and gave me a deck of tarot cards she'd had since the 1950s. My mom never shamed me for always bringing a bag of rocks and antique glass beads everywhere I went or for talking to them instead of people.

So, I want to narrate my path into Lucumí through some lessons that beading has taught me, with the mirrored stories of Spirit woven in. Beadwork and Spirit have given me belonging and guidance for my whole life, teaching me through working with my hands and my intuition. I imagine Spirit and beadwork medicine did the same for my Indigenous ancestors before me. I carry and share those teachings now, both as a Lucumí olorisha crowned to Oshún Ibú Añá and as a respected beadworker in my community.

A Beadwork Teaching: Before anything else, learn to trust your body's knowing. You can learn complicated patterns later, but you need to first trust what your body knows how to do without thinking so that you can navigate tension and undo big knots.

I think I was about three or four years old. I remember lying on the bed, shaking with fever and nausea, staring up at the light fixture above me. I felt like my skin and joints were on fire, but I was wet-cold with sweat at the same time. I had that horrible pre-vomit feeling that my insides were dirty, and something needed to come out. I was crying and pointing up at the ceiling, where it looked like the shadows were shaping themselves into sharp points and coming to slash at me. I remember my mom wiping my tears and sweat away with a damp towel. I was small, and I didn't have words yet for everything I was feeling, but I was scared and in pain, so I just sobbed. But then my paternal grandmother, Ruth, came in and sat next to my bed and started to pray in a low whisper. She passed something small, cool, and pale over my body as she prayed. With each pass, the fever snake that was coiled inside of me loosened its hold, and I could feel the heat and nausea and soreness being pulled out of me, almost as if Gramma Ruth had it lassoed. I didn't know a lot about vacuum cleaners at that age. But later, when I would see one, it felt familiar, because I had felt that same kind of strong whoosh of air pull sickness out of me. When she was done, everything was quiet, and I felt safe inside my body again. The shadows on the ceiling softened. The memory ends there.

When I was older, I asked my mom about this—what was that white stone or something Gramma Ruth used on me? My mom explained that when I had a fever, my gramma would cleanse me with a raw egg. In the Mexican tradition of curanderismo, the belief is that *mal de ojo* (the evil eye) can make children very sick. Afterward, my gramma sometimes broke the egg in a glass of water and left it under my bed overnight. And in the morning, she would read the yolk to see if the *limpia* (cleansing) was complete. Gramma Ruth had lots of stories like this: how a healer named Brother Eli helped cure my *tía's* (aunt's) night terrors, or how a spirit whispered to my great-uncle to put spiderwebs into an open wound after he cut himself badly in a factory accident but didn't have money for the doctor.

This memory is a foundation of my faith, because it came before belief—before I started to consciously decide what ideas I align myself with. I couldn't have just been going along with my gramma's stories and believing that the egg and prayer would heal me, because she didn't explain what she was doing. The healing was real because I felt it. I can still feel echoes of it now as I write this.

So as I grew up, even when there were a million intruding voices telling me that my elders' and ancestors' healing medicines were nothing but superstition and dust, those voices never felt as real as the fever snake sliding out of my body and into the egg in my grandmother's hand.

That bodily knowing cleared the ground for me to trust my feelings and intuition. It taught me to be open to the many healing invitations that Lucumí and Espiritismo would offer later, as I grew out of my teens and into adulthood.

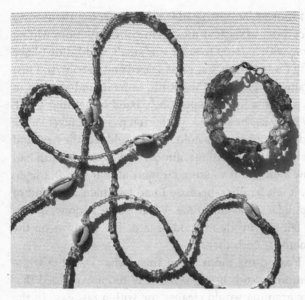

Figure 11.2. Belia Mayeno Saavedra's Oshún *idé* (bracelet) and *eleke* (necklace). Photograph by Belia Mayeno Saavedra, 2018.

A Beadwork Teaching: Even if your hands are the only ones to touch the beads, any beauty that you create is only made possible by the people who shared their knowledge with you. When you bead, remember the godsister who told you the right colors to use for each road of Oshún, or the auntie who showed you how to tie a good knot. When you teach your godchildren, or someone compliments your work, tell them who made it possible.

People often ask me how I started in the Lucumí tradition. When I was seventeen and fresh out of high school, I took a class at Laney College (a community college in Oakland, California) called "African Art and Thought in the Americas." I was allowed to do my final research project and presentation on *anything* Black in the Americas. My classmates did projects on the poetry of Gwendolyn Brooks and Audre Lorde, the Haitian Revolution, Bob Marley, the Negro Baseball Leagues, Malcolm X's trip to Mecca, Black women's hair trends and traditions—anything that excited us and made us want to learn more. And even though the class hadn't covered anything about Afro-Latinxs—the US West Coast is generally terrible about acknowledging the contributions and sometimes even the existence of Black Latinxs—a librarian had shown me an old book about Santería, and I immediately knew I wanted to do my project on the divinatory systems of Lucumí, one name for the African diasporic religion that developed in Cuba. I made a big poster board illustrating all the different ways that four pieces of *obi* (coconut used for divination) can fall to reveal advice or an answer from the Orishas themselves. I learned how to pronounce some of the prayers, even though at that time I didn't know what any of the words meant and I didn't have a lineage of elders whose names I could invoke to complete the prayers properly. I talked for so long and so enthusiastically about what I had learned that eventually the professor started giving very significant head tilt hints toward the clock behind me.

The response to this story (usually from people who were introduced to Lucumí through friends or other network connections, which is common in our community) is often, "Wow! So, you found it on your own?"

No. I took a Black class, with a Black professor, in a historic Black city shaped by Black revolutionaries, and researched books by Black authors, shared with me by a Black librarian. And later, I was connected to my future *madrina* (spiritual godmother) by my Afro-Dominicana coworker and friend (I'll get to that story soon). I made my own choices informed by my experiences to decide what path to follow, but I could not have found Lucumí alone, because no one can find it without the labor, vision, and leadership of Black people—both the ancestors and the living.

I think (and pray) a lot on this legacy now, as Lucumí continues to grow in popularity for non-Black people such as myself. What do we owe to the living descendants of the enslaved African people who kept this tradition alive and who still suffer under the poisons of anti-Blackness and the limits of the white supremacist imagination—both from outside and within the Lucumí community? What do we want to offer, in reverence and reciprocity, for all the Black resilience and resistance and joy and power and song and healing medicine that makes the Lucumí tradition what it is today? I've tried some things on my own or with a few godsisters—such as facilitating a small workshop about challenging anti-Blackness in the *ilé* space, reframing tithing, donating to Black trans–led organizations, and asking others to do the same in honor of my initiation anniversary to Oshún—but there is still so much more to do.

I see another bead metaphor here. In our tradition, we consecrate *elekes* (the sacred beaded necklaces that literally "protect our necks" and identify us as Orisha devotees). It is through the collective washing and steeping of the necklaces in a holy herbal water we call *omiero* that the beaded strands become something more than just decoration. We are being called as non-Black practitioners—by the ancestors and the living—to collectively steep our practice deep in the praxis and history of Black liberation. We're being called to move away from sympathy as an added adornment, toward holding Black liberation as central to making our spiritual work sacred. That calling is the seed inside our faith—the beautiful altars, the divinations, the prayers, the orishamings, the cleansings—and we are ultimately working with the Orishas to grow our souls' freedom. And we can't and won't be free until Black people are free.

A Beadwork Teaching: Have an idea of what you want to make, but let the creation unfold over time. The textures, patterns, and colors might not make sense at the beginning, and most of the time they won't exactly match your vision of what you expect. Beads are tiny, scattered fragments: they take a slow path to build into something harmonious. Hold your threads gently, follow what feels clear and sure to you, and be patient with what doesn't.

After I did the school project, I just *knew* Lucumí was my spiritual home and Oshún was my mother. I think back on myself at seventeen or eighteen, and I'm both amused and in awe of that kid who just trusted herself and what she knew was true. Or rather, that kid who could hear Egún (the ancestors/the departed) and the Orishas, even though she didn't even know yet that it was They who were speaking.

Standard *regla de ocha* (the rule of the Orishas) wisdom would say that I couldn't have known they were speaking without divination or elders to guide me. And it's certainly true that I needed both of those things to know for sure. Without that kind of formal affirmation, I couldn't have moved forward in Lucumí. But that kernel of knowing inside my body was the beginning, and I needed to hold it close and trust it to take me to my eventual teachers.

After reading everything I could find about Lucumí from the school library, and even a few books a light-fingered friend "liberated" from Barnes & Noble, I decided I wanted to offer something to Oshún. I made *oshinshin* (one of Oshún's favorite dishes of eggs, watercress, shrimp, and palm oil) for Her as an entrée, with flan for dessert, along with a bouquet of five sunflowers. I brought all of it as an offering to a creek near my grandparents' house. I didn't know any of the protocol or cautions against doing things like this without elder supervision, so I just prayed to forgive myself, to love myself. Those affirmations are some of Oshún's specialties, those ways of being that felt so mystifying to me at that age. And I swore I felt Her there with me. I wouldn't say I "heard" anything, exactly, but I knew that next She wanted me to find a community.

After the visit to the creek, I went back to my grandparents' house and immediately looked in the phone book for a *botánica* I could go visit. (Reader, if you also remember using phone books, let us pause for a moment to feel hella old together.) There were several botánicas in the yellow pages, because of the Bay Area's large population of people from Mexico, Central America, and South America. I read through their names, saying each one out loud until I read one that felt right: Botánica Caridad del Cobre. I would later learn that La Caridad del Cobre was the patron saint of Cuba, who was syncretized to Oshún, but at that time I just liked the sound of the name. I chose that one as my destination, even though there were probably three others that were closer.

When I walked in, the shop owner greeted me with a loud honk of a laugh. "Here she is, dressed all in blue, but that's a daughter of Oshún coming to visit!" I didn't know if I was supposed to say "thank you," or anything at all—but I thought that maybe I was onto something by listening to the instinct to visit that botánica. I brought a dusty copy of *El Monte* (Cuban ethnologist and writer Lydia Cabrera's famous treatise on herbs in the Lucumí tradition) to the register. When the shop owner saw what I was buying, he asked if I spoke Spanish well enough to read it. I admitted that I wasn't a fluent speaker but I still wanted to try.

He nodded approvingly. "So, you're serious about this then. Good for you. Well, if you want to see the real deal, my godparents are having a *bembe* at their house in East Oakland this Sunday." He wrote something on a slip of paper and handed it to me. "Come to this address, dressed in head to toe white, and see what you think."

I felt awkward about going to a stranger's house without any sense of what to expect, but it was like there was a thread that was pulling me forward, and I didn't feel any question about whether I would follow it.

That *bembe* (a ceremonial orishaming) was the first time I ever saw anyone mounted (possessed) by an Orisha. I arrived late, so I had missed the rounds of songs that call Orishas down into the bodies of their priests. When I walked into the backyard, the orishamers were on break, so everyone was milling around with cigars or sodas, chatting quietly. But the energy and attention of the people was directed differently than at a usual social gathering. People were having their own conversations, but their attention and eyes were also on one Black man, with his waist wrapped in thick gold cloth, and a matching piece of fabric on his head. He was barefoot but moved gracefully over the dirt and rocks in the yard. He seemed to be the center of gravity in the space. I say "he" because, at that time, I didn't know that everyone was watching because Oshún was inhabiting the body of one of Her male priests.

 I tried to take my cues from the way that everyone was watching Oshún without wanting to seem like they were watching, so I mostly looked at the ground with an occasional peep upward. But on one of those furtive glances, I made eye contact with Her, and She immediately spun and walked toward me. She lifted my wrist and turned it in Her hands, examining the collection of hammered gold bangle bracelets I wore. Then She smiled. "I could take these right now if I wanted to. You're one of mine. But I'll let you keep them for a little while. I know you'll give them back to me." She squeezed me in a tight hug and smoothed Her hands all over my face afterward. "Go inside and dance when the orishas start again. It will be good for you." Then She was done with the conversation and turned sharply to advise someone else standing nearby. I stood still, feeling both such reverence and confusion that I somehow didn't mind a total stranger telling me they could jack me for my jewelry and then smearing my makeup. (As any of my exes can testify, I hate it when people tell me what to do or ruin my lipstick.)

 A woman I didn't know, who had been standing nearby doing a terrible job of pretending not to eavesdrop, nudged me toward the house's back door. "If She says go in and dance, go in and dance." But when I got inside, I was too nervous to dance. I didn't know the steps; I didn't know the songs. I wished I hadn't come alone. The anxiety made me have to pee. When I moved out of the room with the orishas, there was a line of people waiting to use the bathroom. The line was so long I had to tuck myself in a little alcove away from the rest of the people who were waiting. But they were doing the same thing that had happened in the yard—pretending not to be tracking another person who was mounted by an Orisha. This time it was a woman with dark curly hair, with a white and silver brocade cloth tied across her chest and over one shoulder. She balanced an *iruke* (a white horsetail with a beaded handle) on her head. But here again, she wasn't female during spirit possession. Similarly, Obatalá, the exalted elder, king Orisha, was visiting us through the body of a female priest.

 A small knot of people hovered around Obatalá, waiting to greet and salute Him. I don't remember what they said, but they must have all asked Obatalá for something. Because suddenly He whipped his iruke over his shoulder and focused in on me. "You! Yes, you." This sudden surge of attention did not help my whole needing-to-pee situation. "Everyone here is

Figure 11.3. Belia Mayeno Saavedra's shrine for Obatalá with beadwork created by her. Photograph by Belia Mayeno Saavedra, 2015.

asking me for this and that. It's a lot of taking for themselves and not a lot of giving to each other. What is it that you want from me?"

I had plenty of things I wanted to ask from Spirit. I still do. But at that moment I just wanted to use the restroom and hide for a while. And since I was not going to tell the living embodiment of an ancient elder mountain deity that I was just waiting to use the bathroom, let's say . . . I told the sweeter part of the truth. "I don't have anything to ask. It is just good to see you." I bowed awkwardly because I didn't know what else to do.

Obatalá cocked His head and considered me, my weird bow, and my nervous sweat mustache. He flicked the iruke out and started to brush it over me from the neck down. My skin tingled. Then he intoned in booming Spanish, "Since you're the only one who didn't ask me for anything today,

I'm going to give you a gift. A big one. But I can't tell you what it is yet because you won't understand." He reached over to His attendant carrying a plate of honey and cocoa butter, grabbed a handful, and smeared it across my face. Then He turned on his heel, sharp as a soldier doing an about-face, and walked away with no other words.

A light-brown-skinned woman with freckles and a kind smile moved closer to me. She gestured to me as I dabbed at the sticky honey on my chin. "You'll get used to it. How are you? Do you need help understanding anything He said in Spanish?"

"I think I got the basic idea, but it's true, I don't understand the gift part yet."

She patted me gently. "That's okay. Be patient. Step by step. You'll understand one day. Oh, look, the bathroom door opened. Your turn!"

I left the bembe soon after that, and I didn't see the botánica owner who had invited me again. But a little over a year later, I started a new job at a rape crisis organization in a city across the bay. My new coworker noticed that I was always tripping, dropping stuff, and breaking things out of nowhere. She told me I should meet her madrina (spiritual godmother), because maybe I needed spiritual help. We arranged to go get dinner all together.

I recognized the madrina as soon as I walked into the restaurant. Obatalá's daughter—the same Obatalá who had cleansed me, mashed honey on my lips, and promised me an enormous blessing that I didn't yet understand. She had no hint of recognition in her eyes, and I didn't mention anything either. Since she and I really hadn't met before, we shook hands like friendly strangers.

I didn't learn what Obatalá's gift was that night. But I learned over the years. I started to learn when that woman became my beloved godmother. I learned a little more when another priest of Obatalá, the kind woman who checked in on me near the bathroom, became my *oyubona* (second godmother). And I understood years later, when both daughters of Obatalá eventually birthed my crown to Oshún and opened the doors for me to become a priest.

A Beadwork Teaching: Notice little delights. The way the light catches a certain facet on a tiny crumb-sized Charlotte-cut bead. The exactly-rightness of when a bead slides exactly into the place you wanted it to land. The smell of warm beeswax to condition cotton thread. The sound of beaded tassels on a mazo clicking together when they're shaken, and how they sound like small river stones moving under flowing water. Be present with those small joys as

much as you notice the inevitable frustrations you'll encounter on your learn-
ing path, so you can remember why you love this work, this art.

A brilliant and kind elder (who also happens to be the editor of this
volume, Martin Tsang) once asked me a joking riddle about the Lucumí
tradition. "What are the first two Orishas everyone receives in Lucumí?" I
guessed Eleguá and Ogún, because, well, according to our theology, that is
the correct answer. "No! A mop and a bucket!" (And then he laughed and
took an elegant sip of his drink, because he is both British and priest of the
princely Orisha Erinle, and basically can't help being elegant.) And it is so
true, y'all. This tradition is Work with a capital W. It was quite a shift to
come to Lucumí from my maternal family's Zen Buddhist spiritual context,
with its quiet, predawn Zazen sessions, slow walking meditations, simple
bowls of rice with pickled vegetables, cups of tea, and minimalism held
sacred at the core of all ceremony and aesthetics.

Lucumí, on the other hand, is often a mix of exalted grandeur, as offerings to the Orishas, and all the mundane labor it takes to make that grandeur possible. Plucking and butchering chickens, mopping floors, washing dishes, cracking open mountains of coconuts and peeling out the white
flesh inside, serving plates to the orishamers and making sure their coffee
cups are always filled and hot, taking out trash, ironing sixteen yards of
fabric for a *trono* (Orisha altar), filling buckets with clear, cool water and
dumping the dirty water and filling the buckets again, running to the store
six or seven times for something we forgot. Any practitioner reading this
knows I'm not even mentioning half the work that goes into a ceremony.
The ceremonies are not particularly fun, sometimes, to be honest. And it
often requires the priests and ceremonial leaders to override the resistance
of their sore backs, swollen feet, or hoarse voices and just keep going—for
the Orishas and Their lifesaving, life-giving ceremonies.

But here is where Buddhism shows up again for me. In the middle of
all the ceremonial work and bustle and rush to get everything done, I remember my grandmother, a Zen priest whose Dharma name was Daishin
Mitsuzen (Magnanimous Mind, Intimate Zen). She was my first and best
teacher of how to slow down, be present, and delight in small things. Every
walk I took with her was punctuated with cries like, "Look at that! Look
how the light is coming through the leaves like that. And isn't that smell
just wonderful?" When we cooked: "Look at that! The bright green of that
spinach! Just beautiful!" She was present in joy for so many little things—
the char on burnt toast, how my hair curled, a good hand of cards in poker,
even the hilarious trumpet sound of a fart or the tuba of a big burp. She told

me her practice as a Buddhist taught her that—to stop wishing for things to be different long enough to notice what *is*.

So, I notice—because my grandmother taught me how.

A bead: My godmother stopping to squeeze me in a hug and ask me how I'm doing, even though we're both sore and dirty and probably smell funky.

A bead: My older Oyá godsister Janet making up a game or song to make the cleaning go faster.

A bead: My goddaughter Jenny glowing after she splashes some omiero onto her face.

A bead: The warm buzz in my chest when the voice of the Obá Oriate (ceremonial leader) starts to sing for Oshún, my Orisha mother, or Aganyu, my Orisha father.

A bead: My godson Cito bringing me back a bag of Haribo gummy bears from the store without being asked, because he knows I like them.

A bead: My Shangó elder *tía* Patricia dancing while she carries a tall stack of *jícara* (dried half gourds) to the *ocha* room, the sacred space where ceremonies take place.

A bead: The pleasure of a freshly cleaned set of Orisha tools (the wooden or metal implements that accompany each deity to symbolize their power and actions). The smell of palm oil and honey and a good cigar. And maybe a rum and coke with my madrina after all the work is done, while all my godsiblings and I sprawl out on the floor, halfway delirious and all the way filthy, hysterically laughing at jokes that won't make sense in the morning after everyone has gotten some rest.

A jewel: Knowing Oshún's love and blessing is real because She led me here.

12

A Hermeneutics of Plurality on the Road of the Orisha

Michael Atwood Mason

In the beginning there was a river. The river became a road and the road branched out to the whole world. And because the road was once a river it was always hungry.

Ben Okri, *The Famished Road*

Orisha Religion Has Real Genius in It

My connections to the orisha religion have been primarily within the Afro-Latinx expressions in Cuba and the United States, where I have been fortunate enough to have support from my teachers and fellow travelers: I was first initiated by Norma Pedroso (Omí Saidé). Ernesto Pichardo (Obá Irawó) has been a patient teacher for nearly thirty years, and Pedro Abreu (Asonyanye) has guided me in the land of the Arará for close to twenty. I have also been in constant dialogue with others, especially David H. Brown (Eguín Koladé), Raquel Fernández (Obá Kedún), Katherine Hagedorn (Ochún Toké), Uma Richardson (Osikán), Ivalú Rodríguez-Gil (Ibú Oñí), Josette Williamson (Oyá Ladé), and Aurora Zulueta (Omí Saidé). I have been blessed to know Nigerian and Brazilian practitioners as well, but my knowledge and practice are rooted in Cuban lineages.

These names—these people and my relationships with them—matter, not just because of the tradition of paying homage to the ancestors and the elders. They matter because they help define what Womanist theologian Linda Thomas has called the "hermeneutics of plurality"[1] and what others have referred to as positionality: I work from my specific social, cultural, and intellectual position, which is a place of tension and complexity. Inherent in this complexity is the lived experience of being an English-speaking European American initiated in Cuba. The fact that I was crowned with Ochún in a well-established Lucumí lineage, initiated to Lucumí Babalú Ayé in the Armando Zulueta lineage, and initiated to Asojoano Arará in the lineage of Pilar Fresneda further complicates my position. Like everyone, I am a multiple presence of infinite layers,[2] and we cannot take the self—even when narrating an autobiography—to be "a thing among other things; it is a function of our involvement with others in a world of diverse and ever altering interests and situations."[3] Orisha religion has living spirits at its core, and thus it endlessly generates these altering interests and focal points. Whether from ancestors or orishas, revelation drives change within the tradition, constantly adding to the already extant diversity. Whether through the divination methods of Ifá, *dilogún, obí,* or possession, the spirits make known the changes that they want to see, guiding the *desenvolvimiento* (spiritual evolution, unfolding, development) as they see fit. Despite many practitioners insisting that some idealized community should adopt a universal set of practices, the religion has always existed with great variations. This multiplicity is part of its genius.

In fact, multiple narrative traditions coexist in the tradition and promise to complicate any autobiography. One tradition says that an individual's past, present, and future are all revealed by the major divination ceremony (Lucumí: *itá*) that happens as part of priestly initiation. In this narrative style, individuals correlate different life events to different divination signs that "come out" in the ceremony. Some elders assert that the key life events will be evident in the sign that comes from the head-ruling orisha. In either case, the life story becomes a series of vignettes, each linked clearly to a specific divination sign and the orisha who gave that sign at the itá. However, a strong cultural tradition against sharing this information widely precludes me from making these details public in a published article.

Another narrative tradition focuses on spiritual evolution or improvement. In this tradition, which is prevalent in many Ifá-centric houses, an individual's original itá is modified by each subsequent itá, and the individual should attempt to live the highest qualities of the most senior divination sign received. Thus, a person who began with Irosun-Sá when he made Ifá would be delighted to receive Baba Eyiogbe when he "received the knife" in a later ceremony. Simply because Baba Eyiogbe is senior to Irosun-Sá in the hierarchy of signs, the person attempts to live from this "higher" place. Again, the tradition of discretion precludes the use of this trope here.

Finally, another widespread narrative tradition comes from Spiritism and posits that an individual will be defined in key ways by the nature of her principal guide spirit. As Diana Espírito Santo has written, "Cuban spiritists and *religiosos* largely rationalize their traits in ways consistent with the biographical characteristics of their *muertos*."[4] While the principal guide spirits, often called the *guía* or the *espíritu de luz,* play the role of coordinator among the other spirits, they also leave a clear mark on the personality or self that is developed by Spiritists. It is through this lens that I will recount one version of my road through the world.

In what follows, I have intentionally alternated between two different narrative styles. The first approximates what might be called my natural storytelling voice. It includes a good bit of detail, many specific time markers, and some personal reflection. This first style is like descriptions I delineated in other publications. The second imitates the style of divination stories recounted again and again in the religion. It is flatter and much less personal. It is almost laconic in that it presents only the most essential details. These two voices again underscore the complex expressive resources that the religion affords.

That we are all on a journey is a truism reflected in most wisdom traditions. But the trope of the road through the world (*ona ayé*) plays a particularly powerful role in orisha tradition. My path has been defined—or can be narrated—through my principal guide spirit. However, I started down the road of orisha before I knew anything about her.

After my second year of college, I took a year off and worked as a baker while I found my way. I spent most of the year in solitude. Five days a week, I rose at three in the morning and worked at the bakery from three thirty until eleven thirty or noon. I returned to my apartment where I lived alone to pray, write, contemplate my dreams, and read. During this time, I began to write down all my dreams, a practice I have never interrupted. When I could, I visited national parks and Native American communities in the American Southwest. As I read about different cultures and their myths, I encountered orisha religion as expressed in Yorùbá communities of Nigeria and their descendants in Cuba and Brazil. The dynamism, vitality, and immediacy of their deities transfixed me. I first encountered the orishas in Luisah Teish's book *Jambalaya,*[5] in which she includes a description of Oyá, a goddess of lightning, storms, and ancestors. The book says that if you asked Oyá to change your house, she would not rearrange the furniture but rather blow away the floorboards, and this image of definite, powerful change excited me.

The same day I read this description, I dreamed that I was holding out my arms and invoking Oyá, but I was saying "OH-ya" (as the book included no guidelines for pronunciation). A strong, feminine voice answered, "No, it is pronounced Oh-YAH." I immediately woke up, filled with excitement: I had called upon this goddess, and she had responded clearly and directly. Yorùbá culture provided a whole living pantheon of gods, each with powerful personality traits, preferences for certain foods and colors, sacred songs, and authority over different aspects of human life. This experience fueled my curiosity and led me to begin researching Yorùbá religion in its various forms.

A couple years later, I found Judith Gleason's book *Oyá: In Praise of the Goddess* (1987). I read it again and again, as I tried to follow the shifting currents of its prose and worked to digest the world it depicted. I still have the original copy whose binding has been broken by wear and double taped for reinforcement. The book is a masterpiece of original, synthetic scholarship that breaks between lived experience, anthropology, depth psychology, textual analysis, and diasporic description. These shifting perspectives imitate the motile quality of Oyá's subjectivity and reveal Gleason's unwillingness to privilege any one perspective. Such was her deep commitment to her vision of wholeness.

Having been pulled (or blown?) into the world of orisha, I needed to find a way to connect to the community, so I sought Judith Gleason out. I found her name and address in *Contemporary Authors* and wrote her a short letter explaining my situation. A week later, I received a short letter in her own hand, explaining that she only knew two diviners but recommended one: Santiago Pedroso.

A month later, in late December 1988, I drove from Washington to Philadelphia, where I visited Pedroso for my first cowrie shell reading. As I entered his old stone house, I was greeted by his Eleguá, who was surrounded by a generous plate of *torrejas,* a traditional offering that resembles French toast. (When they want to tease me, my family still asks periodically about the God of French toast.) The first thing Pedroso told me that Eleguá said was that I was born to serve the orishas and that I would need to make *ocha* (become an initiated priest). I remember telling him that I was not surprised.

I still have a single sheet of paper where Pedroso's wife took notes on the consultation, and two additional pieces of counsel stand out after all these years: He said Babalú Ayé, the orisha of communicable diseases, healing, and miracles, was speaking to me, and he told me that I needed the river "so that everything would be easier" for me. These two orishas continue to be the core of my personal pantheon and therefore my daily practice. But why would their presence be so important over three decades?

Before making ocha, I spent a good deal of time developing spiritually. I received my *bastón de egun*, the staff for honoring the ancestors, and I tended a Spiritist altar, where I sat once or twice a week to draw myself close to the ancestral spirits who guide, heal, and protect me. One night, as I sat at the altar and prayed to meet my spirit guide, I fell into a light trance. I saw a clear image of a dark-skinned woman standing in a cave with a stream of clear water rushing through it. I asked her name. "Clara Luz," she responded without a hint of irony—despite the fact that her name translates as "clear light," a common metaphor in Spiritist circles for spiritual elevation. I asked what orisha she served. "Naná Burukú," she responded without hesitation.

The name Clara Luz translates as "clear light," and light is a major metaphor in Spiritist discourse. In fact, each time I call to my guide by name, I simultaneously invoke clear light, drawing it into my surroundings.

That Clara served Naná Burukú was more surprising. Naná Burukú is a relatively obscure orisha in Cuba, and I had never met anyone with a direct connection to her. However, Naná Burukú does work in caves, and she is said to be the mother of freshwater, which she later gave to Ochún. She is also closely associated with Babalú Ayé. Some communities consider her Babalú's sister, and others his mother. The Sabalú nation of the Arará consider Nanúme to be Babalú's grandmother. So, through her connection to Naná Burukú, Clara links me directly to both Ochún and Babalú Ayé. My relationship with Clara and the orishas connected to her have taken on more subtlety and depth over the years.

When I was initiated as a priest in 1992, it was Pedroso's sister Norma who crowned me. While I went to Cuba thinking that I would be crowned with Oyá, when the master of ceremonies determined what orisha I should make, Ochún stepped forward and claimed my head. In itá, she made clear that I am her "legitimate son," but it was Olókun, orisha of the depths, who promised to be the source of all my blessings. Olókun is strongly associated with the ancestors, with mysteries, and with revelation, and so my own natural curiosity was validated as part of my spiritual work. The ceremony itself transformed me as a person: it felt like a rebirth, and I changed many aspects of my life in the following couple of years. I have written extensively about this experience and the sense of release and the reinvigoration it provided remain with me to this day.[6] And the advice provided by the orishas in itá continues to guide me.

In 1993, I met Obá Oriaté Ernesto Pichardo at a conference in Puerto Rico. Pichardo was widely regarded as a very capable priest with an irascible personality. Initiated and trained in South Florida in the early 1970s, one of his godparents was Rogelio Pérez, Talabí, who had been the partner of Armando Zulueta, Omí Toké, who had founded a major lineage of Babalú worshippers. Moreover, Pichardo's maternal grandfather, Antolín Pla, was the first Babalú priest made in the United States, and his family had chartered the Church of the Lukumí Babalú Ayé in Miami.

We spent a few days talking about the religion and specifically about divination. At the end of the conference, we exchanged numbers. About a week after I returned home, the phone rang: Ernesto launched into a series of questions about different divination processes and signs, and I did my best to answer him with the little knowledge that I had. At some point, he asked a question, and my answer did not satisfy him. He said, "Figure it out. That's your homework." And he hung up. It was clear that I was not supposed to call him back till I thought I had a better answer. Our calls became frequent and long. His approach to divination requires careful attention to detail, and he advocated for only taking steps in the religion that are prescribed by divination. However, his cosmovision also makes space for direct revelation from the ancestors and the orishas. He explained to me that the earth-related orishas often communicate through dreams; furthermore, they often suggest more variations in their ceremonies than other orishas. His advice was to divine with Eleguá's shells to see if a dream is a revelation that should be followed. While I am still unsure why Ernesto chose to take me on as a student, he has been a remarkably generous teacher and has become a dear friend.

In late 1997, Eleguá spoke to me through the cowries and told me that I needed to receive Babalú Ayé, though I was not obviously ill. I knew immediately that I would ask Ernesto to give me Babalú Ayé, and after speaking with his orishas, he agreed.

In early 1998, when I traveled to Miami for the ceremony, my new wife did not want to be excluded, nor did she want to be implicated in the ceremony. So, she timed her flight to arrive just after the *awán*, the big cleansing ceremony on the first night of the ceremony, when there would be little danger of the orisha still mounting me or the other participants. On the day of the itá, I had a terrible stomachache—I almost always get sick before an itá, and I was anxious to learn what Babalú had in store for me. Again, my wife did not want to be left out or too involved. Thinking (naively) that a little distance would keep her out of harm's way, she sat in the next room and read a bestselling novel, as the diviner read the shells. Afrá, the Eleguá of Babalú, said that everything sweet turns sour, and Babalú Ayé said that marriage is a palace with two doors, the true one and the false one.

But my wife did not get to hear those messages. That December, the day after the feast for Babalú Ayé, our son was born. When he was seven days old, I brought down Eleguá to chart his path through the world. Eleguá made clear that the boy's life would always be tied up with Babalú Ayé, and with the orishas' blessings, we named him Abiodun, the one born at the time of the annual feast.

In a little more than a year, the sourness of a false marriage had become intolerable: Afrá, Babalú Ayé, and I moved out.

I first met Pedro Abreu in 2001. My friend and godson David Brown had been telling me about this leading Arará priest for a few years at that point, and when David introduced us, I immediately understood his fascination.

The first time we met, Abreu outlined his whole history in the religion. He was born in Los Sitios in central Havana. He had a *prenda* (Congo-inspired sacred object and entity) from the African-inspired Regla de Congo from a young age, but he had not really believed in religion. In 1975, he received Asojano-Afimaye in Havana from Matilde Sotomayor (Asoninque), the famous Asojano priestess who worked with Pilar Fresneda (Asonsíperaco).[7] The famous Ñica Fernández (Onojome) and Victor (Quemafo) were also there.

On February 20, 1992, Abreu made Asojano-Afimaye at the Cabildo Arará Sabalú Nonjó in Matanzas City. It had been thirty-six years since anyone had made Asojano there, but his godmother María Isabel Reyes (Asonsímeneco) did have Asojano made direct as tradition required. At itá, he was given the orisha name Asonyanye, after the famous Havana priest known as El Abuelo (some say Gervasio was his real name). When Asojano spoke through Ifá, as he does in this lineage, he came with the sign Ogunda-Iwori. Abreu immediately added that this sign includes the proverb "el árbol que se poda, retoña" (the tree that is pruned sprouts back again).

While Abreu did not go on about the implications of the proverb, he did recount the slow dissipation of both the Havana lineage and the Sabalú Cabildo in Matanzas. In Havana, Pilar Fresneda's *cabildo* had been in the hands of Ofelia de Pogolotti, an Ochún priestess who used information to continue to honor Asojano. In Matanzas, the famous Michaela Ruiz had left responsibility for the cabildo in the hands of Mayito, whose son Oscarito was now in charge. But neither Mayito nor Oscarito was an Asojano priests. Abreu also traced the other towns where Arará folks lived: Perico,

Jovellanos, Máximo Gómez, and Agramonte neighborhoods of Matanzas Province. But as he put it, "Much has been lost there."

In this gentle, almost indirect way, Abreu positioned himself as the re-blossoming tree of the Arará worship of Asojano, and, in fact, it's true. To date he has initiated at least sixty people directly to Asojano and has given Asojano to thousands more. Like Afimaye, Abreu's vitality and charisma have motivated many people to work together in ceremonies large and small.

A few years later, I had a vivid dream that Abreu was handing me an Asojano vessel. Representing a key step in the ceremony of consecration to the deity, I took the dream to mean that I should ask Abreu to give me Aso-jano, as Babalú Ayé is called in the Arará community. After consulting with Pichardo and my orishas, the time for the ceremony was set. One fine day in 2004, I underwent the elaborate ceremony to receive Afrá, Nanú—for some the wife of Asojano and for others his mother—and Asojano-Adu Kaké. The famous *babalawo* Andrés Kolá (Baba Eyiogbe) presided over the itá, in which it became clear that Nanúme is my *onilé*, the orisha who "owns my house" and defends me from enemies and obstacles. Asojano also charged me to do healing work. But this was just the beginning.

In the following years, Asojano appeared regularly in my dreams to re-veal ceremonies and other information to me.

In one of my dreams, Asojano is on the floor in the corner of a room with nine candles and nine glasses of water around him, as if it were an altar for the ancestors.

I am fabricating the secret that goes inside Asojano, and as I sing his praise songs, I place ingredients into a bowl: hairs from a goat's beard, earth from a cemetery.

Asojano says, "I can feel all the pain in this world."

Asojano says, "I will be your light in the darkness."

Asojano crowns me with his vessel.

Asojano in "human form" pushes my head down against his vessel and feeds them together with two roosters.

On another visit to Havana, I told Abreu about this last dream. I ex-plained that it seemed like I had been initiated again, that Asojano had stepped forward and taken over from Ochún. In his usual masterful perfor-mance, he reminded me that I have Ochún crowned, and he told me that several of his other godchildren had had a similar experience. "You should not forget to feed those roosters to Asojano."

In 2008, while expecting a new daughter with great anticipation, I had another powerful dream: Octavia Zulueta (Jundesi), who gave Armando Zulueta his Asojano, was explaining how to consecrate a special secret altar for Asojano. Afrá had indicated that this secret was appropriate for me in my itá, and Jundesi had given this same secret to Armando near the end of her life.

One day Jundesi appeared at the family house on Calle Juan Domínguez in Perico. She said she had something to give him. She said she needed to plant the secret of Babalú Ayé in the backyard. She went to the back corner of the yard, next to the latrine. From a basket she pulled a long object that was the size and shape of a piece of yucca. She dug a shallow hole and half-buried the secret. On top she placed a coral stone. There it remains. Over the years, the family built a small house around the secret, and someone tried to protect it with a tin can. Every year, at the time of Babalú's feast, they hold a big celebration that always includes feeding the secret. As they feed Babalú Ayé, they catch some of the blood in a gourd with white wine and rum. They pour this mixture over the secret. No one really knows what the secret is or why Jundesi planted it there. In an uncharacteristic moment of uncertainty, one elder wondered out loud if Babalú Ayé helps people heal from illness and the secret helped to cause it. No one knows, and so it remains, like so many things, part of the mystery of Babalú Ayé. In my case, Jundesi provided detail about what should go into the secret, what it should eat, and how I should tend to it. After consulting with Eleguá, I followed her instructions, which included feeding this secret with the Lucumí Babalú Ayé and Asojano Arará. They had finally come together.

In September 2008, on the seventh day of my daughter's life, Eleguá made clear that Babalú Ayé was standing in the room to welcome this child, who was also his daughter. Her naming ceremony included a orishaming to give thanks to him, and her name is Olu Dupé (We Give Thanks to Babalú).

In 2015, I had the following dream.

Asojano is standing in front of me in human form. He reaches into my heart and pulls out the vessel in which my Ochún lives. From the floor, he picks up his vessel and places it in my heart.

While Asojano had previously suggested his new authority in my life by crowning me in a dream, this time he went further. When I was initiated, Ochún gave me the name Ocán-Oñí (Heart of Honey). And here Asojano was removing Ochún from the center of my being and replacing her with himself. Of course, this fits with the transgressive nature of Asojano, who was exiled from the land of the Lucumí for not following the rules.

This experience and its spiritual implications unnerved me, as I love Ochún and would never want to disrespect her. So, I decided to bring her down to understand her perspective on the situation. She gave me the same Odu she had given at my initiation nearly twenty-five years before, suggesting that I was continuing to live my destiny as she saw fit. However, there was one significant change: when I was initiated, the blessings in this sign came through Olókun, and now they were coming through Asojano. Ochún not only accepted his active presence in my life; she also endorsed and blessed it.

That same year, based on revelations from Clara Luz, I took another step into the land of the Arará when I received Dandá-Jueró—the Rainbow Serpent—from Pedro Abreu. According to Abreu, Jueró is married to Naná Burukú, who is the mother of Ogún, Ochún, and Nanúme. Since Nanúme is the mother of Babalú Ayé, Jueró is the grandfather of Babalú Ayé, though we do not want to be too literal when discussing the paternity of the gods.

In fact, Abreu is fond of pointing out that it is Jueró—and not Asojano—who is the patron of the Cabildo Arará Sabalú Nonjó in Matanzas City where he was initiated. And Milagros Siqueira Palma, one of the oldest living members of the cabildo whom I met before her death, told me about the same thing in 1998, comparing Jueró to Oduduwá rather than Oshumaré and describing how they used to celebrate his festival each year in June with Arará orishaming and a procession through the streets of the city.

According to Pedro, Jueró came to Earth in Osá-Ojuani. This sign includes a long story in which Olofi created the world covered in water. However, he asked his children to do all they could to gather the waters so people could have a place to live on Earth. Since Jueró was a *majá* (a snake) and had no hands, he was worried that he could not do his part. So, he visited the diviner, who told him to make an *inché Osain* (an herbal preparation made for a particular purpose) in a long-necked medicine gourd to help himself. Then the diviner set him afloat in the water atop the gourd, and Jueró did not climb down till he had created solid ground. After sixteen days, all the deities had to report to Olofi. Other orishas had created rivers, but Jueró had created Earth and the great oceans that surround it. Olofi gave gold and jewels to other orishas, but to Jueró he gave a deformed woman with reddish hair.

When Jueró complained about that, the diviner Orula explained that Olofi had given Jueró his daughter. Orula said he should add some things to the long-necked gourd, and he did. Jueró and his wife lived together, but one day they were broke, and Jueró began a conversation with his wife.

She said that he should not worry, that he would have a fortune. She asked him to turn his back, and when he did, she whistled loudly. In that instant, strong winds began to blow from the north, south, east, and west, and living things—plants, animals, human beings—appeared all over the world. And his wife, who was Aida-Jueró, became beautiful. Then Jueró understood the great prize that Olofi had given him, and he too became beautiful. Together they became the rainbow. Since then, they have lived on high and other orishas envy them. Oshosí even tried to kill the rainbow, but Jueró lit it up with his light, and the orishas said, "Jueró is like Olofi himself." And Jueró continued his path through the skies.

There is so much to say about this story that I am not sure where to begin. Dandá-Jueró and his wife, Aida-Jueró, reiterate the Dahomean inclination to see the beginning of things in twins, a powerful way to image the dynamic polarity necessary for creation. And what could be more opposite than the fearsome, earthly snake and the beautiful, celestial rainbow. In this story, Jueró is none other than the creator of the Earth, and Pedro is fond of remarking that "Jueró is a kind of Obatalá." The comparison of Jueró to Olofi also strikes me as particularly fascinating. In 1948, Esteban Baró waxed poetic about Jueró, saying that the rainbow is supreme because it cannot be measured and that the other orishas worshipped him.[8]

Jueró brought more blessings into my life, and I give thanks.

In 2018, I had the following dream.

I am riding on the back of a huge white serpent as it flies through the sky. The snake says, "I have been carrying you for eons and eons."

Jueró, the patron of the Arará, claims me here, asserting that his support for me is very long-standing, indeed.

The plurality of religious traditions and specific relationships that make up my experience of my road with the orisha is complex, and as I pointed out, there are many ways to tell this story. However, the mediating role of my guide spirit, Clara Luz, provides one salient lens through which to view the unfolding of my religious path. Having been a priestess of Naná Burukú in life, Clara connects me to Ochún and Babalú Ayé. Having guided me for the last thirty years, she has mediated between these specific orishas and between the Lucumí and Arará traditions. With her guidance, protection, and healing, I hope to continue to praise her and the orishas for another good thirty or forty years.

Maferefún egun. Maferefún Ochún. Safalú Asojano. Safalú Jue.

Glossary

Abakuá – the Efik/Ekpe religious fraternal association in Cuba associated with Cross River Ejagham and Calabar derived rites.

abebe – a hand fan, also punned to mean "we beseech/pray."

abian – noninitiated Candomblé participants.

aborisha – Lucumí adherent/worshipper, "one who worships orisha." Often used to describe a worshipper who has not undergone priesthood initiation.

adimu – nonanimal sacrifice offerings given to the orishas, such as cooked food.

adimu orisha – satellite or auxiliary deities that relate to fundamental or initiation orishas such as Obatalá, Yemayá, Oshún, Shangó, and Oyá. Adimu orisha are consecrated for orisha worshippers.

Afrá – the Eleguá associated with Babalú Ayé.

Afrosamba – a Brazilian music genre.

Agayú – orisha of the volcano.

Agua Florida – Florida Water, a commercial cologne used in various religious practices, especially Spiritism.

ahijado – godchild, refers to an orisha initiate or affiliate of an *ilé* orisha.

akará – a Yorùbá and Yorùbá-diasporic food made from black-eyed peas and offered to Oyá.

aleyo – stranger, someone not formally aligned with the Lucumí religion.

amalá ilá – a Yorùbá and Yorùbá-diasporic food offering of cornmeal and okra stew.

Añá – (also *Àyàn, Anyá*) set of three hourglass-shaped orishas consecrated and ritually activated. Also refers to the orisha contained within the orishas.

anba dlo – under the water, the Vodou realm of the lwa and wisdom/ truth.

apetebi – ritual title for women in Ifá, often children of Oshún.

apón – Lucumí lead singer in call-and-response chants.

Arará – Afro-Cuban religious descendants of enslaved Fon, Mahi, Adja, Evhe, and other groups of the former Kingdom of Dahomey (now the Republic of Benin) and present-day Togo.

arrecife – sea reef/coral stone.

ashé – divine power, energy, akin to prana or chi.

ashere – maraca musical instruments used in orisha worship.

asiento – "seating" used to denote the Lucumí priesthood initiation ritual wherein the orishas are symbolically placed on the initiate's head.

asogwe – highest rank of manbo/houngan Vodou initiation.

Asojano – a name for Babalú Ayé, especially among the Arará.

assentamento – a seat, the physical consecrated manifestation of an orixá in Candomblé.

asson – sacred beaded gourd rattle that is a badge of initiation in Haitian Vodou.

atabaque – Candomblé sacred orisha.

atiponlá – hogweed. A plant used in Lucumí.

awán – a Babalú Ayé communal healing and cleansing ceremony involving food.

awó – secret, priest. Also a response to a greeting.

awofaca – an Ifá initiation relating to the worship of the orisha Orunla given by babalawos to men. See also *mano de Orunla* and *icofa*.

Awo Ifá – priest of Ifá, babalawo.

Ayizan – Vodou lwa.

babalawo – a (male) priest of the deity Orunla/Orunmila. Specialist in Ifá divination.

babalorishá/babalorixá – father of orisha, initiatory godfather, an olorisha who has initiated one or more persons to the orisha priesthood. Variations in spelling include *babalorisa, babalocha, babaloricha,* and *babalosha.*

Babalú Ayé – orisha of healing, miracles, communicable illness, and virology.

Balogún – title for a priest of the orisha Ogún. Also the name of the ritual slaughterer/butcher.

baptem – part of the Vodou initiation process when new initiates are welcomed as full members of the society.

barracão – large, consecrated space/hall where Candomblé activities such as celebrations are held.

barro – clay or terracotta.

bastón de egun/opa egun/pagugu – the staff used in Lucumí rituals for honoring the ancestors.

batá – the set of three hourglass-shaped orishas. When consecrated and activated, the batá orishas and orisha who reposes in them is called *Añá*.

batalero – a person proficient in playing the batá/Añá/Àyàn/Anyá orishas.

bendición – blessing.

bledo blanco – white amaranth. A plant used in Lucumí.

Bondyé – supreme deity, God, in Haitian Vodou.

botánica – retail store that caters to Afro-diasporic religious communities.

bóveda – ritual apparatus and altar used in Spiritism.

brujería – witchcraft. Sorcery that is often but not exclusively seen as negative.

brujo – male witch/sorcerer.

cabildo – mutual aid society for freed and enslaved Africans in Cuba to provide Catholic education and recreation.

camino – road or path. Refers to avatar-like depictions of specific orishas.

camión – a modified truck used as transport in some parts of Cuba.

Candomblé – Brazilian orixá religion.

capoeira – a Brazilian martial art.

carga – charge or load, the hidden organic ingredients that spiritually animate a Lucumí or Palo religious item.

casa particular – privately run home-style lodging in Cuba.

cascarilla – a white chalklike substance made from pulverized eggshell, used in Lucumí, Ifá, Palo, and Espiritismo. Also called *efún*.

chispa de tren – a toxic alcohol made from gasoline.

cimarrones – Africans who escaped enslavement in Cuba.

cinturitas – a type of seashell used for the orishas in place of money cowries in Cuba (*monetaria moneta*).

clave – a rhythmic pattern used as a tool for temporal organization in Afro-Cuban music.

collar de mazo – large, beaded necklaces for the orishas utilized in the initiation ceremony and to adorn orisha shrines.

collares – sacred necklaces and a fundamental initiation in Lucumí.

conga – a tall, narrow, single-headed orisha used in Afro-Cuban religious worship.

consulta – a divination session.

cuadro espiritual – the number or group of spirits/spirit guides that are known or connected to a practitioner of Spiritism.

cuchillo – knife, also called *obé* or *pinaldo*. See also *kuanaldo*.

cumpleaños – orisha initiation anniversary or birthday.

curanderismo – folk healing, incorporating spiritual and herbal medicine.

derecho – right. Refers to the monetary payment given to priests to perform or participate in a Lucumí ceremony.

desenvolvimiento – spiritual evolution, unfolding, development.

didgeridoo – an Indigenous Australian/Aboriginal wind instrument.

dilogún – from *merindinlogun* (sixteen), referring to the sixteen-cowrie-shell oracular system used by olorishas to determine Odu.

diri ak pwason – Haitian rice and fish.

djevo – Haitian Vodou sacred ritual/initiation chamber.

du – Beninois Fa divination verse, akin to Yorùbá Ifá odu.

ebó – ritual orisha offering, often prescribed in Odu/divination to remedy a situation.

ebó de entrada – offering of entry, the divination and offerings that begin the orisha priesthood initiation process.

efún – white chalklike substance made from pulverized eggshell, used in Lucumí, Ifá, Palo, and Espiritismo. Also called *cascarilla*.

egun – ancestors. Can denote departed religious or biological family and is also used in Cuba to denote spirit guides.

Egungun – ancestral masquerade.

ekede – a female initiate and title holder in Candomblé.

eku – bush rat.

Eleguá – warrior orisha of communication and divination.

eleke – beads or beaded necklaces. Called *collares* in Spanish.

el monte – the bush, forest, or grove. Home to many deities and spirits.

epó – red palm oil.

Erinlé – an orisha of the hunt, medicine, and wealth.

escoba amarga – bitterweed. A plant used in Lucumí.

Eshú – an orisha or an aspect of Eleguá, often referred to as Eshú Eleguá.

eşin òrìşà ibile – Yorùbá religion practiced today in West Africa.

Espiritismo – Spiritism, based on nineteenth-century French/European mediumistic development.

Espiritista – a Spiritist or spirit medium based on nineteenth-century French/European Spiritism philosophy and doctrine.

Espiritismo cruzado – a type of Spiritism that mixes elements of Lucumí or Palo.

estera – straw mat.

ewé – plants, herbs, or trees used in Lucumí rituals.

ewé ikoko – purslane. A plant used in Lucumí.

Fa – Vodún divination system.

festa – celebration or feast.

fèt – a Vodou celebration or party.

firma – signature. A sacred diagram or cosmogram used in Palo rituals.

flamboyán/framboyán – royal poinciana tree. A tree sacred to the orisha Oyá.

frevo – a Brazilian music genre.

fundamento – foundation. The often secret or hidden ashé-laden, consecrated material objects of the orishas.

garro – false buttonweed. A plant used in Lucumí.

Gede – a group of Vodou lwa who govern death, resurrection, and fertility.

Ginen – mythologized Africa as imagined/referred to in Haitian Vodou.

gris-gris – a West African Vodún charm or amulet.

guataca – hoe blade used as a musical instrument.

Guerreros (los) – the orishas Eleguá, Ogún, Oshosí, and Osun received by Lucumí worshippers as a group of consecrated deities.

guía espiritual – spirit guide.

hacer santo – to make saint, or to be initiated as an orisha priest.

helecho – fern. A plant used in Lucumí.

herramientas – tools. Used here to refer to metal and wooden stylized implements such as swords, shields, axes, and arrows, often in miniature used to adorn the shrines of orishas.

hierba fina – a plant used in Lucumí.

higuereta – castor oil plant used in Lucumí.

hijra – a person whose gender identity is neither male nor female in the Indian subcontinent.

houngan – male Vodou priest.

houngenikon – Vodou ritual lead singer.

hounsi – Vodou initiate.

ibayé tonú/ibá é t'orun – from the Yorùbá *iba e, iba e, eni tó nù*, similar to "may they rest in peace." A Lucumí phrase said after mentioning the name of a deceased priest as a sign of respect.

ibú – river eddy or pool of water, referring to the knowable aspects of female orishas such as Oshún and Yemayá. An ibú is similar to *camino*— a road or pathway referring to knowable aspects of orishas connected to land.

ibulosa – the confluence where a river flows into the ocean.

icofá – an Ifá initiation relating to the worship of the orisha Orunla given by babalawos to women. See also *mano de Orunla* and *awofaca*.

idé – bracelet, either beaded or metal. Consecrated religious jewelry signifying the protection of the orishas.

Ifá – a metonym for Orunla/Orunmila, the process of divination that results in Odu being cast.

igbodu – sacred Lucumí initiatory space where the majority of orisha ceremonies and initiations are performed.

ijexá – a Candomblé rhythm played on the orishas.

ikin – palm nuts that are consecrated and used for divination by babalawos.

ilé – house. Both physical structure and members of a house/religious family.

ilé tutu – cool house.

iliminasyon – a Vodou lamp illumination ceremony.

inche Osain – work of Osain. Osain is an orisha of herbalism, medicine, and witchcraft. Small emblems and talismans are made for a variety of purposes under the guidance of specific orishas.

invento – an invention, something made up.

iré – blessings, benedictions.

iruke/irukere – horsetail fly whisk.

ise'fá – Yorùbá Ifá initiation similar to icofá and awofaca.

itá – formal divination session with the orishas.

itótele – the middle-sized orisha of the batá/Añá trio.

itutu – Lucumí funeral ceremonies conducted for olorisha.

Iyá – mother. An honorific title to women who have initiates. Also the name for the largest orisha of the batá/Añá trio.

iyalorisha – mother of orisha, initiatory godmother. An olorisha who has initiated one or more persons to the orisha priesthood. Variations in spelling include *iyalosha, iyalorisa, iyalocha,* and *iyaloricha.*

iyawó – junior bride/wife. Male and female initiates are referred to as *iyawó* during the first year and seven days of their initiation journey in Lucumí.

jekua jei – Hail orisha, or Behold. A praise epithet for various orishas including Oyá and Obatalá.

jícara – dried hollow half gourd used as a container/bowl. Also called an igba.

jogo de búzios – playing the shells. A reference to performing divination in Candomblé using dilogún.

judío – Jewish/a Jewish man.

Jueró – patron Arará deity.

kami – Shinto deity.

kanzo – Vodou initiation process.

kariocha – to place ocha/orisha on the head. A term for Lucumí priesthood initiation.

kawo kabiye sile – Welcome, your majesty. A phrase relating to the worship of Shangó.

kuanaldo – an initiatory grade attained by a babalawo and signified by a consecrated knife.

la plas – a Vodou ritual orishamer.

lakou – a Vodou religious space also designating religious members/community.

Legba – Vodún god of communication between the worlds.

Leve Kanzo – ceremony to rise or lift kanzo, to lift the initiates undergoing kanzo.

licencia – Palo term for "license," "permission," "authority." Used to call and communicate with the spirits.

limpia/limpieza – a spiritual cleansing prescribed in Afro-Cuban and Spiritist religious practice.

Logunedé/Logun Edé – warrior and riverine orisha/orixá of wealth. Son of Erinle and Oshún worshipped extensively in Candomblé.

Lucumí – an Afro-Cuban religion or orisha worship. Alternative spelling: Lukumí.

lwa/loa – Haitian Vodou deity/spirit.

madrina – godmother. A Lucumí religious kinship term given to the female initiator/mentor/instructor.

mãe de santo – Candomblé term for a female priestess who initiates others.

maferefún – an expression of thanks or praise.

majá – snake.

mal de ojo – the evil eye.

mama ounyo – priest in charge of taking care of new Vodou initiates.

manbo – female Vodou priestess.

mano de Orunla – the hand of Orunla. An Ifá initiation relating to the worship of the orisha Orunla given by babalawos to women (*icofá*) and men (*awofaca*).

Mariel Boatlift – a mass emigration of 125,000 Cubans who traveled from Cuba's Mariel Harbor to the United States between April 15 and October 31, 1980.

Marielito – A Cuban who arrived in the United States in 1980 with Mariel Boatlift.

maryaj lwa – a ceremony in which selected lwa arrive in possession to marry their spouses.

mar pacífico – hibiscus. A plant used in Lucumí.

matanza – ritual animal sacrifice.

mazo – large, multistranded, bunched sashes of beads with beaded tassels.

medsin fèy – Haitian Vodou herbalist/botanist.

mesa blanca – white table. Denotes both the physical focus of an Espiritismo mass and a type of Espiritismo.

misa – spiritual mass. A communal séance performance in Espiritismo.

mi-tama – the spirit of a kami or the soul of a dead person in Japanese Shinto.

mpaka – a Palo Monte assemblage.

mpungo – Palo/Kongo term for "deity" or "spirit."

muerto – the dead, deceased. Can refer to spirits and guides in Espiritismo and ancestors and departed family members in Lucumí.

mulata – mixed-race woman in Cuba.

nan peyi a – in the country (Haiti).

Naná Burukú – elder matriarch orisha of underground rivers. Mother of Babalú Ayé.

Nangareo – a ceremony conducted outside before noon honoring the sun and performed on the day of an itá divination.

Nanú/Nanúme – female orisha and Arará deity closely linked to Babalú Ayé.

ngueyo – the name given to a person prior to and during initiation in the Palo tradition.

nkisi – Palo/Kongo term for "spirit" or "ancestor."

obá oriaté – religious title for senior Lucumí olorisha, the master of ceremonies and religious protocol for Lucumí rites and initiations.

Obatalá – orisha, male deity of intelligence, justice, and creation.

obé – knife. See *cuchillo, kuanaldo,* and *pinaldo.*

obi – nut. Refers to coconut (*obi agbon*) in Lucumí, which is used for offerings and divination.

obi abata – divination instrument made with a cowrie shell on a coconut shell backing.

obi agbon – coconut used for offerings and divination.

ocana – also known as okana, an Odu chapter and one of the signs in obi or coconut divination.

ocha – a contraction of *oricha,* an alternative spelling of *osha* and orisha. Can refer to both the orishas and the initiation of orisha priests.

Odu/odù – divination chapter or verse. Odu is the female orisha of divination.

Ogún – orisha of technology, metal, and war.

ofrenda – religious material offering.

ojubona – Lucumí secondary initiatory co-godparent.

okónkolo – the smallest orisha of the batá/Añá trio.

Olodumaré – Lucumí/Yorùbá idea of supreme god. Envisioned as remote and whose emissaries are the orishas.

Olofi/Olofin – supreme deity or god. In Lucumí religion, "One Who Has Sovereign Rule."

Olókun – orisha, deity of the depths of the ocean. Related to Yemayá, deity of water.

olorisha – orisha priest, "one who has orisha."

Olórun – owner of heaven, a praise name for God.

oluwo – an elder babalawo, often a person who was initiated as an olorisha/orisha priest and has also undergone the initiation to become a babalawo.

omiero – a sacred mixture of plants and water that is used for orisha consecrations and initiation rites.

omí tutu – cool water used for orisha and ancestor libations.

ona ayé – road through the world.

ona tutu – cool road.

onilé – owner of the house or earth.

Onishegun – doctor/healer.

opele – a chain with eight sections of dried opele tree (*Schrebera golundensis*) seed pods used by babalawo as a divination instrument.

Orí – physical and spiritual head, personal orisha, and keeper of a person's destiny.

Oriaté – olorisha who is a ritual and divination specialist.

orisha – Lucumí deity of West African Yorùbá origin.

orixá – Candomblé orisha.

oro seco – a Lucumí batá/Añá orishaming sequence for the orishas without singing accompaniment.

orukó – the term for a Lucumí initiatory name.

Orun – sun, sky, heaven.

Orunla – orisha of divination, patron of babalawo/Ifá diviners. Also called Orunmila, Orula.

Osain – orisha of plants, medicine, and religious consecration.

Osainista/Olosain – a person initiated and trained in the healing and herbal arts of Osain.

osha – a contraction of orisha, an alternative spelling of *ocha* and *oricha*. Can refer to both the orishas and the initiation of orisha priests.

oshinshin – a cooked food offering of shrimp, eggs, and greens often given to Oshún at the river.

Oshosí – Orisha, deity of the hunt and justice.

Oshumaré – orisha linked to the boa constrictor, rainbows, rain, and the cycle of life/death.

Oshún – an orisha or Lucumí deity of fresh waters and survival. Also called Ochun, Òsun.

osobo – negative, blocking, challenging energy connected to Odu and divination.

Osun – a deity/orisha received with the warriors Eleguá, Ogún, and Oshosí. Described as a watchman and takes the form of a silver-metal chalice topped by a metal rooster and four jingle bells.

otá – stone. Refers specifically to the stones consecrated to "seat" an orisha, becoming the tangible manifestation of the orisha's ashé received through initiation.

oungan – male Vodou priest.

ounkó – male goat.

owe – proverb.

owó – money, prosperity, wealth.

Oxalá – Candomblé orixá patriarch of purity and wisdom. Correlates to Obatalá.

Oxóssi – Candomblé orixá of the hunt. Correlates to Oshosí.

Oxum – Candomblé orixá of rivers. Correlates to Oshún.

Oyá – orisha, deity of the marketplace, transformation, and atmospheric phenomena.

Oyekun Meyi – an Ifá odu chapter/verse.

oyubona – second godfather or godmother to an initiate. In charge of caring for the initiate during the initiation process.

padrino – godfather. A Lucumí religious kinship term given to the male initiator/mentor/instructor.

pagan – a follower of a polytheistic, nature-based religion. A neo-pagan is a person who practices re-created or revived ancient polytheistic religions.

pai de santo – Candomblé male priest who initiates others.

palenque – a remote settlement or encampment created by *cimarrones*.

Palo, Palo Monte, Palo Mayombe – Congo/Kongo-derived religion in Cuba and its diaspora. Also called Regla de Congo.

paño, panuelo – colorful cloth panel used to adorn orisha vessels and shrines and work by the orishas while in possession.

papa ounyo – male priest in charge of taking care of new Vodou initiates.

patakí, patakín – divinatory narratives of the orishas.

peregún – dragon tree. A plant used in Lucumí.

perfuré – a Candomblé ritual dance.

pinaldo – knife. See also *cuchillo, kuanaldo,* or *obé.*

plante – a convention of babalawos to carry out an initiation or divination ceremony.

plaza – marketplace.

prenda – vessel of material substances consecrated and dedicated to a specific Palo deity.

promesas – promises.

rama – Lucumí initiation lineage/religious family tree/branch/clan.

rayamiento – type of Palo initiation, often translated as "scratching" or being "scratched in Palo," referring to the marks made on the person's body during the ritual process.

Regla de Congo – see *Palo.*

Reiki – a Japanese hands-on healing art.

resguardo – an amulet or talisman prepared for the inquirer by a babalawo or santero according to divination.

roda – Candomblé dance.

ronkô – Candomblé initiation space.

rumba – a Cuban music genre. Can also describe a musical performance/gathering.

Sakpata – Vodún deity of the earth and of healing, medicine, and divine justice. Correlated with Babalú Ayé.

Sakpatasi – initiates of the Vodún, Sakpata.

salud – health.

samba – an Afro-Brazilian dance and music genre.

Santería – colloquial name of Afro-Cuban religion or orisha worship.

santero/a – colloquial term for an olorisha or male or female orisha initiate.

santo – saint. Can refer to the orisha (*un santo*), or the initiation process (*hacer santo,* "to make the saint"; become initiated as an orisha priest).

saraecó – a cornmeal porridge/beverage used as part of the Lucumí and Ifá nangareo ritual.

sèvis lwa – to serve the lwa.

shaba – ritual metal chain with twenty-one miniature tools of Ogún attached to it.

Shangó – an orisha or Lucumí deity of justice, thunder, and royalty. Derived from the Yorùbá, Ṣàngó. The Hispanicized spelling is Changó.

shaworó – brass bells added to the batá/Añá orishas.

sheketé – a fermented beverage made from sour oranges that is used as an offering.

sistrum – a musical instrument of ancient Egypt.

sitar – a stringed musical instrument that is popular in northern India.

sopera – ceramic soup tureen or porcelain lidded vessel used to house emblems of the orishas. See also *tinaja.*

sosyete – Vodou family/community.

sou pwen/si pwen – a grade of Haitian Vodou priesthood initiation.

tambor – orishaming ceremony for the orishas.

tarot – a deck of cards originated in Europe to play games and for divination.

tata nganga/tata nkisi – ritual title in Palo, the male caretaker/owner of a prenda or nganga.

tatuado – tattooed.

terreiro – Candomblé communal sacred space that is used for ceremonies and celebration.

ti fèy – little leaves. Refers to initiates in Haitian Vodou.

tinaja – covered vessel used to house emblems of the orishas. See also *sopera.*

trono – throne. Lucumí orisha altar erected for an initiation or celebration.

Umbanda – Afro-Brazilian orixá religion originated in Rio de Janeiro that blends African traditions with Roman Catholicism, Spiritism, and Indigenous beliefs.

vaina – dried seed pod of the flamboyán/framboyán tree, used as a musical instrument for the orisha Oyá.

verbena – vervain. A plant used in Lucumí rituals.

verdolaga – purslane. A plant used in Lucumí.

vèvè – Haitian Vodou religious symbol or sigil.

vida despreocupada – carefree lifestyle.

Vodou – an Afro-Haitian worldview and practice that combines philosophy, healing, the ancestors, and deities (lwa).

Vodún – Beninois religion, spirit.

Vodouisant – Vodou adherent, practitioner, priest.

Yayi nganga – ritual title in Palo. The female caretaker/owner of a prenda or nganga.

Yemanjá – Candomblé orixá or deity of water, motherhood, and fertility.

Yemayá – Lucumí orisha or deity of water, motherhood, and fertility.

Yeye – mother.

yeza – scarifications made on the face.

Yorùbá – African ethnic group of southwestern Nigeria and adjacent countries.

Zonbi – the Vodou undead.

Notes

Foreword

1 Good Indian, brave Indian, where are you going with that cross? I am going to Mount Calvary to deliver it to Jesus.

2 Édouard Glissant, *Poetics of Relation,* trans. Betsy Wing (Ann Arbor: University of Michigan Press, 1997), 21.

3 Glissant, *Poetics of Relation,* 20.

Introduction. "Why Are You Here?"

1 See 'Wándé Abímbọ́lá, "Lagbayi: The Itinerant Wood Carver of Ojowon in Abiodun Rowland Abiodun," in *The Yoruba Artist: New Theoretical Perspectives on African Arts,* edited by Henry John Drewal and John Pemberton (Washington: Smithsonian Institution Press, 1994), 137–142.

2 Marloes Janson, *Crossing Religious Boundaries: Islam, Christianity, and 'Yoruba Religion' in Lagos, Nigeria* (Cambridge: Cambridge University Press, 2021).

3 Janson, *Crossing Religious Boundaries,* 186.

4 Maxine Kamari Clarke, "New Spheres of Transnational Formations: Mobilizations of Humanitarian Diasporas," *Transforming Anthropology* 18, no. 1 (2010): 48–65.

5 Kevin A. Yelvington, "The Invention of Africa in Latin America and the Caribbean: Political Discourse and Anthropological Praxis, 1920–1940," in *Afro-Atlantic Dialogues: Anthropology in the Diaspora,* edited by Kevin Yelvington, 35–82 (Oxford: James Currey, 2006), 67.

6 Stefania Capone, *Searching for Africa in Brazil: Power and Tradition in Candomblé* (Durham, NC: Duke University Press, 2010), 13.

7 Capone, *Searching for Africa,* 13.

8 See Solimar Otero's chapter, "Afrolatinx Folklore and Representation: Interstices and Anti-Authenticity," in *Theorizing Folklore from the Margins: Critical and Ethical Approaches,* edited by Solimar Otero and Mintzi Martínez-Rivera (Bloomington: Indiana University Press, 2021), 83–102.

9 Maurice Halbwachs and Lewis A. Coser, *On Collective Memory: The Heritage of Sociology* (Chicago: University of Chicago Press, [1925] 1992).

10 See chapter 1, "Herskovits's Heritage," in Andrew H. Apter, *Oduduwa's Chain: Locations of Culture in the Yoruba-Atlantic* (Chicago: University of Chicago Press, 2018), 17–38.

11 See Yelvington, *The Invention of Africa*, 76–79.

12 See Stephan Palmié, *The Cooking of History: How Not to Study Afro-Cuban Religion* (Chicago: University of Chicago Press, 2013).

13 J. D. Y. Peel, *Religious Encounter and the Making of the Yorùbá* (Bloomington: Indiana University Press, 2000), 10.

14 J. Lorand Matory, *Black Atlantic Religion: Tradition, Transnationalism, and Matriarchy in the Afro-Brazilian Candomblé* (Princeton, NJ: Princeton University Press, 2005), 2.

15 Matory, *Black Atlantic Religion*, 7.

16 Martin Holbraad, *Truth in Motion: The Recursive Anthropology of Cuban Divination* (Chicago: University of Chicago Press, 2012), 11.

17 Joseph M. Murphy, "Objects That Speak Creole: Juxtapositions of Shrine Devotions at Botánicas in Washington, DC," *Material Religion* 6, no. 2 (2010): 91–92.

18 Matory, *Black Atlantic Religion*, 1.

19 Matory, *Black Atlantic Religion*, 21.

20 For an in-depth ethnographic account of an initiation of a priest of Oshún, see Michael Atwood Mason, *Living Santería: Rituals and Experiences in an Afro-Cuban Religion* (Washington, DC: Smithsonian Institution Press, 2002).

21 Carole Boyce Davies, "Re-/Presenting Black Female Identity in Brazil: "Filhas d'Oxum" in Bahia Carnival," in *Representations of Blackness and the Performance of Identities*, edited by Jean Muteba Rahier (Connecticut: Bergin & Garvey, 1999), 49–67.

22 For the use of gendered tropes in initiation, see J. Lorand Matory, *Sex and the Empire That Is No More: Gender and Politics of Metaphor in Òyó Yorùbá Religion* (London: University of Minnesota Press, 1994).

23 Trans-Atlantic Slave Trade – Estimates from https://www.slavevoyages.org/assessment/estimates, accessed January 2023.

24 For an extensive examination of the origins and etymology of Vodún (and its many derivations, such as vodu, vodou, voudou, voodoo, vudu), see Suzanne Preston Blier, *African Vodun: Art, Psychology, and Power* (Chicago: University of Chicago Press, 1996).

25 Melville J. Herskovits, *Dahomey: An Ancient West African Kingdom*, 2 vols. (New York: J. J. Augustine, 1938).

26 Leslie G. Desmangles, *The Faces of the Gods: Vodou and Roman Catholicism in Haiti* (Chapel Hill: University of North Carolina Press, 1997), 2.

27 Allan Kardec, *Le livre des esprits, contenant les principes de la doctrine spirite sur la nature des esprits, leurs manifestations et leurs rapports avec les hommes* (Paris: E. Dentu, 1857).

28 Joseph M. Murphy, *Botánicas: Sacred Spaces of Healing and Devotion in Urban America* (Jackson: University Press of Mississippi, 2015), 172.
29 See for an in-depth description and analysis of the misa de coronación, see chapter 3, "Flows," in *Archives of Conjure: Stories of the Dead in Afrolatinx Cultures*, by Solimar Otero, 99–139 (New York: Columbia University Press, 2020).

Chapter 2. Death and Rebirth in African Vodún and Haitian Vodou

1 Claude Lévi-Strauss, *Tristes Tropiques* (London: Jonathan Cape, 1973).
2 William Buehler Seabrook, *The Magic Island* (New York: Harcourt, Brace, 1932).
3 Jean Malaurie, *Hummocks: Journeys and Inquiries among the Canadian Inuit* (Montreal: McGill-Queen's University Press, 2007).
4 The book was published in 2020 by Plon Publishers in Paris, through the Terre Humaine book collection over which I now preside.

Chapter 3. Crossed Paths

1 *Batucada* is a Brazilian substyle of samba, played by a large group of percussionists with different instruments.
2 Natalia Bolívar Aróstegui, *Los orishas en Cuba* (Havana: PM, 1994).
3 Vagner Gonçalves da Silva, *Intolerância religiosa: Impactos do neopentecostalismo no campo religioso afro-brasileiro* (Sao Paulo: EDUSP, 2007).
4 ADICA (Associazione Diffusione Candomblé), http://www.adica.info.
5 Mattijs van de Port, *Ecstatic Encounters: Bahian Candomblé and the Quest for the Really Real* (Amsterdam: Amsterdam University Press, 2011).

Chapter 4. The Scattering and Sharing of Wisdom around the World

1 The website still exists at the time of writing (www.orishanet.org/); however, the guestbook is no longer available.
2 Clayton D. Keck Jr. (1968–2009) was a *babalorisha* and priest of Yemayá whose initiation name was Afolabí Awoyoyomi. He also went by Shloma Rosenberg in honor of his Jewish heritage. See also chapter 6 of this volume for a fuller description and more information on Afolabí.
3 I have written about being a priest of Erinle, an anthropologist, and a Lucumí beadworker. The article can be accessed here: Martin A. Tsang, "Jubilant Coral and Jade: How Afro-Cuban Beaded Art Reflects Religion, Heritage, and Anthropology," *Chiricú Journal: Latina/o Literatures, Arts, and Cultures* 2, no. 1 (2017): 143–52.
4 Lydia Cabrera, *Yemayá y Ochún* (Madrid: C.R., 1974).
5 Some popular and actively celebrated Cuban–Catholic-orisha saint day celebrations are September 7, Nuestra Señora de Regla Yemayá; September 8, Nuestra Virgen de la Caridad del Cobre and Oshún; September 24, Virgen de las Mer-

cedes and Obatalá; December 4, Santa Bárbara and Shangó; and December 17, San Lázaro and Babalú Ayé.

Chapter 5. Making Ocha in Havana

1 Instead of rites of passage, sociologist Pierre Bourdieu used the phrase "rites of Institution," since the process "transforms the person consecrated: first because it transforms the representations others have of him and above all the behaviour they adopt towards him . . . and second, because it simultaneously transforms the representation that the invested person has of himself." Pierre Bourdieu, "Rites of Institution," in *Language and Symbolic Power,* edited by J. B. Thompson, translated by G. Raymond and M. Adamson (Cambridge, MA: Harvard University Press, 1994), 119.

2 Black and White in Color gallery was directed by Renny Molenaar. It also acted as a community center and a place to gather for poetry readings, political meetings, Sunday rumbas, and art exhibitions. There was always the offer of a home-cooked meal. Here, artists and activists from all over the world met to share their work.

3 Ivor Miller, *Aerosol Kingdom: Subway Painters of New York City* (Jackson: University Press of Mississippi, 2002).

4 Lydia Cabrera, *Anaforuana: Ritual y símbolos de la iniciacíon en la sociedad secreta Abakuá* (Madrid: Ediciones Madrid, 1975).

5 The Cuban phrase "to make saint" uses the Catholic "saint" to mean "orisha" while referring to the process of fabricating a shrine for the new initiate, as described in West Africa by Karin Barber, "How Man Makes God in West Africa: Yoruba Attitudes toward the Orisa," *Africa* 51, no. 3 (1981): 724–45.

6 Instead of "mounting" or "possessing," anthropologist Luc de Heusch used the term "adoricism" to describe the phenomenon as "voluntary, desired, and curative possessions," versus the monotheist's understanding of possession as demonic and deserving of exorcism. Luc de Heusch, "Cultes de possession et religions initiatiques de salut en Afrique," in *Annales du centre d'etudes des religions* (Brussels: Université Libre de Bruxelles, Editions de l'Institut de Sociologie, 1962), ii, 226–44.

7 Ivor Miller, "No More Carnivals: Cubans Struggle to Survive Their Economic Crisis," *International Forum at Yale* 12, no. 1 (1992): 23–27.

8 Lydia Cabrera, "Ikolé: Plumas de aura tiñosa," in *Se confeccionan ikolé abebé, abanicos de plumas de aura, para la diosa Oshún; Anagó: Vocabulario Lucumí* (Miami: CR Cabrera y Rojas, 1970), 159.

9 In "Lucumí: Abebe Osún 'the Fan of Oshún'"; "Abebé . . . Fan." Both in Cabrera, *Anagó,* 22.

10 David Brown, *Santería Enthroned: Art, Ritual, and Innovation in an Afro-Cuban Religion* (Chicago: University of Chicago Press, 2003), 101.

11 Because Oyá is considered "owner of the cemetery," she would protect me from its deathly influences. Thus, until I had received her, I was told I should stay away for my own well-being.

12 I was told that the Plaza was where enslaved Africans were auctioned during the colony. Although this is false—the Plaza was built in the 1900s, and the early slave market, now demolished, was at another site—this belief reveals the consciousness of enslaved Africans within Afro-Cuban initiation systems.

13 When local markets were reopened in 1994, this ebó was also revived. Cabrera, "Ebó: Offering, sacrifice, purification," in *Anagó*, 98.

14 Ivor Miller, "Jesús Pérez and the Transculturation of the Cuban Batá Drum," *Diálogo*, no. 7 (Spring 2003): 70–74.

15 Margaret Thompson Drewal, *Yorùbá Ritual: Performers, Play, Agency* (Bloomington: Indiana University Press, 1992), 64–72.

16 Considered a twin because they were "born" or initiated together.

17 Pedro Saavedra, former singer with the National Folklore Ensemble of Cuba.

18 William Bascom, *Shango in the New World* (Austin: African and Afro-American Research Institute, University of Texas, 1972) 3–4, 21.

19 This percussion group used consecrated batá orishas made by Jesús Pérez and was directed by Regino Jiménez Sáez (1948–2005), musical director of the National Contemporary Dance Company.

20 In this exchange, the elder called out my status as "initiate," and I responded with hers as "one already consecrated." One Cuban babalawo interpreted the santeros' salute, with arms crossed, as a physical representation of the cowrie shells used for the oracle. The face of the cowrie shell curves inward, closing in upon itself, and likewise santeros cross arms as if reaching inward. Their greeting symbolically confirms their status as agents of sacred knowledge through the *dilogún*. Arístides Vasecchoncelo, persoal communication, November 1995.

21 Church of the Lukumí Babalú Ayé, Inc., and Ernest Pichardo, v. City of Hialeah, U.S. 91–948 (1991).

22 Ivor Miller, "Belief and Power in Contemporary Cuba" (PhD diss., Northwestern University, 1995).

23 Lula Buarque de Hollanda, dir. *Pierre Verger: Mensageiro Entre Dois Mundos (Messenger between Two Worlds)* (Brazil: Grande Premio Cinema Brasil, 2000), DVD, 83 min.

24 Many of these narratives are published in Ivor Miller, "Religious Symbolism in Cuban Political Performance," *TDR: A Journal of Performance Studies* 44, no. 2 (2000): 30–55.

Chapter 6. Finding Home in the River

1 *Ibayé tonú* is a Lucumí term that is stated after mentioning the name of a deceased religious elder. Babalawo and scholar 'Wándé Abímbólá provides the full Yorùbá expression "ìba e, ìba e, enì tó nù," which translates to "I salute you; I salute you, you who have disappeared" or "who can no longer be seen." The word *nù* means "to be lost" or "to disappear." 'Wándé Abímbólá and Ivor Miller, *Ifá Will Mend*

Our Broken World: Thoughts on Yorùbá Religion and Culture in Africa and the Diaspora (Roxbury, MA: Aim Books, 2003), 124.

2 J. Lorand Matory, *Sex and the Empire That Is No More: Gender and the Politics of Metaphor in Oyo Yorùbá Religion* (New York: Berghahn Books, 2005).

3 James H. Sweet, "Male Homosexuality and Spiritism in the African Diaspora: The Legacies of a Link," *Journal of the History of Sexuality* 7, no. 2 (1996): 184–202.

4 David H. Brown, *Santería Enthroned: Art, Ritual, and Innovation in an Afro-Cuban Religion* (Chicago: University of Chicago Press, 2003), 59.

5 Brown, *Santería Enthroned*, 69.

6 George Brandon, *Santería from Africa to the New World: The Dead Sell Memories* (Bloomington: Indiana University Press, 1997), 115.

7 Brandon, *Santería from Africa to the New World*, 115.

8 For more on transnationalism, see Aisha M. Beliso-De Jesús, *Electric Santería: Racial and Sexual Assemblages of Transnational Religion* (New York: Columbia University Press, 2015).

Chapter 7. How I Came to the Tradition

1 'Wándé Abímbọ́lá, *Ifá: An Exposition of Ifá Literary Corpus* (Ibadan: Oxford University Press Nigeria, 1976).

Chapter 8. Practicing Ifá in Tokyo

1 Harry Mathews, *Cigarettes* (London: Dalkey Archive Press, 1998).

2 "Animism (n.)," Online Etymology Dictionary, accessed August 19, 2021, https://www.etymonline.com/search?q=animism.

3 Edward B. Tylor, *Primitive Culture: Researches into the Development of Mythology, Philosophy, Religion, Art, and Custom*, 2 vols. (London: John Murray, 1871), 1:377–453, 2:1–327.

4 Welcome to Ifá Divination, Tokyo, https://ifa-tokyo.jimdofree.com/, accessed August 19, 2021.

5 "Ifá Divination in Japan. Meet Professor (Babalawo Yoshiaki) of Meiji University, Tokyo, Japan," Adulawo, YouTube, filmed March 16, 2021, video, 14:45 min.

6 Yoshiaki Koshikawa, *Orisha Divination* (Tokyo: Sarue-shokai, 2019). Also on the web: "Orisha Divination 2023," http://www.saruebooks.com/oricha/index.html.

7 W. G. Aston, *Shinto: The Ancient Religion of Japan* (London: Constable & Co. Ltd., 1921), 13.

8 Aston, *Shinto*, 5.

9 Nelly Naumann, "The State Cult of the Nara and Early Heian Periods," in *Shinto in History: Ways of the Kami*, edited by John Breen and Mark Teeuwen (New York: Routledge, 2000), 63.

10 John Breen and Mark Teeuwen, "Introduction: Shinto Past and Present," in *Shinto in History: Ways of the Kami*, 7.

11 For a detailed description of kami, see Reiko Chiba, *The Seven Lucky Gods of Japan* (Rutland, VT: Charles E. Tuttle, 1995).

Chapter 9. On Seeking Guidance

1 For further reading, see Ellen W. Sapega, "In Search of a Creole Voice: Baltasar Lopes, *Chiquinho*, and the *Claridade* Generation," introduction to *Chiquinho: A Novel of Cabo Verde*, by Baltasar Lopes, trans Isabel P.B. Fêo Rodrigues and Carlos A. Almeida with Anna M. Klobucka (Dartmouth, MA: Tagus Press of UMass Dartmouth, 2019).

2 Margot Adler, *Drawing Down the Moon: Witches, Druids, Goddess-Worshippers, and Other Pagans in America Today* (Boston: Beacon Press, 1979).

3 Elizabeth Pérez, "Spiritist Mediumship as Historical Mediation: African-American Pasts, Black Ancestral Presence, and Afro-Cuban Religions," *Journal of Religion in Africa* 41, no 4 (2011): 330–65.

4 Séances are commonly referred to as *misas* and are part of the practice of Spiritism.

5 Wade Clark Roof, *A Generation of Seekers: The Spiritual Journeys of the Baby Boom Generation* (San Francisco: Harper, 1993).

6 When I use the term "historical actor," it is important to note that I see history as what the present is made of and the future as an abstraction to give the present vision. We are never *in* the future (or the past). To refer to ancestors as "historical actors" is not to displace them from the present, or the future, for that matter; it is to say that we do not interact with those who have completed a given lifetime in the same way that we interact with those who have not yet completed a given lifetime.

7 Elizabeth Pérez, *Religion in the Kitchen* (New York: New York University Press, 2016).

8 Pérez, *Religion in the Kitchen*, 6.

9 "Santería" is considered by many to be a derogatory term. "La regla de ocha" (the rule of the ocha) or "Lucumí," which is also the sacred language used in ritual and music, are more appropriate terms.

10 An *ilé*, in this instance, refers to a temporary sacred space put together for an orisha and a new initiate during the seven-day initiation cloistering, and for an orisha during a sacred orisha ritual (these are also referred to by the Spanish *trono*). However, the term can also refer to the house, or space within a house, where religious activities take place and/or to a religious family. For more on the subject, see David H. Brown, *Santería Enthroned: Art, Ritual, and Innovation in an Afro-Cuban Religion* (London: Routledge, 2003).

11 In Odun's ilé, a "orisha" was the term used colloquially for a *wemilere*. This is a formal ritual where three *batá* orishas consecrated to Añá (the orisha of orishas and music) are played by orishamers initiated to Añá and a designated orisha is called down by an *apón* (singer) to possess an initiate who has been prepared to serve in this function. This is distinct from an informal *güiro* where one or two

conga orishas and shekeré are played to honor an orisha. These orishas may be ritually treated, but they are not consecrated to Añá. For more on this subject, see George Brandon, *Santeria from Africa to the New World: The Dead Sell Memories* (Bloomington: Indiana University Press, 1993); Yvonne Daniel, *Dancing Wisdom: Embodied Knowledge in Haitian Vodou, Cuban Yoruba, and Bahian Candomblé* (Urbana: University of Illinois Press, 2005); Joseph M. Murphy, *Santeria: African Spirits in America* (Boston: Beacon Press, 1993); and Miguel "Willie" Ramos, "The Empire Beats On: Oyo, Batá Drums and Hegemony in Nineteenth-Century Cuba" (master's thesis, Florida International University, 2000).

12 Thomas Csordas, ed., *Transnational Transcendence: Essays on Religion and Globalization* (Berkeley: University of California Press, 2009); Roof, *A Generation of Seekers.*

13 Elizabeth Pérez, "Willful Spirits and Weakened Flesh: Historicizing the Initiation Narrative in Afro-Cuban Religions," *Journal of Africana Religions* 1, no 2 (2013): 151–93.

14 George Brandon, "From Oral to Digital: Rethinking the Transmission of Tradition in Yorùbá Religion," in *Òrìṣà Devotion as World Religion: The Globalization of Yorùbá Religious Culture,* edited by Jacob K. Olupona and Terry Rey (Madison: University of Wisconsin Press, 2008), 448–69.

15 Pérez, *Religion in the Kitchen.*

16 While some Lucumí rituals can be performed solely with initiated members of the religious household, a number of rituals require a ritual expert (an Oriaté) to conduct the ritual. An Oriaté must go through extensive training and an initiation specific to that position in order to become an Oriaté.

17 Santa Bárbara is the Catholic saint associated with the orisha Shangó.

18 For further insight, see Steven Gregory, *Santería in New York City: A Study in Cultural Resistance* (New York: Garland, 1999); Tracey E. Hucks, *Yorùbá Traditions and African American Religious Nationalism* (Albuquerque: University of New Mexico Press, 2012); and Stephan Palmié, "Against Syncretism: 'Africanizing' and 'Cubanizing' Discourses in North American Òrìṣà Worship," *Counterworks* (1995): 73–104.

Chapter 12. A Hermeneutics of Plurality on the Road of the Orisha

1 Linda Thomas, "Embracing the Other: A Womanist Perspective," review in *Grace Ji-Sun Kim ~ Loving Life,* blog post, December 23, 2016, https://gracejisunkim .wordpress.com/2016/12/23/syndicate-embracing-the-other-reviewed-by-linda -thomas/.

2 Trinh T. Minh-ha, *Woman. Native. Other* (Bloomington: Indiana University Press, 1989), 104.

3 Michael Jackson, *Paths Toward a Clearing: Radical Empiricism and Ethnographic Inquiry* (Bloomington: Indiana University Press, 1989), 3.

4 Diana Espírito Santo, *Developing the Dead: Mediumship and Selfhood in Cuban Espiritismo* (Gainesville: University of Florida Press, 2015), 194.

5 Luisah Teish, *Jambalaya: The Natural Woman's Book of Personal Charms* (New York: Harper Collins, 1985).
6 Mason, *Living Santería;* Michael Atwood Mason, "Initiation in Cuban Santería," *Anthropology and Humanism* 29, no. 2 (2008): 186–89.
7 Michael Atwood Mason, "Pilar Fresneda—Asonsiperaco," *Baba Who . . . Babalú!,* blog post, March 19, 2011, http://baba-who-babalu-santeria.blogspot.com/2011/03/pilar-fresnedaasonsiperaco.html.
8 William Bascom Papers, 1933–1981, Bancroft Library, University of California–Berkeley, Berkeley, California, https://oac.cdlib.org/findaid/ark:/13030/kt5p3035gz/.

Suggested Further Reading

The following are recommended readings on African and African Atlantic religions, diasporic practices, interviews, as well as descriptions of visual arts, ethnographies, and personal religious experiences.

Abímbọ́lá, 'Wándé, and Ivor Miller. *Ifá Will Mend Our Broken World: Thoughts on Yorùbá Religion and Culture in Africa and the Diaspora*. Roxbury, MA: Aim Books, 2003.

Beliso-De Jesús, Aisha M. *Electric Santería: Racial and Sexual Assemblages of Transnational Religion*. New York: Columbia University Press, 2015.

Brandon, George. *Santería from Africa to the New World: The Dead Sell Memories*. Bloomington: Indiana University Press, 1993.

Brown, David H. *Santería Enthroned: Art, Ritual, and Innovation in an Afro-Cuban Religion*. Chicago: University of Chicago Press, 2003.

Brown, Karen McCarthy. *Mama Lola: A Vodou Priestess in Brooklyn*. Berkeley: University of California Press, 1991.

Carr, C. Lynn. *A Year in White: Cultural Newcomers to Lukumí and Santería in the United States*. New Brunswick, NJ: Rutgers University Press, 2016.

Conner, Randy P., and David Sparks. *Queering Creole Spiritual Traditions: Lesbian Gay Bisexual and Transgender Participation in African-Inspired Traditions in the Americas*. Hoboken, NJ: Taylor and Francis.

Cosentino, Donald. *Sacred Arts of Haitian Vodou*. Los Angeles: UCLA Fowler Museum of Cultural History, 1998.

Daniel, Yvonne. *Dancing Wisdom: Embodied Knowledge in Haitian Vodou, Cuban Yorùbá and Bahian Candomblé*. Urbana: University of Illinois Press, 2005.

Deren, Maya. *Divine Horsemen: Voodoo Gods of Haiti*. London: Thames and Hudson, 1970.

Drewal, Margaret Thompson. *Yorùbá Ritual: Performers, Play, Agency*. Bloomington: Indiana University Press, 1992.

Gleason, Judith. *Oyá: In Praise of the Goddess*. Boston: Shambhala, 1987.

Gleason, Judith Illsley. *Santería, Bronx*. New York: Atheneum, 1975.

Hucks, Tracey E. *Yoruba Traditions and African American Religious Nationalism*. Albuquerque: University of New Mexico Press, 2012.

Hurston, Zora Neal. *Mules and Men*. New York: Harper, 1970.

Landes, Ruth, and Sally Cole. *The City of Women.* Albuquerque: University of New Mexico Press, [1947] 2005.

Landry, Timothy R. *Vodún: Secrecy and the Search for Divine Power.* Philadelphia: University of Pennsylvania Press, 2019.

Mason, Michael Atwood. *Living Santería: Rituals and Experiences in an Afro-Cuban Religion.* Washington, DC: Smithsonian Books, 2016.

Matory, J. Lorand. *Black Atlantic Religion: Tradition, Transnationalism, and Matriarchy in the Afro-Brazilian Candomblé.* Princeton, NJ: Princeton University Press, 2005.

Matory, J. Lorand. *Sex and the Empire That Is No More: Gender and Politics of Metaphor in Òyó Yorùbá Religion.* London: University of Minnesota Press, 1994.

Murphy, Joseph M. *Santería: African Spirits in America.* Boston: Beacon Press, 1993.

Murphy, Joseph M., and Mei-Mei Sanford. *Ọ̀ṣun Across the Waters: A Yoruba Goddess in Africa and the Americas.* Bloomington: Indiana University Press, 2001.

Ochoa, Todd Ramón. *A Party for Lazarus: Six Generations of Ancestral Devotion in a Cuban Town.* Oakland: University of California Press, 2020.

Olupọna, Jacob Obafẹmi Kẹhinde, and Terry Rey. *Òrìṣà Devotion as World Religion: The Globalization of Yorùbá Religious Culture.* Madison: University of Wisconsin Press, 2008.

Otero, Solimar. *Afro-Cuban Diasporas in the Atlantic World.* Rochester, NY: University of Rochester Press, 2010.

Otero, Solimar. *Archives of Conjure: Stories of the Dead in Afrolatinx Cultures.* New York: Columbia University Press, 2020.

Pérez, Elizabeth. *Religion in the Kitchen: Cooking, Talking, and the Making of Black Atlantic Traditions.* New York: New York University Press, 2016.

Román, Reinaldo L. *Governing Spirits: Religion, Miracles, and Spectacles in Cuba and Puerto Rico 1898–1956.* Chapel Hill: University of North Carolina Press, 2007.

Thompson, Robert Farris. *Flash of the Spirit: African and Afro-American Art and Philosophy.* New York: Vintage Books, 1984.

Wafer, Jim. *The Taste of Blood: Spirit Possession in Brazilian Candomblé.* Philadelphia: University of Pennsylvania Press, 2009.

Warner-Lewis, Maureen. *Central Africa in the Caribbean: Transcending Time, Transforming Cultures.* Kingston: University of the West Indies Press, 2004.

Contributors

Michael Atwood Mason (Ocán-Oñí) is an American folklorist and museum professional. He currently serves as CEO and executive director of President Lincoln's Cottage and was, up to February 2021, the director of the Smithsonian Center for Folklife and Cultural Heritage. Mason earned his MA and his PhD at the Folklore Institute at Indiana University Bloomington. Mason is a Lucumí priest of Oshún. Since 1992, Mason has published many articles on the religion and culture of the African diaspora. His research focuses on the processes through which people deploy elements of the cultural heritage to construct their personal histories and identities, and he has focused extensively on the social construction of human subjectivity and experience. His book *Living Santería: Rituals and Experiences in an Afro-Cuban Religion* was published by the Smithsonian Institution Press in 2002 and was nominated for the Victor Turner Award for Ethnographic Writing. Mason is also the author of the cultural blog dedicated to Babalú Ayé, *Baba Who? Babalú!*

Alex Batagi (Bonkira Bon Oungan) was initiated into sèvis lwa (Haitian Vodou) at the hands of Manbo Marie Maude Evans of Sosyete Nago in 2016 in Jacmel, Haiti. Alex has been writing about their experiences with the lwa as a convert and gender-nonconforming individual for a decade, casting an introspective lens on their pursuit of a life lived with the sacred. Alex serves their spirits at home and in the temples of Sosyete Nago in Boston and Haiti and brings their experiences into their work as an artist and social worker.

Giovanna Capponi is a postdoctoral researcher at the University of Roehampton. She is trained as a social anthropologist with a particular interest in environmental anthropology, human-animal studies, and more-than-human ontologies. She conducted multisited fieldwork in Italy and Brazil looking at animal sacrificial practices and perception of the environment in Afro-Brazilian Candomblé, developing perspectives in the fields of anthropology of ritual and material culture. She is currently working on more-than-human ecologies and animal-feeding practices in urban settings. She is the co-convenor of the Human and Other Living Beings EASA Network and secretary of the Environment and Anthropology Committee of the Royal Anthropological Institute.

Philippe Charlier earned his MD in forensic medicine and pathology, his PhD in archaeo-anthropology, and his LittD in bioethics. He is head of the Department of Research and High Education at the Musée du quai Branly–Jacques Chirac (Paris, France) and of the Laboratory Anthropology, Archaeology, Biology (LAAB) at Paris-Saclay University. He is the director of the well-known anthropology book collection Terre Humaine.

Terri-Dawn González (a.k.a. T-D.), whose ritual name is Okántomí, is an ordained priestess of the Orisha Oshún within the Afro-Cuban Lucumí system of Orisha worship, which derives from the traditional Yorùbá religion of West Africa. She was ordained in 1999 in San Miguel del Padrón, Havana, Cuba, by the late Alejandrina Herrera-Thompson (Oshún Ibu Coromí) Iba'é, and the late Gladys Ela Prieto (Elufandeí), Iba'é. T-D. resides in Los Angeles, California, where she is the presiding Iyalorisha of a small ilé. She has been a functioning member of the Lucumí community in Los Angeles for more than twenty-three years and is the widow of Tata Nkisi and Babalorisha Félix González Hernández, Oshá L'Ashé, Iba'é. Her active elder and teacher is her mother-in-law, Iyalorisha María-Antonia Hernández, Oshún Koyimí. T-D. was trained in the art of confecting spiritual baths and propagating esoteric herbs by her religious elders and has developed a great love for this endeavor. She is passionate about working with sacred herbs to effect healing, and after twenty-five years of creating spiritual baths, she is dedicated to continuing her botanical work as a lifelong educational journey of discovery and wonder. T-D. is also an accomplished Lucumí beadworker and a dedicated student of Lucumí history, cosmology, and ritual protocols.

Yoshiaki Koshikawa (Babalawo Ifá Ashé Iwori Batrupon) was born in 1952 in a traditional fishing village in Chiba, a prefecture located on Japan's eastern Pacific coast. Growing up, the family household contained both Buddhist and Shinto altars, and dual worship was part of everyday life. He attained a PhD in language and literature at Tsukuba University and is a professor of literature at the Department of English, Meiji University. His specialism is in Caribbean and American literature with a focus on Cuba. Yoshiaki first visited Cuba in 2008 and became initiated in the Afro-Cuban Lucumí and Ifá traditions there. After he engaged in prolonged fieldwork in Cuba for more than ten years, he recently wrote a book on Afro-Atlantic religions and people in the Caribbean and its diaspora. The book will be published first in Japanese with the hope that it will later be translated into English and Spanish. Yoshiaki resides in Tokyo, where in addition to his faculty role at Meiji University, he is a practicing babalawo who divines, teaches, and writes about Ifá for the growing Japanese community of those interested in the orishas.

Sue Kucklick-Arencibia (Oshúnmilaya) is a licensed counselor, artist, and writer based in Cleveland, Ohio. She was crowned Oshún in 1996. She works as a behavioral health manager on the near west side of Cleveland. She is the author of *Obì Abata Divination,* which was published in Santiago de Cuba and the United States.

Belia Mayeno Saavedra (Ochún Bumí) is a somatic practitioner, beadwork artist, and Lucumí Ochún priest based in Lisjan Ohlone lands, also known as Oakland and Berkeley, California. Her two decades of work with survivors of violence (with a special focus on transformative justice and incarcerated youth) ground both her professional and spiritual paths in trauma-sensitive embodiment practices and collective resilience. She credits her contribution in this volume to the teachings of her elders: Reiko Hanae, Ruth Belia, Rebecca Joy, Odu Fora, and Igbin L'ete.

Ivor Miller is a cultural historian specializing in the African diaspora in the Caribbean and the Americas. He was a Senior Fellow at the National Museum of African Art at the Smithsonian Institution and a Fulbright Scholar to Nigeria, and he taught for several years in the Department of History at the University of Calabar, Cross River State, Nigeria. His book *Voice of the Leopard: African Secret Societies and Cuba* was awarded honorable mention by the Association for Africanist Anthropology. Based upon fieldwork in Nigeria, Cameroon, Cuba, and the United States, it documents ritual languages and practices that survived the Middle Passage and evolved into a unifying charter for those who were enslaved and their successors.

Morgan M. Page (Odofemí) is a Canadian writer, artist, and olorisha based in London. She was crowned to Oshún in 2010. With Chase Joynt, she is the cowriter of the feature film *Framing Agnes* (2022) and the book *Boys Don't Cry* (2022). She also hosts the trans history podcast *One from the Vaults* and executive produced the podcast series *Harsh Reality: The Miriam Rivera Story.*

Eugenia Rainey moved to New Orleans from Chicago in 2001 with her husband and, then, two very young children. Since then, she and her husband have raised four children in New Orleans. Prior to Katrina, she began working as a ghost tour guide in the historic French Quarter of New Orleans. Post Katrina, in 2007, she pursued an MFA in creative writing from the University of Nebraska at Omaha, which led her to teach composition at Delgado Community College in New Orleans for roughly six years. In 2014, she began her graduate work at Tulane, completing her PhD in 2022. She is currently a Mellon Postdoctoral Fellow in the Department of Religion at Dartmouth College.

Martin Tsang (Ayaya) is a cultural anthropologist who has researched, taught, and published on Asian ethnicity, culture, health care, and religion in the Caribbean and in great depth with respect to Cuba. In 2017, he was appointed as the Cuban Heritage Collection Librarian, overseeing print and digital resources for the largest collection of materials on Cuba and its people located outside of the island. He was also the inaugural curator of Latin American Collections at the University of Miami Libraries and regularly teaches classes in anthropology and religious studies at the University of Miami. Martin is an initiated priest of the orisha Inle/Erinle in the Afro-Cuban Lucumí tradition and specializes in the beaded material culture of the religion. His beadwork has been displayed in several exhibitions.

Index